THE HEAVENLY MESSAGE

A History of the Prophets and Messengers

VOLUME ONE

By

Nooralah Troi-Sang Bukhari

The Heavenly Message

THE HEAVENLY MESSAGE

A History of the Prophets and Messengers

BY
NOORALAH TROI-SANG BUKHARI

Volume 1

EDITED BY ISMAEL BUKHARI
INSTITUTE OF MONOTHEISM RELIGION

2016

The Heavenly Message

ALL RIGHTS RESERVED

Copyright 2018 by Al-Waqiah Publishers

No part of this book may be reproduced or utilized in any form or by any electronic or machanical means including photocopying, without permission in writing from the publisher.

Printed in the United States of America

ISBN 978-0-9961768-0-4

THE INSTITUTE OF MONOTHEISM RELIGION

Published by
Al-Waqiah Publishers
P.O. BOX 225112 Dallas, Texas 75222-5112
Tel: 01-214-705-5136
United States of America

Table of Contents

Forward 9-11

Chapter: 1. Story of Adam........................12-22
Chapter: 2. Story of Seth (Sheth)..23-28
Chapter: 3. Story of Idris (Enoch)...29-33
Chapter: 4. Story of Nuh (Noah)..34-47
Chapter: 5. Story of Hud (Hebron)..48-56
Chapter: 6. Story of Salih (Methuselah)..57-64
Chapter: 7. Story of Ibrahim (Abraham)...65-83
Chapter: 8. Story of Ismael (Ishmael)..84-92
Chapter: 9. Story of Ishaq (Isaac)..93-95
Chapter: 10. Story of Lut (Lot)...96-101
Chapter: 11. Story of Yaqoob (Jacob)..102-105

Chapter: 12. Story of Yusuf
(Joseph)..106-123
Chapter: 13. Story of Shu'aib
(Jethro)..124-130
Chapter: 14. Story of Ayub
(Joab)..131-136
Chapter: 15. Story of Musa (Moses) and
Harun (Aaron).......................................137-187
Chapter: 16. Story of Yoshua
(Joshua)..188-192
Chapter: 17. Story of
Ezekiel...193-196
Chapter: 18. Story of Shammil
(Samuel)...197-201
Chapter: 19. Story of
Luqman...202-207
Chapter: 20. Story of Dawud
(David)..208-217
Chapter: 21. Story of Suleiman
(Solomon)...218-231
Chapter: 22. Story of Elias
(Elijah)..232-237
Chapter: 23. Story of Yasa
(Elisha)..238-241
Chapter: 24. Story of
Dhu'l-Kifl...242-246

Chapter: 25. Story of Shia (Isaiah)..................247-251
Chapter: 26. Story of Aramaya (Jeremiah)..................252-256
Chapter: 27. Story of Daniel..................257-261
Chapter: 28. Story of Uzair (Ezra)..................262-266
Chapter: 29. Story of Yunus (Jonah)..................267-277
Chapter: 30. Story of Zachariah (Zacharias)..................278-283
Chapter: 31. Story of Maryam (Mary)..................284-291
Chapter: 32. Story of Yahya (John)..................292-296
Chapter: 33. Story of Isa (Jesus)..................297-310
Chapter: 34. Story of Dhu-l-qarnain..................311-315
Chapter: 35. Story of People of Cave..................316-324
Chapter: 36. Story of Hammed Nagar..................325-329
Chapter: 37. Story of People of Gardens..................330-336

Chapter: 38. Story of People of Saba 337-340

Chapter: 39. Story of Muhammed..341-618

Chapter: 39
The Story of Prophet Muhammed To Be Continued in Volume Two.

Forward

I began with the permission of the most merciful Creator. By the time for the creation, and this publication of the Heavenly Message Vol. I & II. In the light of the Qur'an. For a time in my life as a child of a Muslim scholar, a question came to me that; What does the Qur'an mean to human life, and then I asked my father, he said, the best way to answer my question is to be read, study, contemplate the heavenly scriptures, both in the physical and spiritual revelation.

It is through proper dedication of studying the contextual events in the Qur'an, not only with the tongue, voice and eyes but through own internal light; a purification which is the light of own heart can supply the conscience to give the understanding and the experience on the test of life of the prophets and messengers mentioned in the heavenly scriptures, which result to our spiritual world and becomes the essence in human life.

All praises to the most merciful Creator for a greater help extended to me and my parents. I wish to express my gratitude to individuals and institution that have spent tremendous efforts through translations made easy, the heavenly scriptures available from their original languages to languages in many parts of the world, today.

Particular, I would like to thank my father for his resolution for me and to complete this book. The historical events of the prophets and messengers according to their scriptures from the heaven.

And as a student of Al-Islam and Al-Qur'an learning, I have taken satisfactory notes from my father's teaching of the events of Prophets and messengers from the gracious merciful Creator. But, when I learned that the revelation from the Creator precedes all human knowledge and inventions combined. The essence of the Qur'an in human life is important to total submission to the unseen Creator in the Islam belief.

And to believe in the revelation from the Creator to creates, is the answer to my question concerning heavenly revelations.

The merciful Creator is whom I dedicate my life; to obtain the answers to all my questions adequately. And my answer led me to become a humanist, which allowed my childhood in the compilation of these events.

The scriptures from Prophet Adam to Prophet Muhammed are of a mercy to mankind.

The author and publishers express their glory and gratitude to the most merciful Creator in allowing this work to be within the reach of a greater number of people, so, that they may benefit from it, and have answers to their questions regarding physical and intellectual existence. They may have the understanding of learning and teaching of the heavenly scriptures, both in the academic world and in the community of mankind at large.

Chapter One

The story of Prophet Adam

The Heavenly Message

Chapter One
The story of Prophet Adam

And when the most gracious Creator said to the angels: "I am going to create a mortal of sounding clay, of black mud fashioned into shape. I am going to place him as ruler in the earth." The angels said: "Wilt Thou place in it such as make mischief in it and shed blood? And we celebrate Thy praise and extol holiness." the most gracious Creator said: "Surely, I Know what you know not." So when the most gracious Creator have made him complete and breathed into him of His spirit, named him Adam and taught him all the names, then presented him to the angels; the most gracious Creator said: "Tell Me the names of those if you are right." They said: "Glory is to Thee! We have no knowledge but that which Thou art the Knowing, the Wise." the most gracious Creator said: "O Adam, inform them of their names." So when he informed them of their names, the most gracious Creator said: "Did I not say to you that I know what is unseen in the heavens and the earth? And I know what you manifest and what you hide." the most gracious Creator said to the angels, "Be submissive to Adam, and fall down making obeisance, all of you together." But Iblis did it not, he refused and was proud, he became one who openly disbelieves to the order of his Most Gracious Creator, not to be with those who made obeisance. The most gracious Creator said: "O Iblis, what is the reason that thou art not with those who make obeisance?" Iblis said: "I am better than he; Thou hast created me of fire, while him, Thou didst create of dust." the most gracious Creator said: "Then get forth from this state, for it is not for thee to behave proudly therein. Go forth; therefore, surely thou art of the abject ones." Iblis said: "Respite me till the day when they are raised." the most gracious Creator said: "Thou art surely of the respited ones." Iblis said: "As Thou hast adjudged me to be erring, I will certainly lie in wait for them in Thy straight path, then I shall certainly come upon them from before them and from behind them, and from their right and from their left; Thou wilt not find most of them thankful. I shall certainly make evil fair-seeming to them on earth, and I shall cause them all to deviate, except Thy servants from among them, the purified ones." the most gracious Creator said: "Then go forth, and surely, thou art driven away, and surely on thee is a curse till the Day of Judgment." the most gracious Creator said: "This is a right way with Me. As regards My servants, thou hast no authority over them except such of the deviators as follow thee. And surely, hell is the promised place for them all, it has seven gates. For each gate is an appointed portion of them, some of you, the enemies of others." Adam used to pray to the most gracious Creator for company and comfort. Then The Most Creator created Huwa from Adam's rib, his mate kind as female. The most gracious Creator said: "O Adam, Iblis is an open enemy to thee and to thy wife; so let him not drive you both out of the garden so that thou art unhappy. Surely, it is granted to thee therein that thou art not hungry, nor naked, and that thou art not thirsty therein, nor exposed to the sun's heat." the most gracious Creator Commanded Adam: "O Adam, dwell thou and thy wife in the garden, so eat from whence you desire, but go not near this tree, lest you become of the unjust." But Adam forgot the devil made an evil suggestion to them that he might make manifest to them that which had been hidden from them of their shame. Iblis said: "Your Lord has forbidden you this tree, lest you become angels or become of the immortals. O Adam, shall I lead thee to the tree of immortality and a kingdom which decays not?" And he swore to them both: "Surely, I am a sincere adviser to you." The devil made an evil suggestion to him; so they both ate of it, then their private parts became manifest to them, and they began to cover themselves with the leaves of the garden. And Adam disobeyed his Lord and was disappointed. Thus, Iblis (The devil) caused them to fall by deceit. The devil made him slip from it and caused them to depart from the state in which they were. And the most gracious Creator called to them: "Did not I forbid you that tree, and say to you that the devil is surely your open enemy?" They said: "O Most Gracious Creator, we have wronged ourselves; and if Thou forgive us not, and have not mercy on us, we shall certainly be the losers." the most gracious Creator said: "Go forth; some of you are the enemies of others. And there is for you in the earth an abode and a provision for a time, therein shall you live, and therein shall you die, and therefrom shall you be raised. Surely, there will surely come to you guidance from Me; then whoever follows The My guidance, such persons will not go astray nor be unhappy, no fear shall come upon them nor shall they grieve. And as to those who disbelieve in and reject the My messages, they are the companions of the Fire; in it they will abide." Then the most gracious Creator chose Adam, so He turned to him and guided him. Adam received revelation words from the most gracious Creator and the most gracious Creator turned to him mercifully. Surely, the most gracious Creator is Oft-returning to Mercy, the most Merciful. The most gracious Creator indeed created mankind, in stages, four distinctive methods: the first method was the creation of Adam without a male nor female, the second method is the creation of female from male, the third method is the creation of male without a male but female, and forth method is the creation of male and female from both parents. The most gracious Creator fashioned man and woman, in their respective shapes, each with their own aspiration, so their the most gracious Creator wishes, and there is not a soul but over it is a keeper, and let man consider of what he is created, a soul manlike that was created of clay then water pouring forth, coming from between back and the ribs. "And certainly man was created of an extract clay, Then the most gracious Creator make him a small life-germ in a firm resting-place, Then the most gracious Creator make the life-germ a clot, then the most gracious Creator make the clot a lump of flesh, then the most gracious Creator make in the lump of flesh, bones, then the most gracious Creator clothe the bones with flesh, then the most gracious Creator cause it to grow into another creation. So blessed be the most gracious Creator, the Best of creators! Then after that, you certainly die. Then on the day of Resurrection, you will surely be raised up". The most gracious Creator certainly gave a commandment to Adam before, but he forgot; the most gracious Creator certainly found in him no resolve to deliberately and mentally disobedience to his Most Gracious Creator. "O People, keep your duty to your Most Gracious Creator, Who created you from a single being of a soul kind as male and created its mate kind as female, and spread from these two, many men and women."

So, the life on earth with truth, the story of the two sons of Adam, Abillah (Abel) and Kabillah (Cain) when they offered an offering, but it was accepted from Abillah and was not accepted from Kabillah. So, Kabillah said: "I will certainly kill you Abillah." Abillah said: "the most gracious Creator accepts only from the dutiful. If thou stretch your hand against me to kill me, I shall not stretch out my hand against thee to kill you. Surely, I fear the most gracious Creator, the Lord of the worlds, I would rather that thou should bear the sin against me and thine own sin, thus thou wouldst be of the companions of the Fire, and that is the recompense of the unjust." At length, Kabillah's his mind made it easy to kill his own brother, so he killed Abillah; so Kabillah became one of the losers. Then the most gracious Creator sent a crow scratching the ground to show him how to cover the dead body of his brother. He said: "Woe is I! Am I not able to be as this crow and cover the dead body of my brother? So he became of those who regret."

There is no doubt human being was created by the most gracious Creator, for everything was created independently, no human come from Animal, and human did not form by a chance except by decree of a stated term for men and women in the presence of the most gracious Creator without a doubt. So, the most gracious Creator honored the sons of Adam; provided for them with social amenities, transportation on the land and sea; giving them sustenance things good and pure; and the most gracious Creator bestowed on mankind special favors, above

The Heavenly Message

a great part of the most gracious Creator of all the worlds.

Chapter Two

The story of Prophet Sheth (Seth)

The Heavenly Message

Chapter Two
The story of Prophet Sheth (Seth)

Seth was the third son of Adam, was born when he was 130 years old, he was a gift given by the most gracious Creator after Abel passed away. Seth was very obedient and close to his father, Adam, he used to remind his brothers and nephews about the most gracious Creator. After Adam passed away, he ruled the Children of Adam with justice, in accordance with the most gracious Creator's Laws, and he brought unity between the people around him. On the other hand, Cain and the descendants of Cain grew more than the people around Seth did. Cain decided to leave with his family to the valleys and to the flat land, somewhere further away. Later on, Seth was given an instruction from the most gracious Creator not to mix with the people that had gone to the valleys. Cain's people had their own characteristics so it was prohibited to mix with them. The people obeyed and did not mix, and they were saved to a great degree. Satan had a plan, he wanted to show men how to commit sins, so, he decided to tackle the men. And Satan knew that the people who were with Seth may recognize him because they knew Satan. Then he made himself turn into a form of a young handsome man and went to those who were with Cain and pretended to be those who were banished from Seth. He went to a blacksmith and asked for an employment. So the people looked at him and thought that he seemed to be a good man, so they accepted him. Satan designed a flute with metal. He introduced the flute to everyone, and slowly started making sounds that people had never heard before. Then, Satan created a little drum and beat it, and everyone would come and say, "What is that sound?" They came around him and watched, and then Satan created another instrument, this time a bugle, he blew into it and created a new sound. The people said: "This person is intelligent; he has advanced much more than us." The people were so engaged in it that they slowly started to forget about the most gracious Creator and the commands of Him. They started to dance to the instruments Satan made and partied. Some of the youths of the people of Seth were visited by Satan, he went to them and created doubts in their minds. They thought, 'Why is it prohibited to mix with the people of Cain? What is so bad about them?' It was answered for them because they knew about the crime that Cain committed to his brother Abel. And his character was so different from them. So they moved to the valleys, and the people of Seth were not allowed to mix with them. But the youths were not satisfied with the answer, some of them went to the valleys to look at what is happening. They did not intend to engage in evil, but it attracted them, so the youths also started partying. When it was over, they went back and told the other youths what they were missing out on. So some of the people of Seth used to go quietly to the other side and engage in sin. When Seth heard about this, he went to the people and kept on reminding them what is right and wrong and reminded them of the most gracious Creator. When the time of death came to Seth, he entrusted his most noble son Enos (Anush) to carry on his mission after him. He, in turn, was succeeded by his son Mahlabeel (Mihail); he was the first one to cut down trees to build cities and large forts, which build the cities of Babylonia. When he passed away, his duties were taken over by his son Yard, who after on his death, hands down them to his son Idris (Enoch).

Chapter Three

The story of Prophet Idrisu, Idrisa or Idris (Enoch)

The Heavenly Message

Chapter Three
The story of Prophet Idrisu, Idrisa or Idris (Enoch)

Enoch was born and raised in Babylon following the teachings and religion of Prophet Adam and his son, Seth. When Adam was 840 years old, Idris was born. Enoch was the 5th generation of Prophet Adam. He called the people back to his forefather's religion, but only a few listened to him, while the majority turned away. Prophet Enoch and his followers left Babylon for Egypt. There he carried on his mission, calling people to what is just and fair, teaching them certain prayers, instructing them to fast on certain days and to give a portion of their wealth to the poor. He was the 1st to invent the basic form of writing. Some of his wise sayings are:

"Happy is he who looks at his own deeds and appoints them as pleaders to his Lord, the most gracious Creator."

"None can show better gratitude for the most gracious Creator's favors than he who shares them with others."

"Do not envy people for what they have, as they will only enjoy it for a short while."
"He who indulges in excess will not benefit from it."
"The real joy of life is to have wisdom."

Idris was a truthful man, a prophet, and the most gracious Creator raised him to an elevated state. He used to ponder and reflect and was calm and collected, and very patient. He used to teach about the magnanimity of the most gracious Creator and the excellence of Islam. Idris was told by the most gracious Creator: "O Idris, from those who have followed you, anyone, who does good deeds, at the end of the day, you will have all those good deeds doubled for yourself. Idris was very happy, and he knew that his death was approaching, and had a friend from the angels, so he spoke with his friend: "You know the most gracious Creator has promised me this reward, and I would like to build up a lot of rewards before I go, so why don't we speak to the Angel of Death and see what he has to say to say, to just try and see if you can seek permission to prolong a little bit." So the Angel said: "That is a matter decreed by the most gracious Creator, however, there is no harm in trying. Come, you ride on my wing and let's go." So Idris rode on his wing and he was taken up to the heavens, they crossed the first heaven, the second heaven, the third heaven, and when they entered the fourth heaven, the most gracious Creator instructed the Angel of Death to take the soul of Idris on the fourth heaven. When the Angel of Death saw Idris there, Idris said: "I would like to extend my life." The Angel of Death said: "the most gracious Creator has already instructed me to take your soul." Idris said: "If that is the case, it is fine." So Idris' soul was taken while he was in the fourth heaven.

Chapter Four

The story of Prophet Nuh (Noah)

The Heavenly Message

Chapter Four
The story of Prophet Nuh (Noah)

Noah was raised among his people; in a nation where violence and evildoers spread everywhere, they were worshipping other gods as deities besides the living and only, the most gracious Creator, Lord of all the worlds. They were living evil lives, Noah was known among them to be different for his faith in the unseen Glory, the Creator of everything, the Lord, the cherisher, the source of everything in the heavens and the earth. Noah was known to be a good man among them in his entire life. He loved his people and lived obedient life in serving the most gracious Creator of the entire worlds. The people of Noah rejected the messengers. The most gracious Creator called Noah to his people, and Noah said to them: "Will you not guard against evil?" And so, he remained among them in his ministry for a for nine hundred and fifty years, calling his people to worship none but the most gracious Creator of the heavens and the earth, that you have no other savior but the most gracious Creator, the Owner and the Maker of everything, and said: "O my people serve the most gracious Creator who created you, that you have no god other than your Creator. Indeed I fear for you the chastisement of a grievous day." Noah called them day and night, in public and private but it only made them thrust their fingers in their ears and cover their faces. Surely, Noah said: "I am a faithful messenger to you, so keep your duty to the most gracious Creator and obey me. And I ask of you no reward for it: my reward is only with the most gracious Creator, Lord of the worlds. So keep your duty to Him and obey me." They said: "Shall we believe in thee and the poorest follow thee?" He said: "And what knowledge has I of what they did? Their reckoning is only with my Most Gracious Creator if you but perceive. And I am not going to drive away the believers; I am only a plain warner." They said: "If you desist not, O Noah, thou wilt certainly be stoned to death." Noah said to his people, "Ask forgiveness of your Most Gracious Creator; surely He is ever Forgiving: the most gracious Creator will send down rain upon you pouring in abundance, and help you with wealth and sons, and make for you gardens, and make for you rivers. What is the matter with you that you hope not for greatness from the most gracious Creator who created you? And indeed, He has created you by various stages. See you not how He has created the seven heavens alike, and made the moon therein a light, and made the sun a lamp? And the most gracious Creator has caused you to grow out of the earth as a growth, then He returns you to it, then will He bring you forth a (new) bringing forth. And the most gracious Creator has made the earth a wide expanse for you that you may go along therein in spacious paths." The chiefs of his people said: "Surely we see thee in clear error." Noah said: "O my people, there is no error in me, but I am a messenger from the most gracious Creator of the worlds. "O my people, if my staying with you and my reminding you by the messages of the most gracious Creator is hard on you, except I rely on the most gracious Creator of the entire worlds, and so, decide upon your course of action and gather your associates. Then let not your course of action be dubious to you, so have it executed against me and give me no respite. I ask for no reward from you. My reward is only with my Most Gracious Creator and I am commanded to be of those who submit. But if you turn back my deliver to you the messages of my the most gracious Creator, and I offer you good advice, and I know from the most gracious Creator what you know not. Do you wonder that a reminder has come to you from your Most Gracious Creator through a man from among you, that he may warn you and that you may guard against evil, and that mercy may be shown to you?" But they rejected him and called him a liar. He said: "O my people, surely I am a plain warner to you: That you should serve the most gracious Creator, He is the Creator who created you fashioned you, and keep your duty to Him and obey me as a messenger from your Creator, then He will forgive you some of your sins and grant you respite to an appointed term. Surely the term of the most gracious Creator when it comes, is not postponed if you know! And certainly, I am a plain warner to you, to serve none but the most gracious Creator. Verily I fear for you the chastisement of a painful day." But the chiefs of his people who disbelieved said: "We see thee not but a mortal like us, and we see not that any follow thee but the poorest of us at first thought. Nor do we see in you any superiority over us; nay, we deem you liars." He said: "O my people see you if I have with me clear proof from my Most Gracious Creator, and He has granted me mercy from Himself and it have been made obscure to you. Can we compel you to accept it while you are averse to it? And O my people, I ask you not for wealth in return for it. My reward is only with the most gracious Creator, and I am not going to drive away those who believe. Surely, they will meet their Most Gracious Creator, but I see you are people ignorant. O my people, who will help me against the most gracious Creator, if I drive them away? Will you not then mind? And I say not to you that I have the treasures of Him; and I know not the unseen; nor do I say that I am an angel. Nor do I say about those whom your eyes scorn that the most gracious Creator will not grant them any good? He knows best what is in their souls and for then indeed I should be of the wrongdoers." They said: "O Noah, indeed thou hast disputed with us and prolonged dispute with us, so bring upon us that which thou threaten us with if thou art truthful." Noah said: "Only the most gracious Creator will bring it on you, if He pleases, and you will not escape. And my advice will not profit you, if I intend to give you good advice, if He intends to destroy you. The most gracious Creator is your Lord; and to Him you will be brought back." They said: "O Noah you have forged it." Noah said: "O'my people if I have forged it, on me are my guilt; and I am free of that which you are guilty." And it was revealed to Noah: "None of thy people will believe except those who have already believed, so grieve not at what they do." The chiefs of those who disbelieved from among his people said: "He is nothing but a mortal like yourselves, who desires to have superiority over you. And if the most gracious Creator had pleased, He could have sent down angels that we have not heard of this among our fathers of old. He is only a madman, so bear with him for a time." Then they said: "Forsake not your gods; nor forsake Wadd, nor Suwa', nor Yagthuth and Ya'uq and Nasr." Nuh said, "My Most Gracious Creator, my people called me a liar. So judge between them and me openly, and deliver the believers who are with me. My the most gracious Creator, help me against their calling me a liar. My the most gracious Creator, surely they disobey me and follow him whose wealth and children have increased him in naught but loss. And they have planned a mighty plan. And they say: Forsake not your gods; nor forsake Wadd, nor Suwa', nor Yagthuth and Ya'uq and Nasr. And indeed, they have led many astray. And increase Thou the wrongdoers in naught but perdition, so, they find no helpers besides the most gracious Creator." And Noah said: "My Most Gracious Creator, leave not of the disbelievers any dweller on the land. For if Thou leave them, they will lead astray Thy servants, and will not beget any but immoral, ungrateful ones. I am overcome, so do Thou help." So, the most gracious Creator revealed to Noah, "Make the ark under Our eyes and Our revelation, and speak not to Me on behalf of those who are unjust. Surely they will be drowned." So, Noah began to make the ark. And whenever the chiefs of his people passed by him, they laughed at him. He said: "If you laugh at us, surely we, too, laugh at you as you laugh at us. So you shall know who it is on whom will fall a chastisement which will disgrace him, and on whom a lasting chastisement will fall." At length when the most gracious Creator command came and water gushed forth from the valley, He said to Noah: "Carry in it two of all things, a pair, and thine own family, except those against whom the word has already gone forth and those who believe." And they believed not with him but a few. And he said: "Embark in it, in the name of the most gracious Creator be its sailing and its anchoring. Surely He is Forgiving, Merciful." Then Most Gracious

The Heavenly Message

Creator opened the gates of heaven with water pouring down, and made water flow forth in springs, so the water gathered according to a measure ordained. And the most gracious Creator stood Noah on that which was made of planks and nails, floating on, before the most gracious Creator's eyes a reward for him who was denied. And certainly, the most gracious Creator lifted it as a sign, but is there any who will mind? And it moved on with them on the waves like mountains. And Noah called out to his son, and he was aloof: "O my son, embark with us and be not with the disbelievers." He said: "I will betake myself for refuge to a mountain that will save me from the water." He said: "There is none safe today from the most gracious Creator's command, but he on whom He has mercy." And a wave intervened between them, so he was among the drowned. And Noah cried to his Lord and said: "My Lord, surely my son is of my family, and thy promise is true, and Thou art the Justest of the judges." the most gracious Creator said: "O Noah, his not of your family; he is an embodiment of unrighteous conduct. So, ask not of Me that which thou hast no knowledge, I admonished thee lest thou be of the ignorant, and speak not to Me in respect of those who are unjust; surely they will be drowned." "Then when thou art firmly seated, thou and those with thee, in the ark, say: Praise be to the most gracious Creator, Who delivered us from the unjust people! And say: My Most Gracious Creator, cause me to land a blessed landing and Thou art the Best of those who bring to land." Noah said: "My Most Gracious Creator, I seek refuge in Thee from asking of Thee that of which I have no knowledge. And unless thou forgive me and have mercy on me, I shall be of a loser." It was said: "O Noah, descend with peace from Us and blessing on thee and on nations springing from those with thee." Noah said: "O my Most Gracious Creator, forgive me and my parents and him who enters my house believing, and the believing men and the believing women. And increase not the wrong-doers in aught but destruction!" And the most gracious Creator commanded the earth: "O' earth swallow thy water, O' Cloud, clear away." And water was made to abate, and the affair was decided, and the ark rested on the mount of Judi. And it was said: "Away with the unrighteous people!" And so the most gracious Creator answered Noah and delivered him and his people from the great calamity. And the most gracious Creator helped him against the people who rejected His messages. Surely, they were an evil people, they were a blind people! Because of their wrongs they were drowned, then made to enter Fire. Except those with him in the ark, and the most gracious Creator made them rulers and drowned those who rejected His messages. See, then, what was the end of those who were warned. Surely, there is a sign in this, yet most of them believe not. And surely, thy Lord, Most Gracious Creator is the Mighty, the Merciful. The most gracious Creator is ever trying people. And Noah certainly called upon the most gracious Creator, and excellent Answer of prayers is He! And the most gracious Creator delivered him and his people from the great distress; And made his offspring the survivors, and left for him praise among the later generations, Peace be to Noah among the nations! Thus indeed, does the most gracious Creator reward the doers of good? Surely, he was of His believing servants. And surely of his party was a nation of Ibrahim. Then, after Noah, Most Gracious Creator sent messengers to their people. They came to them with clear arguments, but they would not believe what they had rejected before. Thus, does Most Gracious Creator seal the hearts of those who exceed the limits?

Chapter Five

The story of Prophet Hud (Hebron)

The Heavenly Message

Chapter Five
The story of Prophet Hud (Hebron)

To Ad (Adawa people) their brother Hud was sent to them, he said: "O my people, Serve the most gracious Creator; you have no other deity other than Him. Will you not then guard against evil?" The chiefs of those who disbelieved from among his people said: "Certainly we see thee in folly, and we certainly think thee to be of the liars and fabricators." He said: "O my people, there is no folly in me, but I am a messenger of the most gracious Creator of the worlds. I deliver to you the messages of Him and I am a faithful adviser to you. O, my people, I ask of you no reward for it. My reward is only with Him Who created me. Do you not then understand? And O my people, ask forgiveness of your Most Gracious Creator, then turn to Him, He will send on you clouds pouring down abundance of rain and add strength to your strength, and turn not back, guilty." They said: "O Hud, thou hast brought us no clear argument, and we are not going to desert our gods for thy word, and we are not believers in thee. We say naught but that some of our gods have smitten thee with evil." He said: "Surely I call Most Gracious Creator to witness, and bear witness, and do you, too, bear witness that I am innocent of what you associate besides Him. So scheme against me altogether, then give me no respite. Surely, I put my trust in the most gracious Creator, my Lord, and your Lord. There is no living creature but He grasps by the forelock. Surely, my Most Gracious Creator is on the right path. But if you turn away, then indeed I have delivered to you that with which I am sent to you. And my Most Gracious Creator will bring another people in your place, and you cannot do Him any harm. Surely, my Most Gracious Creator is the Preserver of all things. Do you not wonder that a reminder has come to you from your Most Gracious Creator through a man from among you that he may warn you? And remember when He made you successors after Noah's people and increased you in the excellence of make. So remember the bounties of the most gracious Creator, that you may be successful." They said: "Hast thou come to us that we may serve alone, and give up that which our fathers used to serve? Then bring us what thou threaten us with if thou art of the truthful." Hud said: "Indeed uncleanness and wrath from your Most Gracious Creator have lighted upon you. Do you dispute with me about names which you and your fathers have named? the most gracious Creator has not sent any authority for them. Wait, then; I too with you am of those who wait. Do you build on every height a monument? You only sport. And you make fortresses that you may abide. And when you seize you seize as tyrants. And keep your duty to the most gracious Creator and obey me. And keep your duty to Him Who aids you with that which you know. The most gracious Creator aids you with cattle and children and gardens and fountains. Surely I fear for you the chastisement of a grievous day." They said: "It is the same to us whether thou admonish, or art not one of the admonishers, this is naught but a fabrication of the ancients, and we will not be chastised." So they rejected him, and they were unjustly proud in the land and said: "Who is mightier than we in power?" See they not that it is the most gracious Creator, Who created them, is mightier than they in power are? And they denied His messages. And when Hud warned his people in the sandy plains and reminded them that warners indeed came before him with the same message saying: "Serve none but the most gracious Creator. Surely the messengers recited to them to be fearful of the chastisement of a grievous day." Their people said: "Hast the messengers come to them to turn them away from their gods?" So, they hasten their messengers to bring upon them that with which they referred to as wrath from the most gracious Creator of all the worlds. Hud said: "I will deliver to you that wherewith I am sent, but I see you are an ignorant people." And the chiefs of his people who disbelieved and called the meeting of the hereafter a lie, and whom the most gracious Creator had given plenty to enjoy in this world's life, said: "This is only a mortal like you, eating of that whereof you eat and drinking of what you drink. And if you obey a mortal like yourselves, then surely you are losers. Does he promise you that, when you are dead and become dust and bones, you will then be brought forth? Far, very far, is that which you are promised: There is naught but our life in this world: we die and we live and we shall not be raised again, he is naught but a man who has forged a lie against the most gracious Creator, and we are not going to believe in him." Hud said: "My Most Gracious Creator, help me against their calling me a liar." the most gracious Creator said: "In a little while they will certainly be repenting." So when they saw it a cloud advancing towards their valleys, they said: "This is a cloud bringing us rain." Nay, it is that which you sought to hasten, a wind wherein is a painful chastisement, destroying everything by the command of his Most Gracious Creator. So at dawn naught could be seen except their dwellings. So the most gracious Creator sent on them a furious wind in unlucky days that the most gracious Creator might make them taste the chastisement of abasement in this world's life. And the chastisement of the Hereafter is truly more abasing, and they will not be helped. The most gracious Creator destroyed the Ad people, thus does He reward the guilty people. And certainly the most gracious Creator had given them power in matters in which He had not empowered you, and the most gracious Creator had given them ears and eyes and hearts, but neither their ears, nor their eyes, nor their hearts availed them aught and they denied the messages of Most Gracious Creator, and that which they mocked at encompassed them. Ad denied, so how terrible was His chastisement and My warning! Surely, He sent on them a furious wind in a day of bitter ill-luck, tearing men away as if they were trunks of palm-trees torn up, how terrible was then His chastisement and His warning! And when He sent upon them a destructive wind, it spared naught that it came against, but it made it like ashes. And such were Ad. They denied the messages of their Most Gracious Creator, and disobeyed His messengers. So the punishment overtook them in justice, and He made them as rubbish; so away with the unjust people! Surely, Ad disbelieved in their Most Gracious Creator, now surely away with Ad, the people of Hud! And when the most gracious Creator's commandment came to pass, the most gracious Creator delivered Hud and those with him with mercy from Him; and He delivered them from a hard chastisement, and He cut off the roots of those who rejected His messages and were not believers, Surely there is a sign in this; yet most of them believe not. And surely, thy Most Gracious Creator is the Mighty, the Merciful.

Chapter Six

The story of Prophet Salih (Methuselah)

The Heavenly Message

Chapter Six
The story of Prophet Salih (Methuselah)

Certainly, the most gracious Creator sent to Thamud their brother Salih, saying: "Serve the most gracious Creator, You have no deity other than Him. Clear proof has indeed come to you from your Most Gracious Creator. He has brought you forth from the earth and made you dwell in it, and you hew houses in the mountains, insecurity, so ask forgiveness of the most gracious Creator, and then turn to Him. Surely He is High, Answering." They said: "O Salih, thou wast among us a center of our hopes before this. Dost thou forbid us to worship what our fathers worshipped? And surely we are in grave doubt about that which thou callest us." He said: "O my people see you if I have clear proof from my Most Gracious Creator and He has granted me mercy from Himself, and who will then help me against the most gracious Creator if I disobey Him? So you would add to me naught but perdition." He said: "O my people, why do you hasten on the evil before the good? Why do you not ask forgiveness of the most gracious Creator so that you may have mercy?" They said: "We augur evil of thee and those with thee." He said: "Your evil augury is with the most gracious Creator; nay, you are a people who are tried." So they said: "What! This is a single mortal from among us! Shall we follow him? We shall then be in a big error and distress. Has the reminder been sent to him from among us? Nay, he is an insolent liar!" Salih said to them: "Will you not guard against evil? Surely, I am a faithful messenger to you. So keep your duty to the most gracious Creator and obey me. And I ask of you no reward for it; my reward is only with the most gracious Creator of all the worlds. Will you be left secure in what is here, in gardens and fountains, and corn-fields and palm-trees having fine flower-spikes? And you hew houses out of the mountains exultingly. And obey not the bidding of the extravagant, which make mischief in the land and act not aright." They said: "Thou art only a deluded person. Thou art naught but a mortal like ourselves, so bring us a sign if thou art truthful." Then the most

The Heavenly Message

gracious Creator revealed to Salih, "I Am going to send a she-camel as a trial for them; so watch them and have patience. And inform them that the water is shared between them; every share of the water shall be attended, and this is the most gracious Creator's she-camel, a sign for you so leave her alone to pasture in the most gracious Creator's earth, and do her no harm, lest painful chastisement overtake you. And remember when He made you successors after Ad and settled you in the land, you make mansions on its plains and hew out houses in the mountains. So remember His bounties and act not corruptly in the land, making mischief." Suddenly, the mountains split and a big camel came out, then some of the people started following Salih. And then lo! They became two parties contending. When the believers started to increase, the arrogant chiefs of his people said to those who were weak, to those who believed from among them: "Do you know for certain that Salih is one sent by his Most Gracious Creator?" They said: "Surely we are believers in that wherewith he has been sent." Those who were haughty said: "Surely we are disbelievers in which you believe, surely Salih is a magician." Salih said: "O my people, the camel has come, so do no harm to her; surely a grave punishment will overtake you if you harm the camel. It will drink from the spring one day, and all your cattle, keep them on one side, the camel will drink whatever it can from morning to evening and the next day, it will go out to graze when your cattle can drink, so we are sharing the days. The water will be split between this camel and the rest of the cattle one day this camel and the next day the rest of them." So they were happy and unhappy. They were happy because they had seen the sign, a living miracle; because it was there every day living in their midst, every day a few people were accepting Salih. The community split, some who believed and some who disbelieved. The disbelievers grew tired of the she-camel, every time the she-camel was walking, their cattle ran away. So, the disbelievers among them revolted against their Most Gracious Creator's commandment and called their nine companions, so they took swords and hamstrung the she-camel: "They were proud, and said: "O Salih, bring us that with which thou hast threaten us if thou art of the messengers." Salih said: "Enjoy yourselves in your houses for three days. That is a promise not to be belied." The nine persons who made mischief in the land and did not act aright said: "Swear one to another by our gods that we shall attack him and his family by night, then we shall say to his heir: We witnessed not the destruction of his family, and we are surely truthful. And they planned a plan, and the most gracious Creator Planned a Plan, while they perceived not." Thamud rejected the warning. So the earthquake seized them and leveled them with the ground; and He fears not its consequence. And the cry overtook those who did wrong, so they were motionless bodies in their abodes, as though they had never dwelt therein. So those are their houses fallen down because they were iniquitous. So when the most gracious Creator's commandment came to pass, He saved Salih and those who believed with him

by mercy from Him from the disgrace of that day. Surely, thy Most Gracious Creator is the Strong, Mighty and the Merciful. So Salih turned away from them and said: "O my people, I delivered to you the message of my Most Gracious Creator and gave you good advice, but you love not the good advisers." Surely, the most gracious Creator sent upon them a single cry, so they were like the dry fragments of trees, which the maker of an enclosure collects. Thus Thamud disbelieved in their the most gracious Creator, so away with Thamud!

Chapter Seven

The story of Prophet Ibrahim (Abraham)

The Heavenly Message

Chapter Seven
The story of Prophet Ibrahim (Abraham)

Verily, Ibrahim was called by his Most Gracious Creator, Ibrahim answered to Him, and he came to Him with a secure heart. Surely, he was a truthful man, a prophet. When he said to his father, Azar: "O my father, do you worship that with which you hew out? And the most gracious Creator has created you and what you make. Surely, I see thee and thy people in manifest error. Takest thou idols for gods? Why worshippest thou that which hear not, nor sees, nor can avail thee aught?" Azar said: "We found our fathers worshipping them." Ibrahim said: "O my father, to me indeed Knowledge has come to me which has not come to thee, these are not gods, O my father, serve not the devil. So follow me I will guide thee on a right path. Surely the devil is disobedient to the Most Gracious and Beneficent Creator." Azar said: "Dislikest thou my gods, O Ibrahim?" And Ibrahim said: "O my father, surely I fear lest a punishment from the Most Gracious

Beneficent Creator should afflict thee so that thou become a friend of the devil." Azar said: "O Ibrahim, if thou desist not, I will certainly drive thee away, and leave me for a time." Ibrahim said: "Peace be to thee! I shall pray to my Most Gracious Creator to forgive thee. Surely, He is ever Kind to me. And I withdraw from you and that which you call on besides Him, and I call upon Him. Maybe I shall not remain unblessed in calling upon my Most Gracious Creator." So, when he withdrew from his father and that which he worshipped besides the most gracious Creator. Ibrahim said to his father and his people: "What is it that you worship? Lie gods besides the most gracious Creator do you desire?" They said: "We worship idols, so we shall remain devoted to them." He said: "Do they hear you when you call on them, or do they benefit or harm you?" They said: "Nay, we found our fathers doing so. What is then your idea of the most gracious Creator of the worlds? Then he glanced a glance at the stars, and said: "Surely I am sick of your deities." "Do you not see what you worship, you and your ancient sires? Surely they are an enemy to me, but not so, the most gracious Creator of the worlds, Who created me, then He shows me the way, And Who gives me to eat and to drink, And when I am sick, He heals me, And Who will cause me to die, then give me life, And Who, I hope, will forgive me my mistakes on the day of Judgment." "My Most Gracious Creator, grant me wisdom, and join me with the righteous, And ordain for me a goodly mention in later generations, And make me of the heirs of the Garden of bliss, And forgive my father, surely he is of the erring ones, and disgrace me not on the day when they are raised. The day when wealth will not avail, nor sons, except him who comes to You with a sound heart. The day when wealth will not avail, nor sons, except him who comes to You with a sound heart. And the Garden is brought near for the dutiful, and hell is made manifest to the deviators, and it is said to them: Where are those that you worshipped besides the most gracious Creator? Can they help you or help themselves? So they are hurled into it, them and the deviators, and the hosts of the devil, all. They will say, while they quarrel therein: By You the most gracious Creator! We were certainly in manifest error when we made you equal with You, Lord of the worlds. And none but the guilty led us astray. So we have no intercessors, nor a true friend. Now if we could but once return, we would be believers. Surely there is a sign in this; and surely thy Most Gracious Creator is the Mighty, the Merciful." They said: "Hast thou brought us the truth or art thou of the jesters?" He said: "Nay, your Most Gracious Creator is the Creator of the heavens and the earth; and I am of those who bear witness to this, surely I am sick of your deities." So they turned their backs on him, going away to their festival. Then Ibrahim turned to their gods and said: "Do you not eat? What is the matter with you that you speak not?" So he turned upon them, smiting with the right hand. So he broke them into pieces, except the chief of them that haply they might return to it. Then they came to him hastening. They said: "Who has done this to our gods? Surely he is of the unjust." One group said: "We heard a youth, who is called

Ibrahim, speak of them." They said: "Then bring him before the people's eyes, perhaps they may bear witness." They said: "Hast thou done this to our gods, O Ibrahim?" Ibrahim said: "Surely someone has done it. The chief of them is this; so ask it if it can speak." Then they turned to themselves and said: "Surely we are wrongdoers." Then they were made to hang down their heads: "Thou knowest indeed that they speak not." He said: "Serve you then besides the most gracious Creator what does you no good, nor harms you? Fie, upon you and on what you serve besides Him! Have you no sense? Serve the most gracious Creator and keep your duty to Him. That is better for you, if you did but know. You only worship idols besides Him and you invent a lie. Surely, they are whom you serve besides the most gracious Creator control no sustenance for you; so seek sustenance from Him and serve Him. To Him you will be brought back. And if you reject, nations before you did indeed reject the Truth. And the duty of the Messenger is only to deliver the message plainly. See you not how the most gracious

Creator originates the creation then reproduces it? Surely, that is easy to Him. Travel in the earth and see how He makes the first creation then creates the latter creation. Surely, the most gracious Creator is Possessor of power over all things. He chastises whom He pleases and has mercy on which He pleases, and to Him you will be turned back. And you cannot escape in the earth or in the heaven, and you have no protector or helper besides Him. And those who disbelieve in the messages of the most gracious Creator and the meeting of with Him, they despair of His mercy, and for them is a painful chastisement." But they were stubborn, and they will not believe. They said: "Build for Abraham a building, and then cast him into the flaming fire. Burn him, and help your gods, if you are going to do anything." But the most gracious Creator delivered Abraham from the fire, and He brought them low. The most gracious Creator said: "O fire, be coolness and peace for Ibrahim." And they intended a plan against him, but the most gracious Creator made them the greater losers. And when the

Truth came to them, they said: "This is enchantment, and surely we are disbelievers in it." Surely therein are signs for a people who believe. And he said: "You have only taken idols besides the most gracious Creator by way of friendship between you in this world's life, then on the day of Resurrection some of you will deny others, and some of you will curse others; and your abode is the Fire, and you will have no helpers I am clear of what you worship, Except the most gracious Creator, Who created me, and surely He will guide me. My Most Gracious Creator, grant me a doer of good deeds." So Lot, Ibrahim's nephew, and Sarah believed in him. And he said: "I am fleeing to my Most Gracious Creator. Surely He is the Mighty, the Wise." And when Abraham said, "My Most Gracious Creator, show me how Thou givest life to the dead." the most gracious Creator said: "Dost thou not believe?" Ibrahim said: "Yes, but that my heart may be at ease." He said: "Then take four birds, then tame them to incline to thee, and then place on every mountain a part of them, then call them, they will come

The Heavenly Message

to thee flying; and know that I Am Mighty, Wise." King Namrud heard about Ibrahim when he was safe in the fire and called Ibrahim. Namrud was a man whom the most gracious Creator has given a kingdom but he disputed with Ibrahim about Him, because the most gracious Creator had made him a king and given him kingdom? And people of that town used to worship Namrud. Namrud said: "Who do you worship?" Ibrahim said, "I worship the most gracious Creator, Who gives life and causes to die." Namrud said: "I give life and cause death. Then he took the life of one prisoner and freed another. Ibrahim said: "Surely the most gracious Creator causes the sun to rise from the East, so do thou make it rise from the West." Thus, Namrud who disbelieved was confounded. And the most gracious Creator does not guide the unjust people. Namrud realized that Ibrahim is backed by a Divine power and that a human is unable to destroy him, Namrud released Ibrahim out of fear of becoming disgraced. He ordered, however, that Ibrahim would be expelled from the city lest the people might follow him and convert to his religion. Ibrahim, who was unhappy with Namrud and his followers, and their land, he prepared with his family to depart. So, the most gracious Creator showed him to go up north the Holy Lands, the land of Sham. As Ibrahim, Sarah and Lut were going there; they stopped at a certain place called Haran. Ibrahim said: "Let me stop here and call these people towards the most gracious Creator because only two people have accepted this message." When he got there, the people were worshipping stars. As he was sitting with them when the night overshadowed him, he saw a star. He said: "This is my Most Gracious Creator." So when it set, he said: "I love not the setting ones." Then when he saw the moon rising, he said: "This is my Most Gracious Creator." When it set, he said: "If my the most gracious Creator had not guided me, I should certainly be of the erring people." Then when he saw the sun rising, he said: "This is my Most Gracious Creator. Is this the greatest?" So when it set, he said: "O my people, I am clear of what you set up with the most gracious Creator.

Surely I have turned myself, being upright, entirely to the most gracious Creator, Who originated the heavens and the earth, and I am not of the polytheists." And his people disputed with him. He said: "Do you dispute with me respecting the most gracious Creator and He has guided me indeed? And I fear not in any way those that you set up with Him, unless He pleases. My the most gracious Creator comprehends all things in His knowledge. Will you not then mind? And how should I fear what you set up with Him, while you fear not to set up with the most gracious Creator that for which He has sent down to you no authority? Which then of the two parties is surer of security, if you know? Anyone who believes and mixes not up their faith with iniquity, for them is security and they go aright." Then the people threatened to kill him. So Ibrahim left them. Ibrahim and his family left Haran and went to the closer area of Sham he went into Sham and after some time, there was a drought there. Ibrahim decided: "Let me leave this place with my family. So he instructed Lut to head to a certain area and that area Lut settled in a place known as Sodom." Lut went, and Ibrahim and his wife Sarah headed for Egypt. The king of Egypt was a tyrant and was ruling for many years. The people who were close to the king told him about Sarah who came with Ibrahim. They had a habit: whenever there was a man who was married to someone and they wanted her, they would kill him off and take her away. The king said: "Bring her." As they came to Ibrahim, Ibrahim knew that they had a bad intention. They said: "Who is this woman with you?" Ibrahim said: "She is my sister." They left them and Ibrahim said to Sarah: "They asked who you are and I said that you are my sister. When they ask you who I am, say that I am your brother, we are brother and sister in submission to the most gracious Creator." Then Ibrahim prayed to the most gracious Creator to protect her. When the king asked Sarah: "Who is he?" She said: "He is my brother." Then the king called the women to prepare her in the bedroom to wed the king. Sarah prayed to the most gracious Creator: "O Most Gracious Creator, I have worshipped you and you alone and I

The Heavenly Message

have kept myself clean and pure for my husband, O the most gracious Creator protect me and safeguard me." So when the king reached out to touch her, his hand was suddenly paralyzed, the king said to Sarah: "If you pray to your God to cure me I will release you." She prayed to the most gracious Creator: "O the most gracious Creator, cure him." And the king's hand was cured. Again, the king stretched his hand to touch Sarah, and his hand was paralyzed. Again, the king asked Sarah to call out to her God to cure his hand and he will not touch her. Then it was cured. For the third time the king stretched out his hand to touch Sarah, then his hand was paralyzed. The king asked Sarah to cure his hand and promised to release her. Sarah prayed: "O the most gracious Creator, cure his hand if he is telling the truth." The king's hand was cured. He said to his people: "You have sent me a devil, she is no a human being." Then the king gave her Hagar and said: "You can go." Then Sarah went to Ibrahim and lived as husband and wife. And he had blessings and so much wealth that the people became jealous of him. So Ibrahim left, he went back to Sham after the drought and settled there with Sarah and Hagar. Ibrahim used to pray to the most gracious Creator for offspring, he said: "O the most gracious Creator, grant me offspring who will be pure, and serve your cause, who will surrender to you just like I have." Sarah felt for him, being such a good man always making dua for offspring, Sarah decided to give Hagar to Ibrahim as a wife. So the most gracious Creator then decided to give Ibrahim good news, his first son, Ismael. Ibrahim was 86 years old when Ismael was born. Sarah was tormented by jealousy which saddened and disturbed her. She soon reached the point that she could no longer tolerate seeing Hagar and the child, so she asked her husband to send them to a place so remote that there would be no news of them. Ibrahim, by the command of the most gracious Creator, accepted Sara's request. He took Hagar and Ismael with him and began journeying until, under the guidance of the most gracious Creator, they entered the land which is known later as Mecca. Ibrahim gave them food which would last them a few days, and started walking away. Hagar ran after him, she said: "Where are you going?" Ibrahim did not answer. "Ibrahim!" she said "Where are you going, leaving us alone in this valley?" Still he did not answer. She said: "Ibrahim, has the most gracious Creator commanded you to do this?" Then Ibrahim slowed his steps, he said: "Yes." She said, "Then we will not be lost, since the most gracious Creator is the One who has commanded you will certainly be with us." "Then be in the Care of the most gracious Creator." he cried. He turned to Him, and prayed: "Our Most Gracious Creator; I have settled a part of my offspring in a valley unproductive of fruit near Thy Sacred House, our Most Gracious Creator, that they may keep up prayer; so make the hearts of some people yearn towards them with fruits; haply they may be grateful. Our Most Gracious Creator, surely Thou knowest what we hide and what we proclaim. And nothing is hidden from You, either in the earth, or in the heaven. Praise be to You, Who has given me in old age, Ishmael! Surely, You Are the Hearer of prayer. Make me keep up prayer and from my offspring too, and accept my prayer, grant me protection and my parents and the believers on the day when the reckoning comes to pass." When Ibrahim was with Sarah, three messengers of the most gracious Creator came to Abraham as strangers, he honored them as guests, they said to Ibrahim: "Peace!" Ibrahim said: "Peace!" Then he turned aside to his family and he made no delay in bringing a roasted calf and placed it before them. But when he saw that their hands reached not to it, so, he said: "Will you not eat?" It was then that he conceived a mistrusted fear of them. They said: "Fear not, we are messengers of the most gracious Creator coming with news." And his wife was standing by, so she wondered. Then Ibrahim said: "What is your errand, O messengers?" The messengers said: "We are going to destroy the people of Sodom, for its people are iniquitous." Ibrahim said: "Surely in it is Lot." They said: "We know well who is in it; we shall certainly deliver him and his followers. We shall deliver them all, except his wife: We ordained that she shall surely be of those who remain behind with a guilty people that we may send upon them stones of clay, marked from thy Most Gracious Creator for the prodigal." Then Ibrahim began to plead on behalf of his nephew, Lot and his people. Surely, Abraham was forbearing, tender-hearted, oft-returning to Most Gracious Creator. The messengers said: "O Abraham, cease from this. Surely the decree of thy Most Gracious Creator has gone forth and there must come to them a chastisement that cannot be averted." So when fear departed from Abraham and good news came to him, of Isaac a boy possessing knowledge. Then his wife came up listening. Then they delivered their message from the most gracious Creator, gave Sarah good news of Isaac, and beyond Isaac, of Jacob. Sarah said: "O wonder! Shall I bear a son when I am an extremely old woman, a barren old woman and this, my husband an extremely old man? This is a strange thing indeed!" They said: "We give thee good news with truth, so be not thou of the despairing ones." Ibrahim said: "And who despairs of the mercy of his Most Gracious Creator but the erring ones?" They said: Wonderest thou at the most gracious Creator's commandment? Thus says Him. Surely, He is the Wise, the Knowing." And Jacob will be a son of Isaac, and each of them He made a righteous one and a prophet. And He will give them of His mercy, and He granted them a truthful mention of eminence. So, the most gracious Creator blessed Ibrahim. He granted him a second son Isaac and Isaac offspring from Yaqoob was Israel and his descendants as they are well-known the Children of Israel. Some of them are doers of good, but some are clearly unjust to themselves. Yaqoob-Jacob, Israel was of Ibrahim's grandchildren. The mercy of the most gracious Creator and His blessings on you, people of the house! Surely the most gracious Creator is Praised, Glorious! He has ordained prophethood and the Book among his seed. So, He gave Ibrahim a reward in this world, and in the Hereafter, he will surely be among the righteous. And Ibrahim did enjoin on his sons the same faith of a religion.

Chapter Eight

The story of Prophet Ismael (Ishmael)

The Heavenly Message

Chapter Eight
The story of Prophet Ismael (Ishmael)

Hagar and her child Ismael were alone in the waterless and bare desert far from any city or town. But Hagar learned the way of trust in and reliance on the most gracious Creator from Ibrahim, so with faith in Him, she followed the path of patience and tolerance. She lived on the provisions that she had until they were used up and hunger and thirst overcame her. Her milk dried up, leaving her baby hungry and thirsty also. She was sitting between two hills, so she ran to the top of one hill (As-Safa) to try and see if she could find water. But there was nothing as far as she could see, no tree, patch of green, nothing but hot sand. She went to the top of the other hill, (Al-Maw-rah) still nothing but hot sand. The baby began to cry, so she went to soothe him. She settled Ismael down under the gnarled tree, and cried, "What can I do? Are we to die here?" "O the most gracious Creator! Increase my trust in You!" Then she ran up the first hill and the second hill seven times. She prayed to the most gracious Creator for help. Then she heard a voice. She looked around but saw no one. She said: "Who is it? You have made me hear your voice, now show me that you are here to help us, by the Grace of the most gracious Creator!" She turned and there, near the baby, was an angel. He struck the earth, and water spurted up! The angel said, "Don't be afraid, for you are standing on the site of the House of the most gracious Creator, which will be rebuilt by this boy and his father, and the most gracious Creator never neglects His people." Then she made a basin with clay. And she said, in her language, "Zam, Zam (Stop, Stop) we want to take you and drink you!" She sat down, and Ismael and Hagar drank the refreshing water. "All praise to the One, the most gracious Creator, Most Merciful." Soon birds started coming and drinking from the water. The clan of Jur'hum was passing and they noticed some birds in the middle of nowhere, so they decided to send a person to see where the birds are going. The birds went to the Zam-Zam water where

Hagar and Ismael were, so the messenger went back to his people and told them what he saw. They were amazed and knew that this was a miracle. They asked Hagar, "Do you mind if we live here?" She said: "You can come and live here on one condition: that this water belongs to us, not to you. You can drink and benefit from it, but it is our property." So they stayed there and were happy, they loved Ismael and taught him Arabic. As he grew, Ibrahim used to come and go. Once he had a dream. When Ismael became of age to work with his father Ibrahim, Ibrahim said: "O my son, I have seen in a dream that I should sacrifice thee. So consider what thou seest." Ismael said: "O my father, do as thou art commanded if the most gracious Creator please, thou wilt find me patient." So when they both submitted to his instruction. Ibrahim had taken his knife and took Ismael and they were going. While they were going, Satan came to Ibrahim three times trying to divert him from fulfilling the command of the most gracious Creator. Satan said: "This is the pure, perfect heart but what do you think you are doing? This is your only son!" Ibrahim defied Satan and threw a stone three times at Satan. When Ibrahim had put Ismael down upon his forehead, and he was about to cut Ismael, but the knife would not cut! And the most gracious Creator called out to him saying, "O Abraham, thou hast indeed fulfilled the vision. Thus, do We reward the doers of good? Surely, this is a manifest trial. And We ransomed you with a great sacrifice." And the most gracious Creator granted him among the later generations. Peace be upon Ibrahim! Thus, do the most gracious Creator reward the doers of good? Surely, Ibrahim was one of His believing servants, his Lord tried him with certain commands and he fulfilled them. The most gracious Creator said: "Surely I will make thee, Ibrahim a nation, leader of men." Ibrahim said: "And of my offspring?" the most gracious Creator said, "The Holy Covenant does not include the wrongdoers." And He enjoined Abraham and Ishmael to build a House of the most gracious Creator. And when Abraham and Ishmael raised the foundations of the

House, a place of security, a resort for men to take the place of prayer. Saying: "Purify the House of the most gracious Creator for those who visit it, and those who abide therein for devotion and those who bow down, and those who prostrate themselves only to the most gracious Creator." Abraham said: "My the most gracious Creator, make this a secure town and provide its people with fruits, such of them as believe in the most gracious Creator and the Last Day. Accept from us; surely, Thou art the Hearing, the Knowing. Our the most gracious Creator, make us both submissive to Thee, and raise from our offspring, a nation submissive to Thee, and show us our ways of devotion and turn to us mercifully; surely Thou art the Oft-returning to mercy, the Merciful. Raise up in them a Messenger from among them who shall recite to them Thy messages and teach them the Book and the Wisdom, and purify them. Surely Thou art the Mighty, the Wise." My most gracious Creator, make this city secure, and save my sons me and from worshipping idols, surely they have led man astray. So whoever follows me, he is surely of me; and whoever disobeys me, Thou surely art Forgiving, Merciful." Prophet Ismael was sent by the most gracious Creator, to his people, so he continued teaching the faith of Ibrahim, believe in One Creator and keeping up Salah contact in obedience to the Lord of all the world and be kind to peoples in the Book of Ibrahim, 'Suhufi'. Surely, he was a truthful in promise, and he was a messenger, a prophet. And he was enjoined on his family and his people prayer, 'Salah' and almsgiving, 'Zakat' and he was one in whom the most gracious Creator was well pleased. Ismael, as he was faithful to the most gracious Creator, so, He blessed him and multiply him exceedingly, to have established twelve tribes on earth, all of his twelve children were kings and prophets on the land, they were prophets raced in the land of Canaan for generations after generations, in genealogy related to Isaac and the prophets among the Israelites, Ismael (Ishmael) had twelve sons as follows: 1. Nabajoth. 2. Kedar. 3. Adbeel. 4. Mibsam. 5. Mishma. 6. Dumah. 7. Massa.

8. Hadad. 9. Timah. 10. Jetur. 11. Naphish. 12. Kedeemah.

They all became leaders among leaders beyond Arabia land. Ismael (Ishmael) laid a foundation of twelve (12) leaders (Imams), this was legacy of Ismael (Ishmael) that Musa (Moses) later build upon, and this tradition of twelve tribes and Imams continued after Moses, to Joseph, the establishment of twelve captains or wells for the children of Israel.

Chapter Nine

The story of Prophet Ishaq (Isaac)

The Heavenly Message

Chapter Nine
The story of Prophet Ishaq (Isaac)

When Abraham felt that his life was drawing to a close, he wished to see Isaac married. He did not want Isaac to marry one of the Canaanites, who were pagans, so he sent a trustworthy servant to Haran in Iraq to choose a bride for Isaac. The servants' choice fell upon Rebekah bint Bethuel, Ibn Nahor, who was a brother of Abraham. So, Isaac married her when he was forty years old. And Rebekah gave birth to a set of twins, Esau (Al-Eis) and Jacob (Yaqoob). Prophet Isaac was a believer in the most gracious Creator and only Him. He was a man of power and insight. Ishaq traveled from place to place and taught people about the most gracious Creator and to worship only Him.

Chapter Ten

The story of Prophet Lut (Lot)

The Heavenly Message

Chapter Ten
The story of Prophet Lut (Lot)

When Lot went to Sodom, he found the people doing bad things; they had done a deed that has not been done nations before them. Lot was surely of those sent by the most gracious Creator to his people in Sodom, he called his people to guard against evil. He said: "Surely, I am a faithful messenger to you: So keep your duty to the most gracious Creator and obey me. And I ask of you no reward for it; my reward is only with the most gracious Creator of the worlds." Lot said to his people: "Surely you are guilty of an abomination which none of the nations has done before you. Surely, you come to males with lust instead of females. Do you come to males and commit robbery on the highway, and commit evil deeds in your assemblies? Do you come to the males from among the creatures, and leave your wives whom your Lord has created for you? Nay, you are a people who act ignorantly, a people exceeding bounds." But the answer of his people was only that they said: "If thou desist not, O Lot, thou wilt surely be banished." He said: "Surely I warn you of a punishment from the most gracious Creator, surely I abhor what you do." They said: Bring on us the most gracious Creator's chastisement if thou art truthful. He said: "My the most gracious Creator, help me against the mischievous people, deliver me and my followers from what they do." Then the most gracious Creator sent His messengers to Lot, and when His messengers came to Lot, he greeted them and invited them to his home. He said: "These people of Sodom are certainly devious people; they will do evil to you if you stay here." When Lot and the Messengers went to Lot's house, Lot's wife started telling the people about the Messengers that Lot invited to his house. When the people found out, they came to him, as if driven on towards him, and they were used to the doing of evil deeds before. So the people of the town came, rejoicing. Lot was grieved for the Messengers and he was unable to protect them, and said: "This is a distressful day!" And said: "These are my guests, so disgrace me not, and keep your duty to the most gracious Creator and shame me not." They said: "Did we not forbid thee from hosting people?" Lot said: "O my people, these are my daughters, they are purer for you; so guard against the punishment of the most gracious Creator and disgrace me not about my guests. Is there not among you any right-minded man?" They said: "Certainly thou knowest that we have no claim on thy daughters, and thou knowest what we desire." He said: "Would that I had the power to repel you! Rather I shall have recourse to a strong support." The messengers said: "O Lot, we are the messengers of thy Most Gracious Creator. We have come to thee with that about which they disputed. And we have come to thee with the truth, and we are surely truthful. They shall not reach thee." by thy life! - The people were suddenly struck blind by the most gracious Creator and they blindly wandered on in their frenzy. Then the Messengers said to Lot: "Travel with thy followers for a part of the night – and thyself follow their rear; except Lot's wife. We ordained for her to be of those who remained behind. She rebelled and turned her back to the truth. Surely, whatsoever befalls them shall befall her. Surely, their appointed time is the morning. Is not the morning nigh?" So when the most gracious Creator's decree came to pass, He turned the disbelievers upside down, and rained on them stones, as decreed, one after another, marked for punishment with the most gracious Creator. And it is not far off from the wrongdoers. Surely, He brought down upon the people of this town a punishment from heaven, because they transgressed. So, He delivered Lot and his followers all, except his wife who was among those who remained behind. Surely in this are signs for those who take a lesson. And it is on a road that still abides. Verily therein is a sign for the believers. And surely, you pass by them in the morning, and at night. Do you not then understand? And certainly, We have left a clear sign of it for a people who understand. And surely, thy Most Gracious Creator is the Mighty, the Merciful.

Chapter Eleven

The story of Prophet Yaqoob (Jacob) or Israel

The Heavenly Message

Chapter Eleven
The story of Prophet Yaqoob (Jacob) or Israel

Yaqoob was a pious man. He was born in the Holy Land, now known as Palestine. Yaqoob was a blessing for his grandfather Ibrahim and his grandmother Sarah. The most gracious Creator promised that many righteous leaders were going to come from this family. And the promises of the most gracious Creator always came true. The most gracious Creator blessed Yaqoob with a large family. He had 12 Sons as follows:

1. Reuben. 2. Simeon. 3. Levi. 4. Judah. 5. Zebulun. 6. Issachar. 7. Dan. 8.Gad. 9. Asher. 10. Naphtali. 11. Joseph. 12. Benjamin. They were later known as the 12 tribes of Israel.

Yaqoob and his family lived in the land of Canaan. This place was about 30 miles from north of Jerusalem. On their farm, Yaqoob and his family had a big flock of sheep. They all worked together to care for the flock and to grow food for their family. As the years passed, Yaqoob grew in wisdom and faith in

the most gracious Creator. He taught his people about the One True God, the most gracious Creator. He taught them the same message his father and grandfather had brought to their people. The most gracious Creator made him a Prophet. Yaqoob leads his family and other people from his homeland to love the most gracious Creator. He called on his children: "O my sons, surely the most gracious Creator has chosen for you this religion, so die not unless you are submitting ones." And when death visited Yaqoob at very old age, he said to his children: "What will you serve after me?" They said: "We shall serve thy the most gracious Creator, the Lord of thy fathers, Ibrahim (Abraham) and Ismael (Ishmael) and Isaac; He is the one Lord and only one Most Gracious Creator. And to Him do we submit."

Chapter Twelve

The story of Prophet Yusuf (Joseph)

The Heavenly Message

Chapter Twelve
The story of Prophet Yusuf (Joseph)

Yusuf said: "I had a Dream." And he revealed his dream to his father, and said: "O my father, I saw eleven stars and the sun and the moon – I saw them making obeisance to me." He said: "O my son, relate not your dream to your brethren, lest they devise a plan against thee. The devil indeed is an open enemy to man. And thus will thy Most Gracious Creator choose thee and teach thee the interpretation of sayings, and make His favor complete to thee and to the Children of Jacob, as He made it complete before to thy fathers, Abraham and Isaac. Surely thy the most gracious Creator Knows, Wise." Verily in Joseph and his brethren, there are signs for the inquirers. When they said: "Certainly Joseph and his brother are dearer to our father than we, though we are a strong company. Surely, our father is in manifest error. Slay Joseph or banish him to some other land, so that your father's regard may be exclusively for you, and after that, you may be righteous people." A speaker among them said: "Slay not Joseph, but, if you are going to do anything, cast him down to the bottom of the well. Some of the travelers may pick him up." They said: "O our father, why dost thou not trust us with Joseph, and surely we are his sincere well-wishers? Send him with us tomorrow that he may enjoy himself and play, and we shall surely guard him well." He said: "Indeed it grieves me that you should take him away and I fear lest the wolf devour him, while you are heedless of him." They said: "If the wolf should devour him, while we are a strong company, we should then certainly be losers." So when they took him away and agreed to put him down at the bottom of the pit, the most gracious Creator revealed to him: "Thou wilt certainly inform them of this affair of theirs while they perceive not." And they came to their father at nightfall, weeping. They said: "O our father, we went off racing with one another and left Joseph by our goods, so the wolf devoured him. And thou wilt not believe us, though we are truthful. And they came with false blood on his shirt." He said: "Nay, your souls have made a matter of light for you. So patience is good. And the most gracious Creator is He Whose help is sought against what you describe." And there came travelers, and they sent their water-drawer and he let down his bucket. He said: "O good news! This is a youth." And they concealed him as an article of merchandise, and the most gracious Creator was Cognizant of what they did. And they sold him for a small price, a few pieces of silver, and they showed no desire for him. And the Egyptian who bought him said to his wife: "Make his stay honorable. Maybe he will be useful to us, or we may adopt him as a son." Thus, the most gracious Creator established Joseph in the land, and that He might teach him the interpretation of sayings. And He has full control over Joseph's affair, but most people know not. And when Yusuf attained his maturity, the most gracious Creator gave him wisdom and knowledge. And thus does He reward the doers of good. And she in whose house he was, sought to seduce him, and made fast the doors and said: "Come." Joseph said: "the most gracious Creator forbid! Surely, my Lord made good my abode. The wrongdoers never prosper." And certainly, she desired him, and he would have desired her, were it not that he had seen the manifest evidence of his the most gracious Creator. Thus, it was that He might turn away from Yusuf evil and indecency. Surely, he was one of His chosen servants. And they raced with one another to the door, and she tore his shirt from behind, and they met her husband at the door. She said: "What is the punishment for one who intends evil to thy wife, except imprisonment or a painful chastisement?" Joseph said: "She sought to seduce me." And a witness of her own family bore witness: "If his shirt is torn in front, she speaks the truth and he is of the liars. And if his shirt is torn behind, she tells a lie and he is of the truthful. So when he saw his shirt rent behind, he said: "Surely it is a device of you women. Your device is indeed great! O Joseph, turn aside from this. And O my wife, ask forgiveness for thy sin. Surely thou art one of the sinful." And women in the city said: "The chief's wife seeks to seduce her slave. He has indeed affected her with his love. Truly we see her in manifest error." So when she heard of their device, she sent for them a banquet, and gave each of them a knife, and said to Joseph: "Come out to them." So when they saw him, they deemed him great, and cut their hands in amazement, and said: "Holy God! This is not a mortal! This is but a noble angel." She said: "This is he about whom you blamed me. And certainly, I sought to seduce him, but he was firm with continence. And if he does not what I bid him, he shall certainly be imprisoned, and he shall certainly be of the abject." Yusuf said: "My the most gracious Creator, the prison is dearer to me then that to which they invite me. And if Thou turn not away their device from me, I shall yearn towards them and be of the ignorant." So the most gracious Creator accepted his prayer and turned away their device from him. Surely, He is the Hearer, the Knower. Then it occurred to them after they had seen the signs that they should imprison him till a time. And two youths entered the prison with him. One of them said: "I saw myself pressing wine." And the other said: "I saw myself carrying bread on my head, of which birds were eating. Inform us of its interpretation; surely we see thee to be the doers of good." He said: "The food with which you are fed shall not come to you, but I shall inform you of its interpretation before it comes to you. This is of what my the most gracious Creator has taught me. Surely, I have forsaken the religion of a people who believe not in Him, and are deniers of the Hereafter. And I follow the religion of my fathers, Abraham, Isaac and Jacob, It beseems us not to associate aught with the most gracious Creator. This is by His grace upon us and on mankind, but most people give not thanks." And Joseph said: "O my two fellow prisoners are sundry lords better, or the most gracious Creator, One and Supreme? You serve not besides Him but names which you have named you and your fathers – the most gracious Creator has sent down no authority for them. Judgment is only His. He has commanded that you serve none but Him. This is the right religion, but most people know not. O

The Heavenly Message

my two fellow prisoners, as for one of you, he will serve wine for his master to drink; and as for the other, he will be crucified, so that the birds will eat from his head. The matter is decreed concerning which you inquired." And he said to him whom he knew would be delivered of the two: "Remember to tell about me to thy master." But the devil caused him to forget mentioning it to his him, so Joseph remained in the prison a few years. The king had a dream and said: "I have seen seven fat kine which seven scrawny ones devoured; and seven green ears and seven others dry. O chiefs, explain to me my dream, if you can interpret the dream." They said: "Confused dreams and we know not the interpretation of dreams." And of the two, he who had found deliverance and remembered after a long time said: "I will inform you of its interpretation, so send me." The king sent him and he went to the prison to Joseph and said: "Joseph, O truthful one, explain to us seven fat kine which seven scrawny ones devoured, and seven green ears and seven others dry, that I may go back to the people so that they may know." He said: "You shall sow for seven years as usual, then that which you harvest, leave it in its ear, except a little which you eat. Then after that will come seven years of hardship, which will eat away all you have beforehand stored for them, except a little which you have preserved. Then after that will come a year in which people will have rain and in which they will press grapes." When he informed the king of what Joseph said, the king said: "Bring him to me." So when the messenger came to him, Joseph said: "Go back to thy king and ask him the case of the women who cut their hands. Surely my the most gracious Creator knows their device." The king said: "What was your affair when you sought to seduce Joseph?" They said: "Holy God! We knew of no evil on his part." The chief's wife said: "Now has the truth become manifest. I sought to seduce him, and he is surely of the truthful. This is that he might know, that I have not been unfaithful to him in secret, and that the most gracious Creator guides not the device of the unfaithful. And I call not myself sinless; surely, man's self is want

The Heavenly Message

to command evil, except those on whom my Lord has mercy. Surely my Lord is Forgiving, Merciful." And the king said: "Bring him to me, I will choose him for myself. So when he talked with him, he said: "Surely thou art in our presence today dignified, trusted." Yusuf said: "Place me in authority over the treasures of the land; surely I am a good keeper knowing well." And thus did the most gracious Creator give to Joseph power in the land, he had mastery in it wherever he liked. The most gracious Creator bestows His mercy on whom He pleases, and He wastes not the reward of the doers of good. And certainly, the reward of the Hereafter is better for those who believe and guard against evil. And Joseph's brethren came and went in to him, and he knew them, while they recognized him not. And when he furnished them with their provision, he said: "Bring to me a brother of yours from your father. See you not that I give full measure and that I am the best of hosts? But if you bring him not to me, you shall have no measure of corn from me, nor shall you come near me." They said: "We shall strive

The Heavenly Message

to make his father yield about him, and we are sure to do it." And he said to his servants: "Put their money into their bags that they may recognize it when they go back to their family, so that they may come back." So when they returned to their father, they said: "O our father, the measure is withheld from us, so send with us our brother that we may get the measure, and we will surely guard him." Jacob said: "How can I trust you with him, as I trusted you with his brother before. So the most gracious Creator is the Best Keeper, and He is the Most Merciful of those who show mercy." And when they opened their goods, they found their money returned to them. They said: "Our father, what more can we desire? This is our property returned to us, and we shall bring corn for our family and guard our brother, and have in addition the measure of a camel-load. This is an easy measure." Yaqoob said: "I will by no means send him with you, until you give me a firm covenant in the most gracious Creator's name that you will bring him back to me, unless you are completely surrounded." And when they

The Heavenly Message

gave him their covenant, he said: "the most gracious Creator is Guardian over what we say." And he said: "O my sons enter not by one gate but enter by different gates. And I can avail you naught against the most gracious Creator. Judgment is only His. On Him I rely, and on Him let the reliant rely." And when they entered as their father had bidden them, it availed them naught against the most gracious Creator, but it was only a desire in the soul of Jacob, which he satisfied, surely, he was possessed of knowledge because the most gracious Creator had given him knowledge, but most people know not. And when they went in to Joseph, he lodged his brother with himself, saying: "I am thy brother, so grieve not at what they do." Then when he furnished them with their provision, Joseph told his servant to place the king's drinking-cup in his brother's bag. Then a crier cried out: "O caravan, you are surely thieves!" They said, while they turned towards them: "What is it that you miss?" They said: "We miss the king's drinking-cup, and he who brings it shall have a camel-load, and I am responsible for it." They said: "By the most gracious Creator! You know for certain that we have not come to make mischief in the land, and we are not thieves." The people said: "But what is the penalty for this, if you are liars?" The brothers said: "The penalty for this – the person in whose bag it is found, he himself is the penalty for it. Thus do we punish the wrongdoers?" So he began with their sacks before the sack of his brother, then he brought it out from his brother's sack. Thus, did the most gracious Creator plan for the sake of Joseph? He could not take his brother under the king's law, unless He pleased. The most gracious Creator rises in degree whom He pleases. And above everyone possessed of knowledge is the All-Knowing One. They said: "If he steals, a brother of his did indeed steal before." But Joseph kept it secret in his soul, and disclosed it not to them. He said: "You are in an evil condition, and the most gracious Creator knows best what you state." The brothers said: "O chief, he has a father, a very old man, so take one of us in his place. Surely, we see thee to be of the doers of good." He said: "the most gracious Creator forbid! That we should seize other than him, with whom we found our property, for then surely we should be unjust!" So when they despaired of him, they conferred together privately. The eldest of them said: "Know you not that your father took from you a covenant in the most gracious Creator's name, and how you fell short of your duty about Joseph before? So I shall not leave this land, until my father permits me or the most gracious Creator decides for me; and He is the Best of the judges." They went back to their father and said: "O our father, thy son committed theft. And we bear witness only to what we know, and we could not keep watch over the unseen. And ask the town where we were, and the caravan with which we proceeded. And surely we are truthful." Yaqoob said: "Nay, your souls have contrived an affair for you, so patience is good. Maybe the most gracious Creator will bring them together to me. Surely He is the Knowing the Wise." And he turned away from them, and said: "O my sorrow for Joseph!" And his eyes were filled with tears because of the grief, and then he repressed grief. They said: "By the most gracious Creator! Thou wilt not cease remembering Joseph till thou art a prey to disease or thou art of those who perish." He said: "I complain of my grief and sorrow only to the most gracious Creator, and I know from Him what you know not. O my sons, go, inquire about Joseph and his brother, and don't despair of the most gracious Creator's mercy. Surely none despairs of His's mercy except the disbelieving people." So when they came to him, they said: "O chief, distress has afflicted us and our family, and we have brought scanty money, so give us full measure and be charitable to us. Surely the most gracious Creator rewards the charitable." Yusuf said: "Do you not know how you treated Yusuf and his brother, when you were ignorant?" They said: "Art thou indeed Yusuf?" He said: "I am Yusuf and this is my brother; the most gracious Creator has indeed been gracious to us. Surely he who keeps his duty and is patient, He never wastes the reward of the doers of good." They said: "By the most gracious

The Heavenly Message

Creator! He has indeed chosen thee over us and we were certainly sinners." Joseph said: "No reproof is against you this day. The most gracious Creator may forgive you and He is the Most Merciful of those who show mercy. Take this my shirt and cast it before my father's face – he will come to know. And come to me with all your family." And when the caravan left Egypt, their father said: "Surely I scent the power of Joseph, if you call me not a dotard." The brothers said: "By the most gracious Creator! thou art surely in thy old error." Then when the bearer of good news came, he cast it before his face so he became certain. He said: "Did I not say to you that I know from the most gracious Creator what you know not?" They said: "O our father, ask forgiveness of our sins for us, surely we are sinners." He said: "I shall ask forgiveness for you of my Most Gracious Creator. Surely He is the Forgiving, the Merciful." Then when they went in to Joseph, he lodged his parents with himself and said: "Enter Egypt in safety, if the most gracious Creator please." And he raised his parents on the throne, and they fell prostrate for his sake. And Joseph said: "O my father, this is the significance of my vision of old – my Lord has made it true. And He was indeed kind to me, when He brought me forth from the prison, and brought you from the desert after the devil had sown dissensions between my brethren and me. Surely, my Lord is Benignant to whom He pleases. Truly He is the Knowing, the Wise." "My the most gracious Creator, Thou hast given me of the kingdom and taught me of the interpretation of sayings. Originator of the heavens and the earth! Thou art my Friend in this world and the Hereafter. Make me die in submission and join me with the righteous."

Chapter Thirteen

The story of Prophet Shu'aib (Jethro)

The Heavenly Message

Chapter Thirteen
The story of Prophet Shu'aib (Jethro)

To Midian, the most gracious Creator sent their brother Shu'aib. The people there used to worship a tree. They were very wealthy, but they earned their money through cheating and giving false weight and measures. They were the first people to charge taxes and were the first to commit bribery. Shu'aib said: "O my people, serve the most gracious Creator, you have no god other than Him. Clear proof indeed has come to you from your Most Gracious Creator, so give full measure and weight and diminish not to men their things, and make not mischief in the land after its reform. This is better for you if you are believers. And lie not in wait on every road, threatening and turning away from the most gracious Creator's way him who believes in Him and seeking to make it crooked. And remember when you were few, then He multiplied you, and see what the end of the mischief-makers was! And give not short measure and weight. I see you in prosperity, and I fear for you the chastisement of an all-encompassing day: And if there is a party of you who believe in that wherewith I am sent and another party who believe not, then wait patiently till the most gracious Creator judges between us; and He is the Best of Judges." Then few of the people followed him. The arrogant chiefs of his people said: "We shall certainly turn thee out, O Shu'aib, and those who believe with thee from our town or you shall come back to our religion." He said: "Even though we dislike it? Indeed, we should have forged a lie against the most gracious Creator, if we go back to your religion after He has delivered us from it. And it is not for us to go back to it, unless the most gracious Creator, our Lord, please. Serve Him and fear the Last Day, our Lord comprehends all things in His Knowledge. In the most gracious Creator do we trust." They said: "O Shu'aib, does thy prayer enjoin thee that we should forsake what our fathers worshipped or that we should not do what we please with good to our property? Forsooth thou art the forbearing, the right – directing one!" Shu'aib said: "Our Lord, decide between us and our people with truth, and Thou art the Best of Deciders." And the chiefs of his people, who disbelieved, said: "If you follow Shu'aib, you are certainly losers." He said: "O my people, see you I have a clear proof from the most gracious Creator and He has given me a goodly sustenance from Himself. And I desire not to act in opposition to you, in that which I forbid you. I desire nothing but reform, so far as I am able. And with none but the most gracious Creator is the direction of my affair to a right issue. In Him I trust and to Him I turn. And, O my people, let not opposition to me make you guilty so that there may befall you like of that which befell the people of Noah, or the people of Hud, or the people of Salih. Nor are the people of Lot far off from you. Keep your duty to Him Who created you and the former generations. And ask forgiveness of your Lord, then turn to Him. Surely my Most Gracious Creator is Merciful, Loving, and Kind." Then, more of his family members and a few more others believed him. The arrogant chiefs said: "O Shu'aib, we understand not much of what thou sayest and surely we see thee to be weak among us. And were it not for thy family, we would surely stone thee, and thou art not mighty among us." Shu'aib said: "O my people: is my family more esteemed by you than the most gracious Creator? And you neglect Him as a thing cast behind your backs! Surely my Lord encompasses what you do." They said: Thou art only a deluded person, and thou art naught but a mortal like ourselves, and we deem thee a liar. So cause a portion of the heaven to fall on us, if thou art truthful." He said: "the most gracious Creator knows best what you do. And, O my people, act according to your ability, I too am acting. You will come to know soon who it is on whom the most gracious Creator will light the punishment that will disgrace him and who it is that is a liar. And watch, surely I too am watching with you." And the most gracious Creator delivered Shu'aib and those who believed with him by mercy from Him. And the cry overtook those who were iniquitous, so they were motionless bodies in their abodes, As though they had never dwelt in them. So, away with Midian, just as

Thamud perished! Those who called Shu'aib a liar were as though they had never dwelt therein – they were the losers. And when the most gracious Creator's decree came to pass, Shu'aib turned away from them and said: "O my people, indeed I delivered to you the messages of the most gracious Creator and I gave you good advice; how, then, should I be sorry for a disbelieving people." So the dwellers of the grove were indeed iniquitous: the most gracious Creator inflicted retribution on them. And they are on an open high road. Surely, there is a sign in this; yet most of them believe not. And surely, thy Most Gracious Creator is the Mighty, the Merciful.

Chapter Fourteen

The story of Prophet Ayub (Joab)

The Heavenly Message

Chapter Fourteen
The story of Prophet Ayub (Joab)

Ayub was certainly a servant of the most gracious Creator. He always praised Him in all conditions and he was blessed with livestock and many children. Then the most gracious Creator Decided to test Ayub. He took Ayub's wealth away, his property, and livestock, gone. But Ayub still praised the most gracious Creator. He said: "O Most Gracious Creator, I praise You on all conditions." Not a day did Ayub complain. Thereafter the most gracious Creator decided to test him further, so He took his children away, one after the other, with each of them, Ayub said: "We all belong to the most gracious Creator, whatever He has given to us it was always His, if He took it away, it just returned to who it belonged to always." Then the most gracious Creator decided to test him with the last test, He took his health away on the outside and the inside. Ayub was covered in blisters. People started keeping a distance from Ayub because they were thought the illness will infect them. They said: "the most gracious Creator does not love this man, if He loved him, he would not have this sickness." Even his friends stopped visiting. After some time, nothing was operating, except Ayub's tongue and heart. He still used the tongue to remember the most gracious Creator, and he still used the heart, he never allowed it to lead him to frustration against the most gracious Creator. The sickness lasted for a long time, soon Ayub's wife asked: "How long is this sickness going to last?" That made Ayub so upset because he never wanted to question the Decree of the most gracious Creator; it was not in his nature. He was very upset that his own wife questioned: how long is will this last? Then Ayub asked his wife: "How long the most gracious Creator blessed me with goodness?" She said: "For eighty years, you had health, wealth, and offspring. He said: "And how many years has the most gracious Creator test me?" She said: "The last seven years." Joab said: "How can I lose hope in the most gracious Creator when I have not reached far with what goodness I had and the difficulty I am facing? It is not even equal." Ayub then said: "You can't tell me how long is this sickness going to last, if I get better, I am going to lash you with one-hundred lashes." When his sickness got to an almost breaking point, he said: "The devil has afflicted me with toil and torment and Thou art the Most Merciful of those who show mercy." So the most gracious Creator responded to him, "Strike with thy foot; here is a cool washing-place and a drink." While Ayub drank, his internal organs were cured. And while Ayub was bathing in the cool water, his blisters disappeared, and his health was restored, better than before. And the most gracious Creator said: "Take in thy hand few worldly goods and earn goodness therewith and incline not to falsehood." Then the most gracious Creator sent locusts of pure gold from Heaven. Ayub started gathering them and he was thankful to the most gracious Creator. The most gracious Creator said: "O Joab, you know We will take care of you, why are gathering these locusts?" Ayub said: O Most Gracious Creator, this is Mercy that is from You, I must gather it. Thus, the most gracious Creator restored his health and wealth in a miraculous way. When Ayub came to his home all healthy, Ayub's wife said: "Where is Ayub? Who are you? But you look so similar to him!" Ayub said: I am Ayub, the most gracious Creator has granted me a cure! And then, the most gracious Creator brought back his all family members and multiplied them by two. It was a mercy from Him and a reminder to the worshippers. Now Ayub had one problem when he was ill, he promised to lash his wife one-hundred lashes when he was cured, now he was cured. So the most gracious Creator revealed to him: "Do not break your promise, We will show you a way out. You can take a bundle of a little grass-like branch and use that to whip. It has no pain, but you are not breaking your promise." Because of the most gracious Creator and Ayub's love for Him, the most gracious Creator showed Joab a way out. Surely the most gracious Creator found Ayub patient; most excellent the servant! Surely, he ever turned to Him.

Chapter Fifteen

The story of Prophet Musa (Moses) and Harun (Aaron)

The Heavenly Message

Chapter Fifteen
The story of Prophet Musa (Moses) and Harun (Aaron)

Prophet Musa was sent by the most gracious Creator to King Pharaoh of Egypt who exalted himself in the land, called himself a god, and made his people into parties, weakening one party from among them, (who were foreign, the children of Israel in Egypt). Pharaoh and his advisers feared that the Israelites who were foreign in the land of Egypt might one day become powerful and supreme in the land, therefore king Pharaoh oppressed and persecuted the children of Israel in various ways, and to that extent, he slaughtered their sons and let their women live. Indeed Pharaoh was one of the world's mischief makers. Prophet Musa was sent as a mercy, a Messenger from the most gracious Creator of all the worlds, that when He has desired to bestow a favor upon those who were deemed weak in the land, and in order to grant them power, to make them leaders and inheritors in the land, and Musa was sent to bring about that what Pharaoh and his councilors feared. And to make Pharaoh and Haman and their hosts see from them what they feared. The most gracious Creator revealed to Moses' mother, saying: "Breastfeed him; then when thou fearest for him, put him into a chest, then cast it into the river, the river will cast it upon the shore – there an enemy to Me and an enemy to him shall take him up. And fear not, nor grieve; surely We shall bring him back to thee and make him one of the messengers." So Pharaoh's people took him up that he might be an enemy and a grief for them. Surely, Pharaoh, Haman and their hosts were wrongdoers. And Pharaoh's wife said: "A refreshment of the eye to me and to thee – slay him not; maybe he will be useful to us, or we may take him for a son." And they perceived not. And the heart of Moses' mother was free from anxiety. She would almost have disclosed it, had the most gracious Creator not strengthened her heart so that she might be of the believers. And the most gracious Creator sets forth an example for those who believe – the wife of Pharaoh, when she said: "My the most gracious

Creator, build for me close to Thee a house in the Garden, deliver me from Pharaoh and his work, and deliver me from the iniquitous people." Moses' mother said to his sister: "Follow him up." So she watched him from a distance, while they perceived not. And the most gracious Creator did not allow him to be breastfed before so she said: "Shall I point out to you the people of a house who will bring him up for you, and they will wish him well?" So the most gracious Creator gave Musa back to his mother that her eye might be refreshed, and that she might not grieve and that she might know that, the promise of the most gracious Creator is always true, but most of them know not. And when Moses attained his maturity and became full-grown, the most gracious Creator granted him wisdom and knowledge. And thus does He reward those who do good to others. And Musa went into the city at a time of carelessness on the part of its people, so he found therein two men fighting – one being of his party and the other of his foes; and he who was of his party cried out to him for help against him who was of his enemies, so Moses struck him with his fist and killed him. Moses said: "This is on account of the devil's doing; surely he is an enemy, openly leading astray." Then Moses said: "My Lord, surely I have done harm to myself, so do Thou protect me." So the most gracious Creator protected him. Surely He is Forgiving, the Merciful. He said: "O my Lord, because Thou hast bestowed a favor on me, I shall never be a backer of the guilty." And he was in the city, fearing, waiting, when lo, he who asked his assistance yesterday was crying out to him for help. Moses said to him: "Thou art surely one erring manifestly." So when he desired to seize him who was an open enemy to them both, he said: "O Moses, dost thou intend to kill me as you intend to kill a person yesterday? Thou only desire to be a tyrant in the land, and thou desirest not to be of those who act aright." So the Egyptian who was fighting the man knew that Musa was the man who killed the Egyptian yesterday. When the news reached the Pharaoh and the chiefs, they were planning to slay Musa. Then a man came running from the remotest part of the city. He said: "O Moses, the chiefs are consulting together to slay thee, so depart at once; surely I am of those who wish you well." So Moses went forth therefrom, fearing and waiting. Moses said: "My most Gracious Creator, deliver me from the iniquitous people." And when he turned his face towards Midian, he said: "Maybe my Most Gracious Creator will guide me on the right path. And when he came to the water of Midian, he found there a group of men watering, and he found besides them two women keeping back their flocks. He said: "What is the trouble with you?" They said: "We cannot water until the shepherds take away their sheep from the water; and our father is a very old man." So Musa watered their sheep for them, then went back to the shade, and said: "My most Gracious Creator, I stand in need of whatever good Thou mayest send to me." Then one of the two women came to him walking bashfully. She said: "My father invites thee that he may reward thee for having watered for us." So when Moses came to him and related to him the story, Shu'aib said: "Fear not, thou art secure from the iniquitous people." One of the two women said: "O my father, employ him; surely the best of those that thou canst employ is the strong, the faithful one." said: "I desire to marry one of these two daughters of mine to thee on condition that you serve me for eight years; but, if thou complete ten, it will be of thy own free will, and I wish not to be hard on thee. If the most gracious Creator pleases, thou wilt find me one of the righteous." Musa said: "That is agreed between me and thee; whichever of the two terms I fulfill, there will be no injustice to me; and the most gracious Creator is surety over what we say." Then when Moses had completed the term, and was traveling with his family, he perceived a fire on the side of the mountain. He said to his family: "Wait, I see fire; maybe I will find guidance or a live coal so that you may warm yourselves." When Moses came to the bush, he saw that bush was on fire but the bush was not burning up. And as he came to it, he was called from the right side of the valley in the blessed spot of the bush: "O Moses, surely I am the most gracious Creator, the Lord of the worlds, so take off your shoes; surely thou art in the sacred valley Tuwa. And I have chosen thee, so listen to what is revealed: Surely I am the most gracious Creator, there is no God but I, so serve Me, and keep up prayer for My remembrance, Surely the Hour is coming – I am about to make it manifest – so that every soul may be rewarded as it strives. So let not him, who believes not in it and follows his low desire, turn thee away from it, lest thou perish. And what is this in thy right hand, O Moses?" Moses said: "This is my staff – I lean on it, and I beat the leaves with it for my sheep, and I have other uses for it." the most gracious Creator said: "Cast it down, O Moses." So he cast it down, and lo! It was a serpent gliding. Then Musa turned away retreating, and looked not back. The most gracious Creator said: "O Moses, come forward, seize it and fear not surely thou art of those who are secure. We shall return it to its former state. And press thy hand into thy bosom it will come out white without evil – These two are two arguments from thy

Lord to Pharaoh and his chiefs. Surely, they are a transgressing people. Go to Pharaoh, surely he has exceeded the limits." Musa said: "My the most gracious Creator, I killed one of them, so I fear lest they slay me. My the most gracious Creator, expand my chest for me: And ease my affair for me: And loose the knot from my tongue, that they may understand my word. And my brother, Aaron, he is more eloquent in speech than I, so send him with me as a helper to confirm me and add to my strength by him, And make him share my task So that we may glorify Thee much, And much remember Thee. Surely, Thou art ever Seeing us." Harun was older than Musa, and he was very intelligent, pious, and eloquent. The most gracious Creator said: "Thou art indeed granted thy request, O Moses. And indeed We bestowed on thee a favor at another time, When We revealed to thy mother that which was revealed: Put him into a chest, then cast it into the river, the river will cast it upon the shore – there an enemy to Me and an enemy to him shall take him up. And I shed on thee love from Me;

and that thou mayest be brought up before My eyes. When thy sister went and said: "Shall I direct you to one who will take charge of him?" So We brought thee back to thy mother that her eye might be cooled and she should not grieve. And thou didst kill a man then We delivered thee from grief, and tried thee with many trials. Then thou didst stay for years among the people of Midian. Then thou came hither as ordained, O Moses. And I have chosen thee for Myself. Go thou and thy brother with My messages and be not remiss in remembering Me. Go both of you to Pharaoh, surely he is inordinate; then speak to him a gentle word, and haply he may mind or fear." Moses and Harun said: "Our Lord, we fear lest he hasten to do evil to us or be inordinate." the most gracious Creator said: "Fear not, surely I am with you – I do hear and see. We will strengthen thine arm with thy brother, and We will give you both an authority, so that they shall not reach you. With Our signs, you two and those who follow you will triumph. So go you to him and say: Surely, we are two messengers of thy Most Gracious

Creator; so send forth the Children of Israel with us; and torment them not. Indeed, we have brought to thee a message from thy Lord, and peace to him who follows the guidance. It has indeed been revealed to us that punishment will overtake him who rejects and turns away." So when Aaron and Moses went to Pharaoh they said: "Surely we are two messengers of thy Most Gracious Creator; so send forth the Children of Israel with us; and torment them not. Indeed, we have brought to thee a message from thy Most Gracious Creator, and peace to him who follows the guidance. It has indeed been revealed to us that punishment will overtake him who rejects and turns away." Pharaoh said: "Did we not bring thee up as a child among us, and thou didst tarry many years of thy life among us? And thou didst that deed of yours which thou didst and thou art of the ungrateful ones." Moses said: "I did it then I was of those who err. So I feared you, then my Lord granted me judgment and made me of the messengers. And is it a favor of which thou remind me that thou hast enslaved the Children of

Israel?" Pharaoh said: "And what is the most gracious Creator of the worlds?" He said: "The Lord of the heavens and the earth and what is between them, if you would be sure. Our Most Gracious Creator is He Who gives to everything its creation, then guides it. The most gracious Creator is your Lord and my Lord and the Lord of the fathers of old." Pharaoh said: "What then is the state of the former generations?" Musa said: "The knowledge thereof is with my Most Gracious Creator in a Book; He neither errs nor forgets – Who made the earth for you an expanse and made for you therein paths and sent down water from the clouds. Then thereby He brings forth pairs of various herbs and various plants which you eat and pasture your cattle. Surely, there are signs in this for men of understanding. From it He created you, and into it He shall return you, and from it raise you a second time." Pharaoh said to those around him: "Do you not listen to what he says? Shall we believe in two mortals like ourselves while their people serve us? Surely your messenger, who is sent to you, is mad." Moses said: "the most gracious Creator and the Lord of the East and the West and what is between them, if you have any sense!" Pharaoh said: "If thou takest a god besides me, I will certainly put thee in prison." Musa said: "Even if I show thee something plain?" Pharaoh said: "Show it, then, if thou art of the truthful." So Moses cast down his rod, and lo! It was a clear serpent; and he drew forth his hand, and lo! It appeared white to the beholders. Pharaoh said to the chiefs around him: "Surely this is a skillful enchanter and we never heard of it among our fathers of old! He desires to turn you out of your land with his enchantment." Moses said: "Say you this of the truth when it has come to you? Is it enchantment? And the enchanters never succeed." They said: "Hast thou come to us to turn us away from that which we found our fathers following, and that greatness in the land may be for you two? And we are not going to believe in you." Then Pharaoh said to his chiefs: "What is it then that you counsel?" They said: "Give him and his brother respite and send heralds into the cities that they bring to thee every skillful enchanter. Pharaoh said to Moses and Aaron: "We too can bring to thee enchantment like it, so make an appointment between us and thee, which we break not, neither we nor thou, in a central place." Moses said: "Your appointment is the day of the Festival, and let the people be gathered in the early forenoon." So Pharaoh went back and settled his plan, then came. Moses said to them: "Woe to you! Forge not a lie against the most gracious Creator, lest He destroys you by punishment, and he fails indeed that forges a lie." So they disputed one with another about their affair and kept the counsel secret. They said: "These are surely two enchanters who would drive you out from your land by their enchantment, and destroy your excellent institutions. So settle your plan, then come in ranks, and he will indeed succeed that is uppermost." So the enchanters were gathered together for the appointment of the well-known day, and it was said to the people: "Will you gather? Haply we may follow the enchanters, if they are the vanquishers." And the enchanters came to Pharaoh, saying: "We must surely have a reward if we prevail." Pharaoh said: "Yes, and you shall certainly be of those who are near to me." The enchanters said: "O Moses, wilt thou cast, or shall we be the first to cast?" Musa said: "Cast." The enchanters cast and said: "By Pharaoh's power, we shall most surely be victorious." Then their cords and their rods – it appeared to him by their enchantment as if they ran. They deceived the people's eyes and overawed them, and they produced a mighty enchantment. So Moses conceived fear in his mind. The most gracious Creator said: "Fear not, surely thou art the uppermost. And cast down what is in thy right hand – it will eat up what they have wrought. What they have wrought is only the trick of an enchanter, and the enchanter succeeds not whatsoever he comes from." Moses said: "What you have brought is deception. Surely, the most gracious Creator will make it naught. Surely, the most gracious Creator allows not the work of mischief-makers to thrive. And He will establish the truth by His words, though the guilty are averse." So when Moses cast his rod, lo! It swallowed up their fabrication.

The Heavenly Message

There the magicians were vanquished, and they went back abased. Then the enchanters threw themselves down in prostrate – They said: "We believe in the most gracious Creator of the worlds, The Lord of Aaron and Moses. Pharaoh said: "You believe in him before I give you leave! Surely, he is the chief who taught you enchantment, so you shall know. Certainly, I will cut off your hands and your feet on opposite sides, and I shall crucify you on the trunks of palm-trees, I will crucify you all and you shall certainly know which of us can give the severer and the more abiding chastisement." They said: "We cannot prefer thee to what has come to us of clear arguments and to Him Who made us, so decide as thou wilt decides. Thou canst only decide about this world's life. Surely, we believe in our Lord that He may forgive us our faults and the magic to which thou didst compel us. And the most gracious Creator is Best and ever Abiding. Whoso comes guilty to his Lord, for him is surely hell. He will neither die therein nor live. And whoso comes to him a believer, having done good deeds, for them are high ranks Gardens of perpetuity, wherein flow rivers, to abide therein. And such is the reward of him who purifies himself." And they said: "No harm you will do to us; surely, to our the most gracious Creator we return. And thou takest revenge on us only because we believed in the messages of our Most Gracious Creator when they came to us. Our Most Gracious Creator, pour out on us patience and cause us to die in submission to Thee! We hope that You will forgive us our wrongs because we are the first of the believers." And the chiefs of Pharaoh's people said: "Wilt thou leave Moses and his people to make mischief in the land and forsake thee and thy gods?" Pharaoh said: "Slay the sons of those who believe with him and keep their women alive. And surely we are dominant over them." Because of the fear of Pharaoh and their chiefs persecuting them, none believed in Moses except a few of his people. And Pharaoh was truly high-handed in the land; and surely, he was extravagant. And Pharaoh proclaimed amongst his people, saying: "O my people, is not the kingdom of

Egypt mine and these rivers flowing beneath me? Do you not see? Rather I am better than this fellow who is contemptible, and can hardly express himself clearly. Why, then, have bracelets of gold not been bestowed on him, or angels come along with him in procession?" So he incited the people to levity and they obeyed him. Surely, they were a transgressing people. And the plot of the disbelievers is bound to fail. And Pharaoh said: "Leave me to slay Moses and let him call upon his Lord. Surely, I fear that he will change your religion or that he will make mischief to appear in the land." And Moses said: "Truly, I seek refuge in my Most Gracious Creator and your Most Gracious Creator from every proud one who believes not in the day of Reckoning." And a believing man of Pharaoh's people, who hid his faith, said: "Will you slay a man because he says, My Lord is the most gracious Creator, and indeed, he has brought you clear arguments from your Lord? And if he be a liar, on him will be his lie, and if he be truthful, there will befall you some of that which he threatens you with. Surely, the most gracious Creator guides not one who is a prodigal, a liar. O my people, yours is the kingdom this day, being masters in the land, but who will help us against the punishment of the most gracious Creator, if it comes to us?" Pharaoh said: "I only show you that which I see and I guide you only to the right way." And he who believed said: "O my people, surely I fear for you the like of what befell the parties, the like of what befell the people of Noah and Ad and Thamud and those after them. And the most gracious Creator wishes no injustice for His servants. And, O my people, I fear for you the day of Calling out – The day on which you will turn back retreating, having none to save you from the most gracious Creator; and whomsoever He leaves in error there is no guide for him. And Joseph indeed came to you before with clear arguments, but you ever remained in doubt as to what he brought you; until, when he died, you said: the most gracious Creator will never raise a messenger after him. Thus, does He leave him in error who is a prodigal, a doubter? – They are those who dispute concerning the messages of the most gracious Creator without any authority that has come to them. Greatly hated is it by Him and by those who believe. Thus, does the most gracious Creator seal every heart, of a proud, haughty one?" And Pharaoh said: "O chiefs, I know no god for you besides myself; O Haman, kindle a fire for me, on bricks of clay, then prepare for me a lofty building, that I may attain the means of access – The means of access to the heavens then reach the God of Moses, so that I may obtain knowledge of Moses' God, and surely I think him a liar." And he was unjustly proud in the land, he and his hosts, and they think that they would not be brought back to the most gracious Creator. Thus, the evil of his deed was made fair-seeming to Pharaoh, and he was turned aside from the way. And the plot of Pharaoh ended in naught but ruin. And he who believed said: "O my people, follow me, I will guide you to the right way. O my people, this life of the world is but passing enjoyment, and the Hereafter, that is the abode to settle. Whoever does evil, he is requited only with the like of it;

and whoever does goodness, whether male or female, and he is a believer, these shall enter the Garden, to be given therein sustenance without measure. And O my people how is it that I call you to salvation and you call me to the Fire? You call me to disbelieve in the most gracious Creator and to associate with Him that of which I have no knowledge, and I call you to the Mighty, the Forgiving. Without doubt, that which you call me to has no title to be called to in this world, or in the Hereafter, and our return is to the most gracious Creator, and the prodigals are companions of the Fire. So you will remember what I say to you, and I entrust my affair to Him. Surely, He is Seer of the servants." So the most gracious Creator protected him from the evil they planned; and evil chastisement overtook Pharaoh's people – The Fire. They are brought before it every morning and evening, and on the day when the Hour comes to pass: Make Pharaoh's people enter the severest chastisement. Moses said to his people: "Ask help from the most gracious Creator and be patient. Surely, the land is

His – He gives it for an inheritance to such of His servants as He pleases. And the end is for those who keep their duty." They said: "We were persecuted before thou camest to us." Moses said: It may be that your Most Gracious Creator will destroy your enemy and make you rulers in the land, then He will see how you act." And certainly, the most gracious Creator overtook Pharaoh's people with droughts and diminution of fruits that they might be mindful. But when good befell them, they said: "This is due to us." And when evil afflicted them, they attributed it to the ill-luck of Moses and those with him. Surely, their evil fortune is only from the most gracious Creator, but most of them know not. And they said: "Whatever sign thou mayest bring to us to charm us therewith – we shall not believe in thee." So the most gracious Creator sent upon them widespread death, locusts, lice, frogs and blood, all clear signs. But they behaved haughtily and they were a guilty people. And when the plagues fell upon them, they said: "O enchanter, pray for us to thy Most Gracious Creator as He has made

The Heavenly Message

promise with thee. If thou remove the plagues from us, we will certainly believe in thee and will let the Children of Israel go with thee and we shall surely follow guidance." But when the most gracious Creator removed the plagues from them till a term which they should attain, lo! They broke their promise. And certainly, the most gracious Creator gave Moses nine clear signs, when he came to Pharaoh, Pharaoh said to him: "Surely, I deem thee, O Moses, to be one bewitched." Moses said: "Truly, thou knowest that none but the Lord of the heavens and the earth has sent these as clear proofs; and surely, I believe thee, O Pharaoh, to be lost. Surely, I bring to you a clear authority. And I take refuge with my Lord and your Lord, lest you stone me to death. And if you believe not in me, leave me alone." And Moses said: "O my people, if you believe in the most gracious Creator, then rely in Him if you submit to Him." They said: "On the most gracious Creator, we rely; our the most gracious Creator, make us not a trial for the unjust people. And deliver us by the disbelieving people." And the most gracious Creator revealed to Moses and his brother: "Take houses for your people to abide in Egypt and make your houses places of worship and keep up prayer. And give good news to the believers." And Moses said: "Our Most Gracious Creator, surely Thou hast given Pharaoh and his chiefs finery and riches in this world's life, that they may lead people astray from Thy way. Our Most Gracious Creator, destroy their riches and harden their hearts, so that they believe not till they see the painful chastisement." the most gracious Creator said: "Your prayer is accepted; so continue in the right way and follow not the path of those who know not." And certainly, the most gracious Creator revealed to Moses: "Travel by night with My servants, you will be pursued. Do not fear to be overtaken, nor being afraid." Then Pharaoh sent heralds into the cities proclaiming: "These are indeed a small band, and they have surely enraged us. And we are truly a vigilant multitude." So the most gracious Creator turned them out of their gardens and springs, and treasurers and goodly dwellings – Even so, the most gracious Creator gave them as a heritage to the Children of Israel. Then they pursued them at sunrise. So when the two hosts saw each other, the companions of Moses cried out: "Surely, we are overtaken." Musa said: "By no means; surely, my Most Gracious Creator is with me – He will guide me." Then the most gracious Creator revealed to Moses: "March on to the sea with thy staff." So the sea parted, and each party was like a huge mound. And the most gracious Creator brought the Children of Israel across the sea. Then Pharaoh and his hosts followed them for oppression and tyranny, till, and then, the sea covered them. Pharaoh led his people astray and he guided not aright. So when the drowning overtook him, he said: "I believe that there is no God but the most gracious Creator, in Whom the Children of Israel believe, and I am of those who submit." the most gracious Creator said: "What! Now! And indeed before this, thou didst disobey and thou wast of the mischief-makers! But this day We shall save thee in thy body that thou mayest be a sign to those after thee." Pharaoh was drowned because they rejected the most gracious Creator's signs and were heedless of them. And surely, most of the people are heedless of His signs. How many of the gardens, springs, cornfields, noble places, goodly things wherein they rejoiced, things that they left behind! Thus it was. The most gracious Creator made other people inherit them. So the heaven and the earth wept not for them, nor were they respited. He indeed delivered the Children of Israel from the abasing chastisement, from Pharaoh; Surely, Pharaoh was haughty, prodigal. And certainly, the most gracious Creator chose them above the nations, having knowledge, and gave them signs wherein was clear blessing. These do indeed say: "There is naught but our first death and we shall not be raised again. So bring our fathers back, if you are truthful." Are they better or the people of Tubba' and those before them? the most gracious Creator destroyed them, for surely they were guilty. He did not create the heavens and the earth and that which is between them in sport. He created them not but with truth, but most of them know not. Surely, the day of Decision will be the term for them all, the day when friend will avail friend in naught, nor will they be helped, save those on whom the most gracious Creator has mercy. Surely, He is the Mighty, the Merciful. And He made the people who were deemed weak to inherit the eastern lands and the western ones which He had blessed. And the good word of thy Most Gracious Creator was fulfilled in the Children of Israel – because of their patience. And He destroyed what Pharaoh and his people had wrought and what they had built. When the most gracious Creator took the Children of Israel across the sea, they came to a people who were devoted to their idols. They said: "O Moses, make for us a god as they have gods." He said: "Surely, you are an ignorant people! As to these, that wherein they are engaged shall be destroyed and that which they do is vain. Shall I seek for you a god other than the most gracious Creator, while He has made you excel all created things?" As they got to the other side of the sea, they were hungry and needed water. The land they came into was a desert that was barren. So they said: "O Musa, we are thirsty and hungry, so pray to the most gracious Creator to give us something to eat and drink. When Moses prayed for water for his people, the most gracious Creator said: "March on to the rock with thy staff. So there flowed from it twelve springs. Each tribe knew their drinking-place." And He made the clouds to give shade over them, He sent to them manna and quails. It was said: "Eat and drink of the provisions of the most gracious Creator, and act not corruptly, making mischief in the land. Moses said to his people: "O my people, Remember the favor of the most gracious Creator to you when He raised prophets among you and made you kings and gave you what He gave not to any other of the nations. Call to mind the most gracious Creator's favor to you, when He delivered you from Pharaoh's people, who subjected you to severe torment, and slew your sons and spared your women. And therein was a great trial from your Lord. And your Lord made it known: "If you are grateful, I will give you more, and if you are ungrateful, My chastisement is surely severe." Moses said: " And if you are ungrateful, you and all those on earth, then the most gracious Creator is surely Self-Sufficient, Praised. O my people, Enter the Holy Land, the land of Jerusalem which the most gracious Creator has ordained for you and turn not your backs, if you do, you will turn back losers." They said: "O Moses, Therein are a powerful people, and we shall not enter it until they go out from it; if they go out from it, then surely we will enter." Two men of those of those who feared, on whom the most gracious Creator had bestowed a favor, said: "Enter upon them by the gate, for when you enter it you will surely be victorious; and put your trust in the most gracious Creator, if you are believers." They said: "O Moses, we will never enter it so long as they are in it; go therefore thou and thy Lord, and fight; surely here, we sit." Musa said: "My Most Gracious Creator, I have control of none but my own self and my brother; so distinguish between the transgressing people and us." the most gracious Creator said: "It will surely be forbidden to them for forty years — they will wander about in the land. (The land was called At-Te, The land of wandering). So grieve not for the transgressing people." Then the people became stubborn and doing as they please. So Moses prayed to the most gracious Creator: "O the most gracious Creator, I would like some laws, something that they can follow and can succeed." the most gracious Creator said: "We will appoint you thirty nights, and complete them with ten." So the appointed time of his Lord was complete forty nights. And Moses said to his brother Aaron: "Take my place among my people, and act well and follow not the way of the mischief-makers." When Moses came at the most gracious Creator's appointed time and spoke to Him, Moses said: "My Lord, show me Thyself so that I may look at Thee." the most gracious Creator said: "Thou canst not see Me; but look at the mountain; if it remains firm in its place, then you will see Me. So when his Most Gracious Creator manifested His Glory to the mountain, He made it crumble and

Moses fell down in a swoon." Then when he recovered, he said: "Glory is to Thee! I turn to Thee, and I seek forgiveness for having asked what I have just asked, and I am the first of the believers." the most gracious Creator said: "O Moses, surely I have chosen thee above the people by My messages and My words. So take hold of what I give thee and be of the grateful. And what made thee hasten from thy people O Moses?" Musa said: "They are here on my track, and I hastened on to Thee, my Most Gracious Creator, that thou mightest be pleased. The most gracious Creator said: "I ordained for you in the tablets (Torah) admonition of every kind and clear explanation of all things. So take hold of them with firmness and enjoin thy people to take hold of what is best thereof. I shall show you the abode of the transgressors. I shall turn away from My Messages those who are unjustly proud in the earth. And if they see every sign, they will not believe in it; and if they see the way of rectitude, they take it not for a way; and if they see the way of error, they take it for a way. This is because they reject My messages and are heedless of them. And those who reject My messages and the meeting of the Hereafter – their deeds are fruitless. Can they be rewarded except for what they do? And certainly, Bring forth thy people from darkness into light and remind them of the days of Me. In this are surely signs for every steadfast, grateful one." the most gracious Creator said: "Surely, We have tried thy people in thy absence and the Samiri has led them astray." So Moses returned to his people angry, sorrowing, he said: "Evil is that which you have done after me! Did you hasten on the judgment of your Most Gracious Creator?" And he threw down the tablets and seized his brother by the head and the beard, dragging him towards him. Moses said: "O Aaron, what prevented thee, when thou sawest them going astray, that thou didst not follow me? Hast thou, then, disobeyed my order?" Aaron said: "O son of my mother, seize me not by my beard, nor by my head. Surely, I was afraid lest thou shouldst say: 'Thou hast caused division among the Children of Israel and not waited for my word' the people reckoned me weak and had well-nigh slain me. So make not the enemies to rejoice over me and do not count me among the unjust people." Musa said: "My the most gracious Creator, forgive me and my brother, and admit us to Thy mercy, and Thou art the Most Merciful of those who show mercy." Musa said: "O my people, did not your Most Gracious Creator promise you a goodly promise? Did the promised time, then, seem long to you, or did you wish that displeasure from your Lord should come upon you, so that you broke your promise to me?" They said: "We broke not promise to thee of our own accord, but we were made to bear the burdens of the ornaments of the people, then we cast them away, and thus the Samiri suggest." And Moses' people made of their ornaments a calf before him – a lifeless, hollow body, having a lowing sound. Samiri said: "This is your god and the god of Moses." But he forgot. Could they not see that it spoke not to them, nor guided them in the way? They took it for worship and they were unjust. And Aaron indeed had said to them before: "O my people, you are only tried by it, and surely, your Most Gracious Creator is the Beneficent God, so follow me and obey my order." They said: "We shall not cease to keep its worship until Moses returns to us." Moses said: "O Samiri, What was thy object?" He said: "I perceived what they perceived not, so I took a handprint from the footprints of the messenger then I cast it away. Thus, my soul embellished it to me." Musa said: "Begone then! It is for thee in this life to say: 'Touch me not.' And for thee is a promise which shall not fail." Then Musa said to his people: "Look at thy god to whose worship thou hast kept. We will certainly burn it then we will scatter it in the sea. Your Lord is only the most gracious Creator; there is no god but Him. He comprehends all things in His knowledge. Those who took the calf for a god – wrath from their Lord, and disgrace in this world's life, will surely overtake them. And thus does He recompense those who invent lies. And those who do evil deeds then repent after that and believe – thy Lord after that is surely Forgiving, Merciful. O my people, you have surely wronged yourselves by taking the calf for a god, so turn to your Most Gracious Creator penitently, and kill your passions. That is best for you with your Creator." So when they repented and saw that they had gone astray, they said: "If our Most Gracious Creator have not mercy on us and forgive us, we shall certainly be of the losers." So the most gracious Creator turned to them mercifully. Surely, He is the Oft-returning to mercy, the Merciful. And when Moses' anger calmed down, he took up the tablets; and in the writing thereof was guidance and mercy for those who fear their Lord. And Musa said to his people: "Indeed, the most gracious Creator gave me the guidance, and He made you, Children of Israel, inherit the Book – guidance and a reminder for men of understanding. So be patient; surely, the promise of the most gracious Creator is true; and ask protection for thy sin and celebrate the praises of thy Lord in the evening and the morning." And certainly, the most gracious Creator gave Moses the Book that they might go aright, but differences arose therein. And had not a word already gone forth from thy Lord, judgment would have been given between them. And surely, they are in a disquieting doubt about it. The Children of Israel were lazy to obey the Commandments. They said: "We hear and we disobey." So the most gracious Creator raised the mountain above them, and then the mountain came slowly down, as though it was going to fall on them. The most gracious Creator said: "Are you going to fulfill the Commandments We sent to you?" They said: "Yes indeed, we give You our covenant, we will fulfill these Commandments." the most gracious Creator said: "O Children of Israel, do not go back on your promises, hold on firmly that which We have given you, and be mindful of that which is in it, so that you may guard against evil." When they promised their promises, then the most gracious Creator caused the mountain to return to where it was. Then some people began to follow a few things, some still ignored them and some continued harassing Musa. And Moses said to his people: "O my people, why do you malign me, when you know that I am the most gracious Creator's messenger to you? But when they deviated, the most gracious Creator made their hearts deviate. And He guides not the transgressing people. When the people saw the Signs and the Book was there, they said: "O Moses, we want to talk to the most gracious Creator, when you are speaking to Him; we want to come and listen." So Musa was told by the most gracious Creator: "Select seventy men from amongst your people and bring them." So Musa selected seventy people to come to the appointed place. When they came there, they heard the Message of the most gracious Creator. Then the people said: "O Moses, we will not believe in thee till we see the most gracious Creator manifestly, it is not enough that we hear him. The most gracious Creator was not pleased with this and sent lighting and thunder, together with an earthquake, and the seventy people all died. So when the earthquake overtook them, Moses said: "My the most gracious Creator, if Thou had pleased, Thou destroyed them before and me too. Wilt Thou destroy us for that which the foolish among us have done? It is naught but Thy trial. Thou cause to perish thereby whom Thou pleasest and guidest whom Thou pleasest. Thou art our Protector, so forgive us and have mercy on us, and Thou art the Best of those who forgive. And ordain for us good in this world's life and in the Hereafter, for surely we turn to Thee." the most gracious Creator said: "I afflict with My chastisement whom I please, and My mercy encompasses all things. So I ordain it for those who keep their duty and pay the poor-rate, and those who believe in My messages. Then the most gracious Creator gave them life after they were dead so that they can be thankful. After a while, the people got tired of eating the manna and quails. So they said to Moses: "O Moses, we cannot endure one food, so pray thy Lord on our behalf to bring forth for us of what the earth grows, of its herbs and its cucumbers and its garlic and its lentils and its onions." Moses said: "Would you exchange that which is worse? If you are really asking for that, there is a possibility that the most gracious Creator will return you to Egypt in a condition that you will once again have all of the food and together with it, you will be oppressed. Would you like to be oppressed again?" But they kept asking Musa. So the most gracious Creator said: "Enter a city, so you will have what you ask for, then eat from it a plenteous food whence you wish, and enter the gate submissively, and make petition for forgiveness. We will forgive you your wrongs and increase the reward of those who do goodness to others." But those who were unjust changed the word which had been spoken to them, for another saying, so the most gracious Creator sent upon the wrongdoers a pestilence from heaven, because they transgressed. And abasement and humiliation were stamped upon them, and they incurred the most gracious Creator's wrath. There was a time when the most gracious Creator tested the Children of Israel. He instructed the people from the Commandments that they were not allowed to work at all on the Sabbath. To this day, Jews still follow the Commandment. But there was a time when they violated the Sabbath, when their fish came to them on their Sabbath day on the surface, and when it was not their Sabbath they came not to them. Thus, the most gracious Creator did try them because they transgressed. So they threw their nets on Friday evening and picked them up full of fish on Sunday morning. And when a party of them said: "Why preach you to a people whom the most gracious Creator would destroy or whom He would chastise with a severe chastisement?" They said: "To be free from blame before your Lord, and that haply they may guard against evil." So when they neglected that whereof they had been reminded, the most gracious Creator delivered those who forbade evil and He overtook those who were iniquitous with an evil chastisement because they transgressed. So when they revoltingly persisted in that which they had been forbidden, the most gracious Creator said to them: "Be apes, despised and hated." And when the most gracious Creator declared that, He would send against them to the day of Resurrection those who would subject them to severe torment. Surely thy Lord is Quick in requiting; and surely He is Forgiving, Merciful. And the most gracious

The Heavenly Message

Creator divided them in the earth into parties – some of them are righteous and some of them are otherwise. And He tried them with blessings and misfortunes that they might turn. Three incidents occurred at the time of Musa. There was a wealthy man, he passed away and he left one son, he inherited everything so, the cousins were jealous, and they murdered him. Then there was an argument about who murdered the man. So they went to Musa and said: "We need to know the murderer of this man, it is causing a big problem, and it is splitting communities and causing a rift in the family. So Musa prayed to the most gracious Creator about the matter. When Musa came back to his people, he said: "O my people, surely the most gracious Creator commands you to sacrifice a cow, you sacrifice a cow and then you will see that the most gracious Creator will reveal the name of whoever was the murderer. They said: "Dost thou ridicule us?" Musa said: "I seek refuge to the most gracious Creator from being one of the ignorant." They said: "Call upon thy Lord for our sake to make it plain to us what she is." Moses said: "He says, surely she is not a cow advanced in age nor too young, but of middle age between these two; so do what you are commanded." They said: "Call on thy Lord for our sake to make it clear to us what her color is." Moses said: "He says: She is a yellow cow; her color is intensely yellow delighting the eyes." They said: "Call on thy Lord for our sake to make it clear to us what she is, for surely, to us the cows are all alike, and if the most gracious Creator pleases, we shall surely be guided aright." Moses said: "He says, she is not a cow made submissive to plough the land, nor does she water the tilth, without a blemish in her." They said: "Now thou hast brought the truth. There was a man who passed away, and he left a behind a widow and his one child. And he made a dua: "O the most gracious Creator, I am dying at this age and leaving my wife and my child, O the most gracious Creator, I leave them in your Care, look after them." The man only had one calf, so he instructed his wife before he passed away: "Take this calf and release it into the forest, because I do not trust these people, they are greedy and selfish." So when the boy grew up, the mother said: "Your father left you a calf now a cow in the forest, go and look for it." As he went, only one cow came to him. At that time, the Children of Israel were looking for exactly the same cow. It fitted everything that Musa was told. They said: "We want to buy this cow for five silver coins." But young man and his mother did not want to sell it for that price. So they settled for gold that was the same weight as the cow was. The young man became rich. After The Children of Israel purchased the cow, they slaughtered it and cut it. But they did not have the mind to do it. After that, the most gracious Creator said: "Strike the murdered man with a chunk of meat from this cow." the most gracious Creator was going to bring forth that which they were going to hide. When the man was struck, he came up alive, and said the name of the person who murdered him, and died again. So the problem was solved. Thus, the most gracious Creator brings the dead to life, and He shows you His signs that you may understand. Then the people's hearts hardened after that, so that they were like rocks, rather worse in hardness. And surely there are some rocks from which split asunder so water flows from them; and there are some of them which fall down for the fear of the most gracious Creator. And He is not heedless of what you do. The second incident occurred at the time of Moses. Korah was surely of the people of Moses, but he oppressed them, and the most gracious Creator gave him treasures, so much so that his hoards of wealth would weigh down a body of strong men. When the Children of Israel said to Korah: "Exult not; surely, the most gracious Creator loves not the exultant. And seek the abode of the Hereafter by means of what the most gracious Creator has given thee, and neglect not thy portion of the world, and do good to others as the most gracious Creator has done good to thee, and seek not to make mischief in the land. Surely, He loves not the mischief-makers. Korah said: "I have been given this only because of the knowledge I have." Did he not know that the most gracious Creator had destroyed before him generations who were mightier in strength than he was and greater in assemblage? And the guilty are not questioned about their sins. So he went forth to his people in his finery. Those who desired this world's life said: "O would that we had the like of what Korah is given! Surely, he is possessed of mighty good fortune!" But those who were given knowledge said: "Woe to you! the most gracious Creator's reward is better for him who believes and does goodness and none are made to receive except the patient." So the most gracious Creator made the earth to swallow Korah up and his abode. He had no host to help him against the most gracious Creator, nor was he of those who can defend themselves. And those who had yearned for his place the day before began to say: "Ah! Know that the most gracious Creator amplifies and straitens the means of subsistence for whom He pleases of His servants; had not the most gracious Creator been gracious to us, He would have abased us. Ah! Know that the ungrateful are never successful." The third incident occurred when Musa was asked a question by someone: "O Musa, we want to know who is the most knowledgeable." Musa said: "It's I." So the most gracious Creator revealed to him: "No, O Musa, no one can know everything there is to know in knowledge. But We send down knowledge in pockets. We bless some with more than one, but not every pocket. There is a certain pocket of knowledge which We have granted someone besides you." So Musa was interested to know. He said: "Who is this? I want to see him. If he is around, he must be from my people." Then the most gracious Creator instructed Musa to take his lunch, (which were items in a basket and a live fish). And go to a certain part on the coast. Musa took a certain young man with him whose name was Joshua and told him: "the most gracious Creator has given us a task, I will not cease until I reach the junction of the two rivers, other-wise I will go on for years." So when they reached the junction of the two rivers, while they were resting they forgot their fish, and it took its way into the river being free. But when they had gone further, Musa said to Joshua: "Let us have our morning meal, certainly, we have found fatigue in this our journey." He said: "Sawest thou when we took refuge on the rock, I forgot the fish, and none but the devil made me forget to speak of it, and it took it's way into the river; what a wonder!" Musa said: "This is what we sought!" So they returned retracing their footsteps. Then they found one of the most gracious Creator's servants, his name was Khidir, whom The Most Graacious Creator had granted mercy from Him and whom He had taught knowledge from Himself. Moses said to him: "May I follow thee that thou mayest teach me of the good, thou hast been taught?" Khidir said: "Thou canst not have patience with me. And how canst thou have patience in that whereof thou hast not a comprehensive knowledge?" Moses said: "If the most gracious Creator please, thou wilt find me patient, nor shall I disobey you thee in aught." He said: "If thou wouldest follow me, question me not about aught until I myself speak to thee about it." So they set out until, when they embarked in a boat, the first thing that they saw was a bird, and it dipped its beak into the water, once or twice. Khidir said: "O Musa, did you see this? Did you see the amount of water being displaced when the beak of the bird went into the ocean?" Moses said: "Yes, I saw it." Khidir said: the most gracious Creator's Knowledge is like the whole ocean and we only have a little droplet. Moments later, Musa saw Khidir make a hole in the boat. Moses said: "Hast thou made a hole in it to drown its occupants? Thou hast surely done a grievous thing!" Khidir said: "Did I not say that thou couldst not have patience with me?" Musa said: "Blame me not for what I forgot, and be not hard upon me for what I did." So they went on, until, when they met a boy, he slew him. Moses said: "Hast thou slain an innocent person, not guilty of slaying another? Thou hast indeed done a horrible thing!" Khidir said: "Did I not say to thee that thou couldst not have patience with me?" Musa said: "If I ask thee about anything after this, keep not company with me. Thou wilt then indeed have found an excuse in my case." So they went on, until, when they came to the people of a town, they asked its people for food, but they refused to entertain them as guests. Then they found in it a wall which was on the point of falling, so Khidir put it into a right state. Moses said: "If thou hadst wished, thou couldst have taken a recompense for it." Khidir said: "This is the parting between thee and me. Now I will inform thee of the significance of that with which thou couldst not have patience. As for the boat, it belonged to poor people working on the river, and I intended to damage it, for there was a behind them a king who seized every boat by force. And as for the boy, his parents were believers and we feared lest he should involve them in wrongdoing and disbelief. So we intended that their Lord might give them in his place one better in purity and nearer to mercy. And as for the wall, it belonged to two orphan boys in the city, and there was beneath it a treasure belonging to them, and their father had been a righteous man. So thy Lord intended that they should attain their maturity and take out their treasure – a mercy from thy Lord – and I did not do it of my own accord. Thou couldst not have patience of these significances." And certainly, the most gracious Creator conferred a favor on Moses and Aaron. And He delivered them, and their people from the mighty distress. And He helped them, so they were the vanquishers. And He gave them both the clear Book. And He guided them on the right way. And He granted them among the later generations the salutation, Peace be to Moses and Aaron! Thus, does the most gracious Creator reward the doers of goodness? Surely, they were both of His believing servants.

And certainly, the most gracious Creator lodged the Children of Israel in a goodly abode and provided them with good things. Then they differed not till the knowledge came to them. Surely, thy Lord will judge between them on the day of Resurrection concerning that in which they differed.

Chapter Sixteen

The story of Prophet Joshua (Yusha)

The Heavenly Message

Chapter Sixteen
The story of Prophet Joshua (Yusha)

Yusha was a student and a follower of Musa. Joshua (Yusha) was the young man with Musa when the most gracious Creator gave him a task. "I will not cease until I reach the junction of the two rivers, other-wise I will go on for years." So when they reached the junction of the two rivers, while they were resting they forgot their fish, and it took its way into the river being free. But when they had gone further, Musa said to Joshua: "Let us have our morning meal, certainly, we have found fatigue in this our journey." He said: "Sawest thou when we took refuge on the rock, I forgot the fish, and none but the devil made me forget to speak of it, and it took it's way into the river; what a wonder!" Musa said: "This is what we sought!" So they returned retracing their footsteps.

After Musa passed away, the most gracious Creator appointed Joshua (Yusha) as a messenger. Joshua has a friend Caleb both were men that tried to encourage the Children of Israel to enter Jerusalem in

Moses' time. They were some of the people the most gracious Creator permitted to enter the Promised Land (Palestine). In forty years, there was a new generation of the Children of Israel. Yusha did not allow anyone newly married, or building a new home to live, or if someone is busy with his business, to join the army; Joshua prepared the army and went to attack Jericho, (the first city of Palestine) on Friday. It was a very big fight. At evening Yusha started to worry, as the most gracious Creator's law, they were not allowed to fight after sunset because Saturday (Day of Sabbath) would start. It was prayer day and holy day for the Jews. And the sun was about to set. Then Yoshua prayed to the most gracious Creator to stop the sun. The most gracious Creator heard this and commanded the sun to stop. So the sun as it was setting paused, then, when the Children of Israel achieved victory, the sun set. After the victory, they gathered all the valuable items and put them in one place, these are called spoils of war. A miracle came; fire came to destroy those items but was waiting for something. Joshua realized that some people had hidden some valuables items from their enemies, so Yusha called one man from each tribe to put their hands together. The hand of one man stuck to his hand. So the evil people were in his tribe. He called all the men from that tribe and put their hands with him. Two or three men were stuck to his hand because they were guilty persons; they had collected one bowl of gold which was equal to the head of a cow. Joshua ordered the men to bring back their stolen gold and put them in the place where everyone put. The fire came and all the items disappeared. The Children of Israel lived in Jerusalem for some time; Yusha taught them the Torah and ruled according to it. He lived for 127 years.

Chapter Seventeen

The story of Ezekiel

The Heavenly Message

Chapter Seventeen
The story of Ezekiel

At the time of Yoshua, there was a plague, and there were certain people who tried to run away from that plague, and they were in their thousands. They fled to the top of the mountain, fearing death. And they settled there for a while. Then the most gracious Creator instructed the Angel of Death to cause their death. As Ezekiel was passing this place, which seemed that there was nothing wrong with it. Ezekiel thought: 'No punishment seemed to have overcome it, and there was no one there besides some bones. But the destruction, how did it come? Everyone died all at once.' As Ezekiel was watching, the most gracious Creator said to him: "Would you like to see these people come back to life?" Ezekiel said: "Yes, I want to see." And then the most gracious Creator gave them life. Ezekiel watched, seeing the bones come together, thereafter the flesh coming on the bones. And the people were back. And the most gracious Creator said: "We are very bountiful upon people, We bestow them with so many gifts, but many people are not grateful." When the people came back to life, they started to thank the most gracious Creator and ask Him for Forgiveness, so the most gracious Creator forgave them. After Ezekiel passed away, the Children of Israel deviated from the right way of life and deserted the most gracious Creator's covenant. They worshipped many idols, among them Baal.

Chapter Eighteen

The story of Prophet Shammil (Samuel)

The Heavenly Message

Chapter Eighteen
The story of Prophet Shammil (Samuel)

During the time of Yusha, the Children of Israel took control of most of the area in Palestine. So, the Philistines, who were pagans, had to get together and control some of the small towns around the Children of Israel. But when Yusha passed away, day by day, The Children of Israel lost their focus; they broke their unity among themselves, so, each tribe got separated and got their own land; they even started to follow their pagan neighbors. Because the Children of Israel were doing many sins including idol worshipping, as a punishment, the most gracious Creator united all their pagan neighbors and made them stronger. They fought the Children of Israel and took their women and children. The enemies destroyed The Children of Israel. At that time, the most gracious Creator chose Shammil to be a Prophet and to guide the Children of Israel. After many years of guidance, Samuel finally united The Children of Israel. The Children of Israel said to Samuel: "Raise up for us a king that we may fight in the way of the most gracious Creator." He said: "May it not be that you will not fight if fighting is ordained for you?" They said: "And what reasons have we that we should not fight in the most gracious Creator's way and we have indeed been deprived of our homes and our children?" But when fighting was ordained for them, they turned back, except a few of them. And the most gracious Creator is Knower of the wrongdoers. And Shammil said to them: "Surely the most gracious Creator has raised Saul to be a king over you. They said: "How can he have a kingdom over us while we have a greater right to the kingdom than he does, and he has not been granted an abundance of wealth?" Shammil said: "Surely the most gracious Creator has chosen him above you, and has increased him abundantly in knowledge and physique. And the most gracious Creator grants His kingdom to which He pleases. And the most gracious Creator is Ample-giving, Knowing." And Samuel said to them: "Surely the sign of his kingdom is that there shall come to you the heart in which there is tranquility from your Most Gracious Creator and the best of what the followers of Moses and the followers of Aaron have left, the angels bearing it. Surely, there is a sign in this for you if you are believers." During Samuel's time, he guided his people to the most gracious Creator's law. He also guided Prophet David.

Chapter Nineteen

The story of Prophet Luqman

The Heavenly Message

Chapter Nineteen
The story of Prophet Luqman

Luqman was a scholar and a very wise man. He even used to meet Dawud often and give him words of wisdom and advisement. And certainly, the most gracious Creator gave Luqman wisdom, saying: Give thanks to the most gracious Creator. And whoever is thankful, is thankful for his soul; and whoever denies, then surely the most gracious Creator is Self-Sufficient, Praised. And when Luqman said to his son, while he instructed him: "O my son, ascribe no partners to the most gracious Creator. Surely ascribing partners to Him is a grievous iniquity. And He has enjoined on man concerning his parents – his mother bears him with faintings and his weaning takes two years – saying: Give thanks to Me and to thy parents. To Me is the eventual coming. And if they strive with thee to make thee associate with Me that of which thou hast no knowledge, obey them not, and keep kindly company with them in this world, and follow the way of him who turns to Me;

then to Me is your return, then I shall inform you of what you did." "O my son, even if it be the weight of a grain of mustard-seed, even though it is a rock, or in the heaven or in the earth, the most gracious Creator will bring it forth. Surely, He is Knower of all things, Aware." "O my son, keep up prayer and enjoin good and forbid evil, and bear patiently that which befalls thee. Surely, this is an affair of great resolution. And turn not thy face away from people in disdain, nor go about in the land exultingly. Surely, the most gracious Creator loves not any self-conceited boaster. And pursue the right course in thy going about and lower thy voice. Surely, the most hateful of voices is braying of donkeys." One time, Luqman said to his son, "O my son! Do not tie your heart in seeking the pleasure of people. You are not likely to succeed. Do not pay attention to what people say, instead tell yourself to seek the pleasure of the most gracious Creator." Luqman wanted this lesson to be always remembered, never to be forgotten. He thought of a way. He then told his son to ride a donkey. The son obeyed, and Luqman followed behind on foot. They traveled in this way for some distance, then, they came across a group of people. Seeing the son on the donkey, one of them said, "What an impolite and bad boy. The old father is walking on foot and the young son is comfortably riding on the donkey. This is no manner to show respect to one's father." Father and son heard this, so the son came down from the donkey, and Luqman rode the donkey. After some time they came across another group of people. Seeing the father riding the donkey, the elder of the group said: "Oh you old man! This is not the way to bring up a son. You make him walk in the hot sun, while you sit comfortably on the donkey." Luqman heard what the people said. He came down from the donkey and walked with his son on foot, while the donkey walked in front. They went a little further. People seeing them said: "How foolish you are! You walk behind a donkey! Why don't you ride it?" Luqman and his son again accepted what the people said. They both rode the donkey and went further. They came across a river. There was a bridge to be crossed. Some people were sitting there and saw Luqman and his son riding the donkey. One of them said, "It is very unkind and cruel of you two to ride on the poor donkey. The little animal can hardly take all of your burdens." So taking this advice Luqman and his son dismounted from the donkey. They traveled a little distance further. Looking very lovingly at his son Luqman said, "You have heard and seen what the people said. It must have assured you, by now, that whatever you do or whichever way you move, one is not able to please the people of the world." Luqman pointed at the flowing river and added, "A person can build a wall across the river. It will stop the flow of the water. But it is not possible to stop the mouth of people from criticism."

Chapter Twenty

The story of Prophet Dawud (David)

The Heavenly Message

Chapter Twenty
The story of Prophet Dawud (David)

Hast thou not thought of the leaders of the Children of Israel after Moses? Saul did not allow anyone who was building a new home, newly married, or busy in their business, to join the army; after Saul set out with the forces, he said: "Surely the most gracious Creator will try you with a river. Whoever drinks from it, he is not of my army, and whoever tastes it not, he is surely of my army, except he who takes a handful with his hand." But most of the people drank of it except a few of them. So when he had crossed it, he and those who believed with him, they said: "We have today no power against Goliath and his forces." Those who were sure that they would meet their the most gracious Creator said: "How often has a small party vanquished a numerous host by the most gracious Creator's permission!" And the most gracious Creator is with the steadfast. And when they went out against Goliath and his forces, they said: "Our Lord, pour out patience on us and make our steps firm and help us against the disbelieving people." Goliath challenged any soldier to fight him, he wanted to show off his strength to the people. Because of that, none agreed to fight, but a young man who was Dawud stepped forward, he wanted to fight with Goliath. The people were surprised; Saul did not want Dawud to fight Goliath because he was a young man. But David told Saul to have faith in him; he told him that once, he killed a lion to protect a flock. Dawud also killed a bear. David was not afraid of anyone because he knew that the most gracious Creator would protect him from Goliath. Saul became happy to hear this and tried to put armor on Dawud, but Dawud did not take the armor, instead, he took his sling and some rocks. When Goliath saw David, he laughed: "You are going to fight me? I will simply cut off your head!" David warned Goliath that he had power from the most gracious Creator. Then in the Name of the most gracious Creator, David flung the rock to Goliath using his sling. A rock it Goliath's head. He was dead. Goliaths' army was shocked and scared. So Banu Israel put the rest of Goliath's army to flight by the most gracious Creator's permission. Banu Israel took their land back. Soon, Dawud got married to Saul's daughter and became the Kings' chief advisor. And the most gracious Creator gave Dawud kingdom and wisdom and taught him of what He pleased. Dawud was always very kind to people and the most gracious Creator gave him prophethood. And the most gracious Creator gave Dawud the Book Zabur (Psalms). And were it not for the most gracious Creator's repelling some men by others, the earth would certainly be in a state of disorder; but He is Full of Grace to the worlds. During Dawud's' prophethood, the most gracious Creator gave Dawud a special gift, Dawud had the most beautiful voice in the whole world, when he read from his Book, Zabur, to pray to the most gracious Creator, the mountains would repeat praises with him, and the birds and all the creatures. In a miracle of the most gracious Creator, David could understand the language of all creatures. After a few years, when Saul passed away, David was made a king; he was a wise, strong king. In his time, he controlled all of Palestine and its surrounding areas. Dawud used to always sleep first, half of the night, then wake up and pray for a third of the night, and then, he slept for the rest of the night. Dawud used to fast during the daytime for the most gracious Creator. The most gracious Creator also gave him the gift to be a good judge. And remember the most gracious Creator's servant David, the possessor of power. He ever turned to Him. Truly the most gracious Creator made the mountains subject to Dawud, glorifying the most gracious Creator at nightfall and sunrise, and the birds gathered together. All were obedient to him. And He strengthened Dawud's kingdom and He gave Dawud wisdom and a clear judgment. Once, he was praying in his prayer room, when no one was allowed to be there at that time. To give a special guide and judgment, the most gracious Creator sent two angels to his room. When they made an entry into the private chamber by climbing the wall, they came upon David, so he was afraid of them. They said: "Fear not; we are two litigants, of whom one has wronged the other, so decide between us with justice, and do not act unjustly, and guide us to the right way." One of them said: "This is my brother. He has ninety-nine ewes and I have a single ewe. Then he says: Make it over to me, and he has prevailed against me in dispute." Without hearing the other man, Dawud said, "Make it over to me, and he has prevailed against me in dispute. Surely, he has wronged thee in demanding thy ewe to add to his own ewes. And surely many partners wrong one another save those who believe and do good, and very few are they!" When the two litigants, (who were Angels) disappeared, David knew that the most gracious Creator had tried him, so he asked Him for protection, and he fell down bowing and turned Him. The most gracious Creator had taught him not to judge without hearing both sides of the persons. So the most gracious Creator gave him this protection, and surely, he had a nearness to Him and an excellent resort. The most gracious Creator said to him: "O David, surely We have made thee a ruler in the land; so judge between men justly and follow not desire, lest it lead thee astray from the path of Me. Those who go astray from the path of Me, for them is surely a severe chastisement because they forgot the day of Reckoning." During the nighttime, Dawud used to visit the town in disguise so no one would recognize him. Dawud asked the people about the king. They said that everyone loved him and said good things about him. One night, an angel came to Dawud in a human form. The Angel told him that king Dawud should not take his money from his treasury of his kingdom for his living expenses. David requested the most gracious Creator to give him a special ability so he could earn money and use that money for his living expenses. The most gracious Creator accepted his prayer and made the iron pliant to him, Saying: "Make ample coats of mail, and assign a time to the making of coats of mail to protect you in your wars and do ye good. Surely, I am Seer of what you do." So Dawud made weapons to sell at the market, and used the money for his expenses. Dawud was the first person that discovered how to make the shield in a new way, surely he was taught by the most gracious Creator. During Dawud's time, his soldiers had to join in many wars. The soldier's armors were made from iron which was one piece, so it was not flexible to move in and were very heavy. To make better armors, the most gracious Creator gave the knowledge to Dawud, to make little rings and to put those rings together. Then, the armor became very flexible and light, this was another of David's invention. Dawud was very protective of his family; when he left the palace, he always locked all the gates so no one was allowed to come in. One day when he went out and locked all the doors as usual, suddenly his wife saw a man in the middle of the palace. She said: "How did you enter the house? All the doors were locked! Dawud would not be happy to see you." When Dawud came back, he saw the man and asked him who he was. The man replied that he was not afraid of any king and no one could run away from him. Then king Dawud realized that this was the Angel of Death, so he welcomed the Angel to take his soul. At King Dawud's funeral,

thousands of thousands of people came to pray for him, it was a very hot day, then, thousands of thousands of birds came to create shade for the funeral. Peace and salutation be to Dawud! Surely, he was one of the most gracious Creator's servants!

Chapter Twenty-One

The story of Prophet Suleiman (Solomon)

The Heavenly Message

Chapter Twenty-One
The story of Prophet Suleiman (Solomon)

Suleiman was the son of Dawud, he was born in Jerusalem. Solomon was very talented since childhood. One day, when Solomon was 11 years old, he was with David in the courtroom. Two men came to deal with their problems; one of them said: "His sheep destroyed my field, I want justice." Dawud asked the second man. He said: "Sir, that is true, but I do not have the money to pay for the damage." Hearing this, Dawud ordered the second man to give his sheep to the owner of the field to pay for the damage. But Solomon told his father that he had another idea to solve their problem: "The owner of the sheep would work at the field until the crops grew, while the field owner will take care of the sheep and benefit from its wool and milk. When the crops grew in a good shape as before, the field owner would take back his field and give the sheep back to its owner." Dawud became very happy for his son's judgment. The most gracious Creator had given Solomon knowledge to be a good judge. Thus David and Solomon, when they gave judgment concerning the field when the people's sheep strayed therein by night, and the most gracious Creator was the bearer of witness to their judgment. So the most gracious Creator made Solomon to understand it. And to each of them He gave wisdom and knowledge. After Dawud passed away, Solomon became king. One time, two women who used to take care of their cattle, both of the women each had a baby, and they were both the same age. One day, both of the mothers took their own baby with them and went to the field to take care of the cattle. They put the babies in a spot to play. While the mothers were busy a work, a wolf came and took one of the babies! When the mothers came, they saw that only one baby was alive. Then both of them wanted that baby and each of the women claimed that baby was hers, so they went to Solomon. When Solomon heard their complaints, he then ordered that the baby would be cut in half and give each half the baby to each of the mothers. One of the mothers cried out: "No! Do not cut the baby!

This is not my baby; give the baby to the other mother instead." King Suleiman realized knew that this was the baby's mother because she was full of love for the baby when he ordered to cut the baby in half. So Suleiman gave the baby to its real mother. Solomon was very wise and obedient to the most gracious Creator; because of this, He made Solomon very rich and powerful. He had many great horses for his army. When well-bred, swift horses were brought to Solomon at the evening, he said, "I love the good things because of the remembrance of my Lord" – Until they were hidden behind the veil. He said: "Bring them back to me. So he began to stroke their legs and necks. Certainly, the most gracious Creator tried Solomon, because Solomon missed his prayer, he became very sick, no medicine could cure him, and he was on his throne a mere body, so he turned to the most gracious Creator. He said: "My Lord, forgive me and grant me a kingdom which is not fit for anyone after me; surely, Thou art the Great Giver." So the most gracious Creator made the wind subservient to him, running gently by his command wherever he desired, it made a month's journey in the morning and a month's journey in the evening; and the most gracious Creator made a fountain of molten copper to flow for him. So the workers could make any shape with that copper. And of the jinn, there were those who worked before him by the command of his Lord. And whoever turned aside from the most gracious Creator's command from among them, the most gracious Creator made him taste of the chastisement of burning and the most gracious Creator kept guard over them, and other bad jinn fettered in chains. The jinn, every builder and diver to dive in the ocean to collect things, and they made for him what Solomon pleased, of synagogues, images, bowls large as watering-troughs, and fixed cooking-pots. The most gracious Creator said: "Give thanks, O people of David! And very few of My servants are grateful. This is Our free gift, so give freely or withhold, without reckoning." Solomon had a wish, he wanted a smart son so after his death, he could rule his big kingdom. One time, one of Solomon's wives gave birth to a dead son, and then the servant brought the dead son, and put it on his throne. Solomon realized that the most gracious Creator did not like his wish for his son to be king. Then Solomon asked the most gracious Creator for Forgiveness. Then the most gracious Creator made him king of men, jinn, and the birds. Some people believed that Solomon did all this by magic. But they were miracles from the most gracious Creator. But at that time there were magicians, they were devils, some people started to follow them, the devils fabricated against the kingdom of Solomon. And Solomon disbelieved not, but the devils disbelieved, teaching men enchantment and black magic. During the time of Suleiman, some of the people of Banu Israel commonly used black magic to break other families or to harm others. And it was not revealed to the two angels in Babel, Harut and Marut. Nor did they teach it to anyone, so that they should have said, we are only a trial, so disbelieve not. But they learn from these two sources that by which they make a distinction between a man and his wife. And they cannot hurt with it anyone except with the most gracious Creator's permission. And they learn that which harms them and profits them not. And certainly, they know that he who buys it has no share of good in the Hereafter. And surely evil is the price for which they have sold their souls, did they but know! Then, Solomon decided to stop black magic. He ordered his armies to collect all the writing that teaches black magic from everywhere. When the armies of bird, man, and jinn, collected all the written information of black magic, they buried all of the written magic under Suleiman's throne so none one could touch it. During Solomon's lifetime black magic stopped; but after his death, Satan convinced some people to get what they thought was Solomon's power. They dug under Solomon's throne, to find the written black magic. So the people lost their belief of the most gracious Creator, and started to follow the evil. There was a time when Solomon decided to rebuild and extend Masjid-l-Aqsa. Part of the construction was the Dome of the Rock and Solomon's Temple, Solomon prayed to the most gracious Creator to remove all the sins from anyone who prayed in this Mosque. And surely, Suleiman had a nearness to the most gracious Creator and an excellent resort. One day, when his hosts of the jinn, men, and birds were gathered to Solomon, and they were formed into groups, they were going to a place, until when they came to the valley of the Naml (Ants), a Namlite said: "O Naml, enter your houses, lest Solomon and his hosts crush you, while they know not." So he smiled, wondering at her word, and said: "My Most Gracious Creator, grant me that I may be grateful for Thy favor which Thou hast bestowed on me and on my parents, and that I may do good such as Thou art pleased with, and admit me, by Thy mercy, among Thy righteous servants." Then he ordered his army to be very careful not to crush the ants. And Solomon said: "O men, we have been taught the speech of birds, and we have been granted of all things. Surely, this is manifest grace." When Suleiman reviewed the birds, then said: "How is it I see not Hudhud, or is that he is one of the absentees? I will certainly punish him with a severe punishment, or kill him, or he shall bring me a clear excuse." And Hudhud tarried not long, then said: "I have compassed that which thou hast not compassed, and I have come to thee from Sheba with sure information, I found a woman whose name was Bilquees ruling over them, and she has been given of everything and she has a beautiful and mighty throne. I found her and her people adoring the sun instead of the most gracious Creator, and the devil has made their deeds fair-seeming to them and turned them from the way, so they go not aright, So that they worship not the most gracious Creator, Who brings forth what is hidden in the heavens and the earth and knows what you hide and what you proclaim. The most gracious Creator, there is no God but He, He is the Lord of the Mighty Throne." Suleiman said: "We shall see whether thou speakest the truth or whether thou art a liar. Take this my letter and hand it over to them, then turn from them and see what answer they return." When the letter reached Bilquees, she said: "O chiefs, an honorable letter has been delivered to me. It is from Solomon, and it is in the name of the most gracious Creator, the Beneficent, and the Merciful: Proclaiming, exalt not yourselves against me and come to me in submission." She said: "O chiefs, advise me respecting my affair; I never decide an affair until you are in my presence." They said: "We are possessors of strength and possessors of mighty prowess. And the command is thine, so consider what thou wilt command." She said: "Surely the kings, when they enter a town, ruin it and make the noblest of its people to be low; and thus they do. And surely, I am going to send them a present, and to see what (answer) the messengers bring back." So when the envoy came to Solomon, he said: "Will you help me with wealth? But what the most gracious Creator has given me is better than that which He has given you. Nay, you are exultant because of your present. Go back to them, so we certainly come to them with hosts which they have no power to oppose, and we shall certainly expel them therefrom in disgrace, while they are abased if they do not accept the most gracious Creator." The messenger informed Bilquees about Solomon who did not accept the gift, his powerful army and that no one could defeat them and they was coming to attack them. Bilquees decided to visit Solomon in submission. She ordered her messenger to inform Solomon about her visit. When Solomon heard the message, he decided to welcome her with the highest respect and to show her the Power of the most gracious Creator. He said: "O jinn, which of you can bring me her throne before they come to me in submission?" One audacious among the jinn said: "I will bring it to thee before thou rise up from thy place; and surely, I am strong, trusty for it." One having knowledge of the Book said: "I will bring it to thee in the twinkling of an eye." Then when Suleiman saw, it settled beside him, he said: "This is the grace of my Lord, that He may try me whether I am grateful or ungrateful. And whoever is grateful, he is grateful only for his own soul, and whoever is ungrateful, then surely my Lord is Self-sufficient, Bountiful." "Alter her throne for her; we may see whether she follows the right way or is of those who do not go not aright." So when Bilquees came, Solomon said: "Was thy throne like this?" She said: "It is as it were the same; and we were given the knowledge before about it, and we submitted." And that which she worshipped besides the most gracious Creator prevented her; for she was of a disbelieving people. It was said to her: "Enter the palace." But when she saw it, she deemed it a great expanse of water, and prepared herself to meet the difficulty. Suleiman said: "Surely, it is a palace made smooth with glass." She was amazed and knew that it was done by the most gracious Creator. She said: "My Most Gracious Creator, surely I have wronged myself, and I submit with Solomon to You, the Lord of the worlds." She also told her people to do the same; she went back to Ethiopia to spread the religion of the most gracious Creator and all of her people believed in Him. One day, when Solomon was old, he was checking on the jinns work, when The Angel of Death came and took his soul. Solomon's body was standing while his staff supported it. No one knew that

Solomon was dead, not even the jinn so the jinn worked day and night. After a few days, the most gracious Creator sent some ants that ate away his staff. So when Solomon's body fell down, the jinn saw clearly that, if they had known the unseen, they would not have tarried in humiliating torment. The people quickly came to him and realized that he had died a long time ago. He was buried near Masjid-l-Aqsa. And certainly, the most gracious Creator gave knowledge to David and Solomon. And they said: "Praise be to the most gracious Creator, Who has made us excel many of His believing servants!" And the most gracious Creator gave to David and Solomon, most excellent the servants! Surely, they ever turned to Him.

Chapter Twenty-Two

The story of Prophet Elias (Elijah)

The Heavenly Message

Chapter Twenty-Two
The story of Prophet Elias (Elijah)

After Solomon passed away, his kingdom was divided into two parts, Israel and Judah. Solomon's family controlled the Kingdom of Judah and the capital was Jerusalem. On the other side, another king ruled The Kingdom of Israel, and the capital was Samaria. Day by day, those countries moved further and further from the most gracious Creator's laws and started to do very bad things. But Israel was the worst; they even started to accept idols as their gods. The king of Israel name was Ahab; he married a polytheistic woman named Jezebel. She worshipped an idol, Ba'al, and Ahab started to follow her example. He built a temple for Ba'al in Samaria and convinced his people to worship Ba'al instead of the One God the most gracious Creator. Soon they started to worship Ba'al publicly. Then, the most gracious Creator sent Elijah to guide those people. Elijah tried to guide the people back to the most gracious Creator's way. He said: "Will you not guard against evil? Do you call upon Ba`al and forsake the Best of the creators, the most gracious Creator, your Lord and the Lord of your fathers?" But the people rejected him. One day, he went to Ahab and told him to accept the most gracious Creator as his God and not worship the idols. Ahab also refused him. The most gracious Creator then sent a very long drought to the town. Ahab now realized that Elijah was truly the prophet of the most gracious Creator. He asked Elias to ask the most gracious Creator to remove the drought. But before Elias asked the most gracious Creator to remove the drought, he wanted to show the people that the idol Ba'al, was powerless and not a god. He told the king to get the entire Baal priests together in front of the people. When they all got together, Elias told them that the priests should sacrifice an animal in the name of their Ba'al while he should sacrifice another animal in the name of the most gracious Creator; whichever of the sacrifices are accepted by sending fire, He is the True God. After they sacrificed their sacrifices, a fire immediately came from the Heaven and took Elias's sacrifice. All the people were amazed to see that Ba`l had no power, so the majority of the people and some of the priests accepted the most gracious Creator as their only God. Then Elias gave a punishment to the priests who still believed in Ba'al. Then, Elijah prayed to the most gracious Creator to remove the drought. The most gracious Creator accepted his dua and sent the rain immediately to all of Israel. Everyone was so happy that the most gracious Creator was able to remove the people's drought. On the other hand, queen Jezebel was not happy with Elijah. Because she had a strong faith in Ba'al, she got so angry that she plotted to kill Elijah. When Elias knew the information, he left the Israel Kingdom and moved to Jerusalem in the Kingdom of Judah. At that time, Judah's king had married queen Jezebel's daughter. Day by day those people also started to worship Ba'al. Elias also tried to convince the king and his people to worship the most gracious Creator and not the idol Ba'al or other idols. But they refused his advice. So the most gracious Creator sent outsiders to control the Kingdom of Judah. They fought and the outsiders destroyed the Kingdom of Judah. After that, the king of Judah died from a bad disease. Then Elijah moved back to Israel and tried to convince the king and his people to accept the most gracious Creator and to take lessons from the other kingdom. Elias also said if they do not believe they will be destroyed. But they refused him. During Elijah's Prophethood, the most gracious Creator sent Prophet Yasa (Elisha) to help Prophet Elias. And the most gracious Creator granted Elijah among the later generations the salutation, Peace be to Elias! Even thus, the most gracious Creator rewards the doers of good. Surely, he was one of the most gracious Creator's believing servants.

Chapter Twenty-Three

The story of Prophet Yasa (Elisha)

The Heavenly Message

Chapter Twenty-Three
The story of Prophet Yasa (Elisha)

Elisha was the helper and student of Elijah. One day, Elisha was working in his field and he saw Elijah, he knew that he was a prophet of the most gracious Creator, so Yasa started to follow Elijah. Before Elias' death, he asked Yasa for anything he wished. Yasa wanted blessings from the most gracious Creator and from Elias. So Elias prayed to the most gracious Creator to fulfill Yasa's wish. The most gracious Creator granted his prayer and made Elisha a prophet to guide the people of Israel. Elisha started to invite the people to worship only the most gracious Creator and that Ba'al was just an idol, who did not have any powers. One day, the people of Israel had a food shortage because there was a drought. The people requested Yasa to pray to the most gracious Creator to remove their drought. So Elisha prayed to Him to remove their drought. The most gracious Creator accepted his prayer and removed the drought. At that time Israel had a bad king and queen, they used to worship the idol Ba'al. Yasa tried to convince the king and queen not to worship Ba'al and follow the most gracious Creator's law. But they did not listen to him and rejected him. When Elisha did not see any hope, he sought the help of a young prince, Jehu, to turn against the evil king and queen. Then, the most gracious Creator destroyed the king and his family. So they shall be brought up, but not the servants of the most gracious Creator, the purified ones. Jehu was against the idol Ba'al. Jehu forced the people to stop the Ba'al worship and killed many bad people who were worshippers of Ba'al. During his time, the people started to follow the most gracious Creator's laws. But unfortunately, after his death, the people of Israel returned to their idols and bad deeds. Elisha was now very old, he asked some of his followers: "Who will be successor after me upon certain conditions, and preach the people calmly and never become angry with them?" Owaidya (Dhu'l-Kifl) said to Yasa: "I accept and will follow your terms." Soon, Elisha passed away.

Chapter Twenty-Four

The story of Prophet Dhu'l-Kifl

The Heavenly Message

Chapter Twenty-Four
The story of Prophet Dhu'l-Kifl

Dhu'l-Kifl was a very patient man and a very good judge. He always kept his promises. During the day, he used to fast. And during the night, he used to pray the whole night for the most gracious Creator. He did not sleep during the day or night. Only at noon, he took a nap. He never became angry at anything. One day, Satan decided to make him angry. He disguised himself as an old man, came to Dhu'l-Kifl while he was taking his nap and made up a story. Satan complained that someone was giving him a hard time, and needed help from Dhu'l-Kifl. To tell his story, Satan took a long time on purpose, so Dhu'l-Kifl missed his naptime. Dhu'l-Kifl asked him to bring that person with him. Satan said: "He would not come if I ask." Then, Dhu'l-Kifl gave him his ring to show that person so he would come. Satan took the ring and went away. Because of Satan, Dhu'l-Kifl could not take his nap that day. The next day after Dhu'l-Kifl finished his work, and about to take his nap, again

The Heavenly Message

Satan came to him and said: "The person refused to take the ring and refused to come." And he told his story in a very long way, that Dhu'l-Kifl missed his nap again the second day. Then, Dhu'l-Kifl gave Satan a letter to take to that person. Satan took the letter and went away. Dhu'l-Kifl became very tired because he could not take a nap for two days. On the third day, after Dhu'l-Kifl finished his work and ready to take a nap, Satan came to him. One of Dhu'l-Kifl's servants tried to stop Satan so as not to disturb his nap, and he should wait till Dhu'l-Kifl woke up from his nap. But Satan made a lot of noises so that Dhu'l-Kifl could not take a nap. Then Dhu'l-Kifl came outside and saw that same old person. Satan said to him: "The person refused to come." Dhu'l-Kifl took his hand and started to walk to the person to settle their dispute. It was very hot and Dhu'l-Kifl was walking in the severe heat of the sun. Satan felt ashamed seeing the prophet's patience and became disappointed that he can not have control over Dhu'l-Kifl. Then, Satan disappeared. Dhu'l-Kifl now knew that he was Satan. Thus, the most gracious Creator named him Dhu'l-Kifl because he took responsibility for something and then fulfilled it.

Chapter Twenty-Five

The story of Prophet Shia (Isaiah)

The Heavenly Message

Chapter Twenty-Five
The story of Prophet Shia (Isaiah)

At that time, The Kingdom of Judah had a very bad king, he did not follow the most gracious Creator's laws, and the kingdom was full of idol worshippers. To guide these people, the most gracious Creator sent Isaiah. Isaiah tried to convince the king and his people to follow the most gracious Creator's laws, otherwise, as a punishment, their enemy would attack them and take over their country. But the king refused to accept Isaiah's advice and rejected him as a prophet. After a few years, that bad king died, and the next king was righteous. His name was Hezekiah; he believed in the most gracious Creator and followed Isaiah's advice. Hezekiah destroyed all the idols and told the people to worship the most gracious Creator and do the right deeds. With the help of Isaiah, Hezekiah established the most gracious Creator's law. One time, king Hezekiah became sick, his foot was infected. In this situation, the enemy, the Assyrian Empire, wanted to attack the Kingdom of

Judah with their big army. Hezekiah did not know what to do. So he asked Isaiah about the situation. Isaiah was waiting for the most gracious Creator's instruction and got bad news for Hezekiah, he said that his time was over and that he should choose another king as his successor. Hezekiah started to weep, he prayed to the most gracious Creator to forgive all of his sins, and accept his good work. The most gracious Creator accepted his prayer, and extended his life; He would even protect Hezekiah's country from the enemy. When Hezekiah heard this from Isaiah, he started to give thanks to the most gracious Creator. Isaiah then put fig juice on Hezekiah's infected foot and the most gracious Creator cured his foot infection. At night, when the enemy was about to attack, a miracle happened. Some of the soldiers suddenly died. When the other soldiers saw this, they were scared and ran away. During the time of Hezekiah, there was no idol worshipping at all. But when the king passed away, the people, day by day started to worship idols again and increased their wrongdoing. Isaiah tried

hard to save the people from their evil acts. But the people rejected him and plotted to kill him. But, Isaiah escaped from them.

Chapter Twenty-Six

The story of Prophet Aramaya (Jeremiah)

The Heavenly Message

Chapter Twenty-Six
The story of Prophet Aramaya (Jeremiah)

The People of Israel were getting worse; they forgot the most gracious Creator and worshipped the idol Ba'al again, they even killed many prophets. So the most gracious Creator decided to destroy The People of Israel and their cities. But as a last warning and chance, He sent Jeremiah to guide the people. When the most gracious Creator told Jeremiah that he would destroy the People of Israel, Jeremiah started to weep, he requested the most gracious Creator to forgive Banu Israel (The Children of Israel). The most gracious Creator told Jeremiah to go to the king and Banu Israel to guide them to become good people, to worship only the most gracious Creator, and follow His laws. Jeremiah preached to the people about the most gracious Creator and told them that it was their last chance to believe, otherwise, He will destroy them. The people rejected him and said that he was a liar. They could not believe that the most gracious Creator will destroy Solomon's Temple and the

The Heavenly Message

Dome of Rock. The king was so arrogant that ordered to arrest Aramaya and send him to prison. So that was their final error. The most gracious Creator sent their enemy which was the king of Babylon. When the Babylonian army reached the gate of Banu Israel city, Banu Israel surrendered and opened their gate. The Babylonian army attacked the city and killed almost the entire population. They only set the disabled and old people free; but unfortunately, they arrested the rest of the people as their slaves. They destroyed all of Banu Israel; they burned all their books including the Torah. One day the king, Nebuchadnezzar of Babylon heard that one of Banu Israel's prophets knew about this disaster in advance. The king ordered his men to bring him from the prison. After talking to Jeremiah, the king realized that he really was the prophet of the most gracious Creator. So the king let Jeremiah go as a free man. After the Babylonians destroyed Banu Israel, they went back to their country with valuable goods as well as many men, women, and children. After that, a new beginning started for Banu Israel at that moment. Jeremiah told the people: "Whoever was in the city of Israel, to say sorry to the most gracious Creator and ask for His Forgiveness, and to stay united and rebuild the town." but most of them did not want to stay in that destroyed country; they again refused the prophet's order. And so, Banu Israel spread all over the world.

The Heavenly Message

Chapter Twenty-Seven

The story of Prophet Daniel

The Heavenly Message

Chapter Twenty-Seven
The story of Prophet Daniel

When the Babylonians destroyed Banu Israel, they took the rest of them as their slaves; Daniel was one of them. In Babylon, Nebuchadnezzar was the king, he ordered the sculptors to make a statue of himself he also ordered all the people to worship him as a god. But Daniel did not accept the statue as a god. When the Nebuchadnezzar knew about Daniel, he became very angry. He ordered that Daniel must be killed by feeding him to the hungry lions. So they threw Daniel to the lions. But the most gracious Creator did a miracle; He commanded the lions not to attack him. When the lions did not attack, the people were so amazed to see the miracle. Nebuchadnezzar realized that this was no ordinary person, soon Daniel was known by everyone. After a while, the king had a dream: he saw that his statue was being destroyed, at first, he did not tell his people; he wanted to see if anyone could guess what his dream was about and tell its meaning.

The Heavenly Message

Whoever could tell it would receive a special reward. But no one could guess what the dream was about, then, the most gracious Creator sent Daniel to the king to show him another miracle. Daniel told the king his dream and its meaning. He said that if he did not become a good person, his kingdom would not last for long. So Nebuchadnezzar became a good person. Daniel gave guidance to Banu Israel to keep faith in the most gracious Creator and ask forgiveness from Him for their mistakes. After many years later, Nebuchadnezzar of Babylon died and his son became king. But the new king was a bad person. One time the most gracious Creator sent some warning signs on his wall; no one could read the signs, but Daniel read the signs and told the king that his time was almost over. Their strong enemy, the Persians, would attack his kingdom and the Babylonians would lose. Soon the Persian king took over the Kingdom of Babylon. The Persian king knew about Daniel and Banu Israel, so he let Banu Israel go back to their Holy Land of Palestine. The Persian king even helped Banu Israel rebuild their town and Temple. Daniel continued to invite the people in Babylon to worship the most gracious Creator and to follow His laws.

The Heavenly Message

Chapter Twenty-Eight

The story of Uzair (Ezra)

The Heavenly Message

Chapter Twenty-Eight
The story of Uzair (Ezra)

When Jerusalem was destroyed by the Babylonians, Uzair passed that town; he saw that it was destroyed. Uzair said: "How is the most gracious Creator going to resurrect this?" Then, the most gracious Creator caused him to die one-hundred years. During one-hundred years, Jerusalem was rebuilt with the help of the Persian king. Everything changed. After one-hundred years, the most gracious Creator resurrected Uzair. Uzair could not recognize the place. The most gracious Creator said: "How long did you rest?" Uzair answered: "I have only rested a day or part of a day." He said: in fact, you have been for one-hundred years in that condition, look at your food and your drink, it has not yet become stale, it is as fresh as it was. Now, look at something else, to prove how long you have been sleeping. Look at your donkey, it is only bones, but watch how We will bring it back to life." Uzair watched. The most gracious Creator said: "Look at how We put the bones together, the bones came together. Look how We clothe it with flesh, the bones were clothed with flesh once again. The donkey came to life." When Uzair saw this clearly, he said: "I declare and I know sound knowledge, I have seen with my eyes, that the most gracious Creator is definitely Able and capable to do anything. Nothing is impossible for Him." When Uzair went back to his people, there was a new generation of the Children of Israel, so they were in doubt as to whom this man was. But there was an old lady, who was blind, beyond one-hundred years old. The people asked her: "Do you know this man known as Uzair?" She said: "Yes he was a pious man, saintly man. All the prayers he made were accepted." She said: "But wait, if he is the same Uzair, every prayer he made were accepted, so tell him to make prayer to the most gracious Creator that my eyesight and health is restored." So Uzair made the prayer: "May this woman's eyesight and health be restored." And they were restored by the gift of the most gracious Creator. When the woman's eyesight and health were restored, she saw him and said: "Indeed this is the man, this is the same Uzair." When the woman took Uzair to his family, his elder son at that time was old. When the woman introduced Uzair to his family, they were shocked. They said: "How can that young man be our father?" Uzair's son knew there was a certain mark on Uzair. When Uzair showed them, they recognized their father. The people told him that the Babylonians destroyed all their books including the Torah. They did not have the knowledge of the Torah anymore. Uzair was the only man that had memorized the Torah, so he dedicated the entire Torah at that stage, and taught it to the Children of Israel, he also united them. Banu Israel was good people for the next 200 years. But, the people in Northern Palestine, Samaria, rejected Ezra as a prophet. They build a new worship center of idols to attract other people. So the people of Ezra and the people of Samaria started to hate each other. Later on, some of the Jews say that Ezra is the son of God. In Uzair's time.

Chapter Twenty-Nine

The story of Prophet Yunus (Jonah)

The Heavenly Message

Chapter Twenty-Nine
The story of Prophet Yunus (Jonah)

One day the most gracious Creator spoke to Jonah, son of Amittai. He said: "Go to Nineveh, that great city, and speak out against it; I am aware of how wicked its people are." Jonah, however, set out in the opposite direction in order to get away from the Lord. He went to Joppa, where he found a ship to go to Spain. He paid his fare and went aboard with the crew to sail to Spain, where he would be away from the Lord. But the most gracious Creator sent a strong wind on the sea, and the storm was so violent that the ship was in danger of breaking up. The sailors were terrified and cried out for help, each one to their own god. Then, in order to lessen the danger, they threw the cargo overboard. Meanwhile, Jonah had gone below and was lying in the ship's hold, sound asleep. The captain found him there and said to him: "What are you doing asleep? Get up and pray to your god for help. Maybe he will feel sorry for us and spare our lives." The sailors said to each other: "Let's draw lots and find out who is to blame for getting us into this danger." They did so, and Jonah's name was drawn. So they said to him: "Now then, tell us! Who is to blame for this? What are you doing here? What country do you come from? What is your nationality?" "I am a Hebrew," Jonah answered. "I worship the most gracious Creator, the God of heaven, who made land and sea." Jonah went on to tell them that he was running away from the Him. The sailors were terrified, and said to him: "That was an awful thing to do!" The storm was getting worse all the time, so the sailors asked him, "What should we do to you to stop the storm?" Jonah answered, "Throw me into the sea, and it will calm down. I know it is my fault that you are caught in this violent storm." Instead, the sailors tried to get the ship to shore, rowing with all their might. But the storm was getting worse and worse, and they got nowhere. So they cried out to the most gracious Creator, "O Lord, we pray: do not punish us with death for taking this man's life! You, O Lord, are responsible for all this; it is your doing." Then they picked Jonah up and threw him into the sea, and it calmed down at once. This made the sailors so afraid of the most gracious Creator that they offered a sacrifice and promised to serve Him. At the most gracious Creator's Command, a large fish swallowed Jonah, and he was inside the fish for three days and three nights. From deep inside the fish, Jonah prayed to the most gracious Creator: "In my distress, O the most gracious Creator, I called to you and you answered me. From deep in the world of the dead, I cried for help and you heard me. You threw me down into the depths, to the very bottom of the sea, where the waters were all around me, and all your mighty waves rolled over me. I thought I had been banished from your presence and would never see your Holy Temple again. The water came over me and choked me; the sea covered me completely, and seaweed wrapped itself around my head. I went down to the very roots of the mountains, into the land whose gates locked shut forever. But You, O the most gracious Creator, my God, brought me back from the depths alive. When I felt my life slipping away, then, O Lord, I prayed to you, and in

The Heavenly Message

your Holy Temple, you heard me. Those who worship worthless idols have abandoned their loyalty to you. But I will sing praises to you; I will offer You a sacrifice and do what I have promised. Salvation comes from the Lord!" Then the most gracious Creator ordered the fish to vomit Jonah up on the beach, and it did. Once again, He spoke to Jonah. He said: "Go to Nineveh, that great city, and proclaim to the people the message I have given you." So Jonah obeyed the most gracious Creator and went to Nineveh, a city so large that it took three days to walk through it. Jonah started through the city, and after walking a whole day, he proclaimed, "In forty days Nineveh will be destroyed!" The people of Nineveh believed the most gracious Creator's message. So they decided that everyone should fast, and all the people, from the greatest to the least, put on sackcloth to show that they had repented. When the king of Nineveh heard about it, he got up from his throne, took off his robe, put on sackcloth, and sat down in ashes. He sent out a proclamation to the people of Nineveh: "This is an order from the king and his officials: No one is to eat anything; all people, cattle, and sheep are forbidden to eat or drink. All people and animals must wear sackcloth. Everyone must pray earnestly to the most gracious Creator and must give up their wicked behavior and their evil actions. Perhaps He will change His mind; perhaps He will stop being angry, and we will not die!" the most gracious Creator saw what they did; He saw that they had given up their wicked behavior. So He changed his mind and did not punish them as He had said He would. Jonah was very unhappy about this and became angry. So he prayed, "the most gracious Creator, did not I say before I left home that this is just what You would do? That's why I did my best to run away to Spain! I knew that You were a Loving and Merciful God, always Patient, always Kind, and always ready to change your mind and not punish. Now then, Lord, let me die. I am better off dead than alive." the most gracious Creator answered, "What right do you have to be angry?" Jonah went out east of the city and sat down. He made a shelter for himself and sat in its shade, waiting to see what would happen to Nineveh. Then the most gracious Creator made a plant grow up over Jonah to give him some shade, so that he would be more comfortable. Jonah was extremely pleased with the plant. But at dawn the next day, at the most gracious Creator's Command, a worm attacked the plant, and it died. After the after the sun had risen, God sent a hot east wind, and Jonah was about to faint from the heat of the sun beating down on his head. So he wished he were dead. "I am better dead than alive," he said. But the most gracious Creator said to him, "What right do you have to be angry about the plant?" Jonah replied, "I have every right to be angry – angry enough to die!" the most gracious Creator said to him: "This plant grew up in one night and disappeared the next day; you did not make it grow – yet you feel sorry for it! How much more, then, should I have pity on Nineveh, that great city, after all, it has more than 120,000 innocent children in it, as well as many animals!"

Yunus was sent to Nineveh, the biggest city in Iraq. The most gracious Creator sent him to a hundred thousand people or more. He instructed Yunus to guide these people, call them towards the most gracious Creator, and to warn them of the previous punishments of the previous nations. And to tell them that the most gracious Creator is Able to send them punishments if they would not believe. So Yunus started calling them towards the most gracious Creator, but they did not listen, they started mocking him and doing what the previous nations had done. Yunus was very irritated by them and his patience was running out. Yunus decided: "I am not winning with these people, so, I will go away, I might find other people somewhere very far away and might call those people towards the most gracious Creator, they might listen. The most gracious Creator had not instructed Yunus to go away, but Yunus really wanted to spread his Da'wa and really wanted these people to accept his Da'wa but no one was accepting. So he went to the laden ship and went into it. As the ship was sailing on calmly, soon the wind started blowing, a storm started gathering, then the ship started rocking, and after a while, the ship started sinking. When it started sinking the people in the ship decided to throw all their goods into the sea to make the ship lighter. But the boat was still sinking. Then, the people decided to draw lots, "Whoever's name is drawn, we will throw him into the sea. It is the only way to save the ship." When Yunus's name was drawn, they said: "No, he is a good man, a blessed man, so let us try again." Then, Yunus's name was drawn the second time. They said: "No, it can't be, let's try again." For the third time, Yunus's name was picked out. Then, the people said, "Sorry, but we have to throw you off this ship." Yunus said: "In the name of the most gracious Creator." And he jumped out of the ship. Then the most gracious Creator instructed a whale to swallow Yunus. So the whale took him into its mouth unconscious, in the belly of the whale while he was blamable. He gets up, after a while, and he thought that the most gracious Creator would not straiten him, so he called out among afflictions: There is no God but Thou, glory be to Thee! Surely, I am of the sufferers of loss. But had he not been of those who glorify Him, he would have tarried in its belly till the day when they are raised. So He responded to Yunus and instructed the whale to put Yunus out on the shore. And thus does He deliver the believers. Yunus's skin was quite eaten, and the sun was affecting him. So, the most gracious Creator caused a gourd to grow up for him to give him shade and health. And when Yunus went back to Nineveh, he was shocked; the people were worshipping the most gracious Creator! While Yunus was away, the most gracious Creator sent dark clouds to the people, when they saw the dark clouds, they remembered the punishments of the previous nations. They decided that this was a punishment sent to them, so they all repented and worshipped the most gracious Creator. And why was there not a town which believed, so that their belief should have profited them, but the people of Yunus? Then the most gracious Creator removed from them the chastisement of disgrace in this world's life, and He gave them provision till a time.

Chapter Thirty

The story of Prophet Zechariah (Zacharias)

The Heavenly Message

Chapter Thirty
The story of Prophet Zechariah (Zacharias)

After Uzair passed away, about 100 years later, a Greek king, Alexander, took control over Palestine. Then, around 130 years later, Greece had an awful king; he tried to control Banu Israel with different ways. After his death, another awful Greek king took over, he was worse than the others. He tried to destroy the most gracious Creator's laws he forced Banu Israel not to worship the most gracious Creator or follow the Torah; he built idols inside Masjid-l Aqsa and forced the people to accept those idols as their gods. He made it a law: Whoever worships the most gracious Creator or follow the Torah, they would be executed. Because of this, some of the good Banu Israel got together and fought back against the Greek king. Banu Israel won and got back their kingdom of Maccabees. At first, Banu Israel were very good people and worshiped the most gracious Creator and followed the Torah; Then Rome controlled Palestine, the Roman government chose a puppet king from Banu Israel to rule Palestine. His name was Herod;

The Heavenly Message

he was very sly and bad. To run his kingdom he kept all of the priests happy to get support from Banu Israel, he also kept the Roman king happy to get his support so he could stay as the king of Palestine. Banu Israel became greedy and selfish, they were using the religion as their business, they made a lot of money from people and gave some of their share to King Herod. They also were changing the most gracious Creator's laws for their own benefit. They even divided themselves. So within 100 years, they lost their kingdom. To guide Banu Israel, the most gracious Creator sent Prophet Zachariah; he was a priest and a religious leader of Banu Israel. He tried hard in his whole life to guide the people; he was a carpenter for his living expense. Soon after, Zachariah adopted Maryam, who was later the mother of Isa; in his old age, he was worried that after his death, who would guide Banu Israel? There in the sanctuary did Zacharias pray to his Lord, crying in secret. He said: My the most gracious Creator, my bones are weakened, and my head flares with hoariness, and I have never

The Heavenly Message

been unsuccessful in my prayer to Thee, my Lord. And I fear kinsfolk after me, and my wife is barren, so grant me from Thyself an heir who should inherit me and inherit of the Children of Jacob, and make him, my Lord, acceptable to Thee. Surely, Thou art the Hearer of prayer. So the angels called to him as he stood praying in the sanctuary: "the most gracious Creator gives thee good news of a boy, whose name is John (Yahya), verifying a word from the most gracious Creator, honorable and chaste and a prophet from among the good ones. He has not made before anyone his equal." And the most gracious Creator made Zachariah's' wife fit for him. Surely, they used to compete, one with another, in good deeds and called upon Him, hoping and fearing; and they were humble before Him. He said: "My Lord, how can I have a son when old age has already come upon me, and my wife is barren?" The angels said: "Thy Lord says: It is easy to Me, and indeed I created thee before when thou was nothing." Zachariah said: "My Lord, appoint a sign for me." He said: "Thy sign is that thou speak not to men for three days, except by signs, being in sound health, and remember thy Lord much and glorify Him in the evening and early morning." So Zacharias went forth to his people from the sanctuary and proclaimed to them: "Glorify the most gracious Creator morning and evening." Soon, Yahya was born; Zachariah guided and taught him about the most gracious Creator and His Laws during his childhood. Both father and son tried hard to guide Banu Israel. They hated the idea of using religion for business. But some of the people and the priests started to hate Zachariah and Yahya. For their benefit, the bad Banu Israel decided to kill Zachariah and Yahya. And sadly, they did.

Chapter Thirty-One

The story of Mary (Maryam)

The Heavenly Message

Chapter Thirty-One
The story of Mary (Maryam)

Zachariah's wife and Mary's mother were both sisters. Mary's mother was a wife of Imran. When she said: "My Most Gracious Creator, I vow to Thee what is in my womb, to be devoted to Thy service, so accept it from me; surely Thou, only Thou, art the Hearing, the Knowing." So when she brought it forth, she said: "My Lord, I have brought it forth a female – and You know best what I bring forth – and the male is not like the female, and I have named it Mary, and I commend her and her offspring into Thy protection from the accursed devil." The daughter of Imran, Maryam, she was one who guarded her chastity. The most gracious Creator breathed into her of His inspiration, and she accepted the truth of the words of her Lord and His Books, and she was of the obedient ones. After Mary was born, her father, Imran passed away. As a promise, the wife of Imran gave Maryam up to the Temple. Because Maryam's father, Imran was a very good priest, many people wanted to adopt Maryam, even her uncle

Zachariah, wanted to adopt her and they contended one with another. So, they cast their pens to decide which of them should have Mary in his charge, they wrote their names on a wooden pen and placed them in a container, and then they let a random child select one of the pens from the container. The child picked Zacharias' name, but the others were not happy with it. So, they decided to put their wooden pens into a river they said that whoever's name on the pen floats against the river flow, then, that person would be the one to adopt Maryam. With the most gracious Creator's Plan, Zachariah's pen floated against the river flow. So, Zacharias took care of Maryam in the Temple. She had a special place in the Temple to live and to worship the most gracious Creator. So her Lord accepted her with a goodly acceptance and made her grow up a goodly growing, and gave her into the charge of Zacharias. Whenever Zacharias entered the sanctuary to see her, he found food and out of season fruits with her. He said: "O Mary, whence comes this to thee?" She said: "It is from the most gracious

The Heavenly Message

Creator. Surely, He gives to whom He pleases without measure; when she drew aside from her family to an eastern place; so she screened herself from them." Then the most gracious Creator sent to her His Spirit and it appeared to her as a well-made man. She said: "I flee for refuge from thee to the Beneficent, the most gracious Creator, do not come near, if thou art one guarding against evil." He said: "I am only a bearer of a message of thy Lord: That I will give thee a pure boy whose name is the Messiah, Jesus, son of Mary, worthy of regard in this world and the Hereafter, and of those who are drawn nigh to the most gracious Creator, he will speak to the people when in the cradle and when of old age, and he will be one of the good ones." She said: "How can I have a son and no mortal has yet touched me, nor have I been unchaste?" He said: "So it will be. Thy Lord says: It is easy to Me; the most gracious Creator creates what He pleases. When He decrees a matter, He only says to it: Be. And it is. And that the most gracious Creator may make him a sign to men and a mercy from Him. And He will teach him the

Book and the Wisdom and the Torah and the Gospel." And the angel said: "O Mary, surely the most gracious Creator has chosen thee and purified thee and chosen thee above the women of the world. O Mary, be obedient to thy Lord and humble thyself and bow down with those who bow. This is of the tidings of things unseen which We reveal to thee." Day by day, a few people started to guess that Mary was pregnant. To avoid the public shame of carrying a child without a husband, she left the house and started to walk to a remote place where there were no people who could see her in that condition. And the pains of childbirth drove her to the trunk of a palm-tree. She said: "Oh, would that I had died before this, and had been a thing quite forgotten!" So a voice came to her from beneath her: "Grieve not, surely thy Lord has provided a stream beneath thee. And shake towards thee the trunk of the palm-tree, it will drop on you fresh ripe dates. So eat and drink and cool the eye. Then if thou seest any mortal, say: Surely, I have vowed a fast to the Beneficent, so I will not speak to any man today." And the most gracious Creator made the son of Mary and his mother a sign, and He gave them refuge on a lofty ground having meadows and springs. Then Maryam came to her people with Isa, carrying him. They said: "O Mary, thou hast indeed brought a strange thing! O sister of Aaron, thy father was not a wicked man, nor was thy mother an unchaste woman!" But Mary pointed to him. They said: "How should we speak to one who is a child in the cradle?" But, as a miracle from the most gracious Creator Isa spoke to them in the cradle! He said: "I am indeed a servant of the most gracious Creator. He has given me the Book and made me a prophet: And He has made me blessed wherever I may be, and He has enjoined on me prayer and poor-rate so long as I live: And to be kind to my mother; and He has not made me insolent, unblessed. And peace on me the day I was born, and the day I die, and the day I am raised to life." Such is Jesus son of Mary – a statement of truth about which they dispute. When the people saw and heard this, they knew that this was a very special baby. Some of them believed in

Maryam and Isa and some did not like that. The event reached king Herod, they thought that Jesus would be bad for them, so, they plotted to kill baby Isa. But with the most gracious Creator's Plan, Maryam took her baby, and moved to another place. When Herod died, Mary and Jesus moved to Nazareth, a small town in Northern Palestine, where Jesus spent his childhood. And Maryam who guarded her chastity, the most gracious Creator breathed into her of His Inspiration, and made her and her son a sign to the nations.

Chapter Thirty-Two

The story of Prophet Yahya (John)

The Heavenly Message

Chapter Thirty-Two
The story of Prophet Yahya (John)

When Yahya was born; Zachariah guided Yahya and taught him about the most gracious Creator and His laws during his childhood. And the most gracious Creator granted him wisdom in his childhood and kind-heartedness from Him and purity. And he was dutiful, And kindly to his parents, and he was not insolent, disobedient. With the most gracious Creator's guidance, Yahya learned the Torah and the Psalms, and it was said to him, "O John, take hold of the Books with strength." Yahya started to spread the most gracious Creator's laws since his childhood. He could explain to the people in very depth about their laws. Yahya always asked forgiveness from the most gracious Creator. One day, when he did not come home, his parents were looking for him; they found him crying next to the Jordan River. They asked him why he was crying. Yahya replied: "I was crying for the most gracious Creator's mercy and forgiveness. Sometimes we make mistakes without perceiving. Even for small and big mistakes, we should ask Him for His Forgiveness." Yahya was always humble and was kind to all creatures. After Herod's death, all of the lands were divided between three of his sons. One of his bad sons was Antipas, who ruled part of Palestine. Yahya and his father Zachariah tried to guide the people to follow the most gracious Creator's laws so they would become good. When they saw any wrongdoing, they would try to stop it. But some of the people and the priests started to hate Zachariah and Yahya. One time, Antipas wanted to marry his own niece. And his niece also wanted to marry her uncle, so she would become queen of Palestine. But according to the most gracious Creator's laws, they could not marry each other because their relationship between them was uncle and niece. Unfortunately, some of the bad priests supported the king in marrying his niece for money. Yahya and Zachariah tried to stop that marriage. Yahya told the people how the king was trying to destroy the most gracious Creator's Laws. So the king, the bad priests, and some of the bad Banu Israel became very angry with the two prophets. Antipas ordered his men to arrest Yahya and put him in prison. Antipas' niece became very angry with Yahya, because of him she could not become queen. She still wanted to become queen, so, she went to Antipas and asked for a special gift. The king promised to give her anything that she wanted. When she got the king's promise, she asked for the head of Yahya. To fulfill the promise that he made, the king ordered his men to kill Yahya and bring his head on a plate. This was one of Banu Israel's evil activities and worst mistakes. But the most gracious Creator was so Merciful, that he sent Isa (Jesus) to guide Banu Israel to become good people. Peace is on Yahya the day he was born, and the day he died, and the day, he is raised to life!

Chapter Thirty-Three

The story of Prophet Isa (Jesus)

The Heavenly Message

Chapter Thirty-Three
The story of Prophet Isa (Jesus)

Isa and Yahya were born as miracles at the same year. During his childhood at Nazareth, Banu Israel celebrated a special event called Passover. So, a lot of people came to Masjid-l-Aqsa from different places. When Isa was 12 years old, he came to Aqsa with his mother, Maryam on Passover. He used to hear the speeches of the priests. He would ask the priests questions that even the priests could not answer. As Jesus grew up, he noticed that some of the people were doing terrible deeds in the name of religion. Some of the bad priests made their Sabbath law harder and harder and made it difficult for people. Sometimes during Sabbath, the bad priests would not even allow calling the doctor for a very sick person. That is why many of times, people cheated and broke the most gracious Creator's laws. So the most gracious Creator cleared some of the Laws. He chose Isa as a Prophet to guide Banu Israel. He taught Isa the Torah and the Psalms, and Isa understood the depths meaning of the Laws the most gracious Creator also gave him a new book of Laws, and that was the Injil (Gospel). In his hometown in a gathering, Jesus declared: "I have come to you indeed with wisdom, and to make clear to you some of that about which you differ. This is the right path." But parties among them differed, so woe to those who did wrong for the chastisement of a painful day! Wait they for aught but the Hour, that it should come on them all of a sudden, while they perceive not? Friends on that day will be foes one to another, except those who keep their duty. But most of Banu Israel did not accept Isa as a Prophet or his message. Soon, it became very difficult for him to make others worship the most gracious Creator and follow His Laws. So Isa asked the people: "Who are my helpers in the cause of the most gracious Creator? 12 disciples said: "We are helpers in the cause of the most gracious Creator, and bear thou witness that we are submitting ones. Our Lord, we believe in that which Thou hast revealed and we follow the messenger, so write us down with those who bear witness."

So a party of the Children of Israel believed and another party disbelieved; then the most gracious Creator aided those who believed against their enemy, and they became predominant. So only a few people of the Banu Israel accepted his Prophethood and message. The disciples and Jesus traveled from place to place to teach the Children of Israel to worship the most gracious Creator and follow His Laws. During Jesus' work, he used to show Banu Israel his miracles by the most gracious Creator's leave, he said to the people: "I have come to you with a sign from your Lord, that I determine for you out of dust the form of a bird, then I breathe into it and it becomes a bird with the most gracious Creator's permission, and I heal those born blind, and the lepers, and I wake up the dead with His Permission. And I inform you of what you should eat and what you should store in your houses. Surely, there is a sign in this for you, if you are believers. And I am a verifier of that which is before me of the Torah, and I allow you part of that which was forbidden to you; I have come to you with a sign from your Lord, so keep your duty to the most gracious Creator and obey me. Surely, the most gracious Creator is my Lord and your Lord, so serve Him. This is the right path." One day, he and his disciples went into a marketplace and saw a blind man begging, saying that he had been blind his whole life. Isa felt sorry for that man, so he prayed to the most gracious Creator to cure the blind man's eyes. So when Isa touched the blind man's eyes, as a miracle from the most gracious Creator, his eyes were cured! Then, many people instantly knew that he was truly was a Prophet sent by the most gracious Creator. One time, Jesus was giving a speech to a small town when a man with a bad skin disease, requested Jesus to cure his disease. So Jesus prayed to the most gracious Creator to cure this person. As another miracle, the most gracious Creator cured the man's disease in front of many people. Having seen that miracle, many people started to worship the most gracious Creator and follow His laws. On his way, Isa saw a dead child, and the family was weeping. The family asked Isa to bring him back to life. Jesus told them that he did not have the power to bring the life back from the dead except by the most gracious Creator's Permission. So Jesus prayed to the most gracious Creator to bring this child to life. So the most gracious Creator brought the child to life. Many people realized that Isa was the real prophet of the most gracious Creator and they accepted him as a messenger. Some of the Banu Israel could not believe the miracle; they thought that Jesus could only give life back to those who only died recently; maybe they did not even die. To prove his ability, they took him to a grave and bring back the life of someone who died a long time ago. Isa prayed to the most gracious Creator to bring back a dead person. And by His Permission, the person came back to life. After seeing extraordinary miracles, some people began to think that he is god. But Jesus said to them: "O Children of Israel serve the most gracious Creator, my Lord and your Lord. Surely, whoever associates others with Him, He has forbidden him the Garden and his abode is the Fire. I heal those born blind, and the lepers, and I wake up the dead by the most gracious Creator's Permission. And for the wrongdoers there will be no helpers. One day Isa and his disciples came to a town hungry, and the people of the town also did not have any food. So the disciples said: "O Jesus son of Mary, is thy Lord able to send down food to us from heaven?" He said: "Keep your duty to the most gracious Creator if you are believers." They said: "We desire to eat of it, and that our hearts should be at rest, and that we may know that thou hast indeed spoken truth to us, and that we may be witnesses thereof." Isa said: O, the most gracious Creator, our Lord, send down for us an ever-recurring happiness to the first and last of us, and a sign from Thee, and give us sustenance and Thou art the Best of sustainers. The most gracious Creator said: Surely, I will send it down to you, but whoever disbelieves afterwards from among you, I will chastise him with a chastisement with which I will not chastise anyone among the nations. So when the most gracious Creator sent down the food, the people ate and thanked Him. Day by day

Jesus' followers became bigger and bigger, even some of the rich people started to give their money to the poor. On Friday night, Jesus saw some children and they were so hungry, that they were crying, so Isa picked out some fresh fruit, for the hungry children. Some of the people did not like this because it was breaking the Sabbath law. On another Friday night, it was cold, Jesus saw elderly ladies who were shivering from the cold, so Jesus made some fire for the old ladies. The priests also thought that this was breaking the Sabbath law. On the big celebration, Passover, Isa and his disciples went to Aqsa to preach to the people. By that time, Isa had enemies; the priests were planning to kill him. At that time, to go inside the Temple, the people had to pay a lot of money. The priests would even waste a lot of food, even if they knew that there were poor people outside hungry. Isa became very sad after seeing the situation, he knew that the priests were changing or misunderstood the most gracious Creator's Laws. Jesus tried to explain to the people that in order to save them from punishment of the mistakes that they were making, the most gracious Creator sent new laws for them the Injil to correct some of the old laws. But most of the priests did not like Isa because his teaching will affect the benefit of the bad priests. The bad priests started to say that he was not a prophet. So Isa showed the people another miracle to prove that he was a prophet of the most gracious Creator. He took some clay, molded it into a shape of a bird, blew into it, and by the most gracious Creator's permission, it became a live bird! More people realized that this was the prophet of the most gracious Creator. But some of the people thought that Isa came to destroy the Laws of Musa. Jesus said: Children of Israel, "Surely I am the messenger of the most gracious Creator to you, verifying that which is before me of the Torah giving the good news of a Messenger who will come after me, his name being Ahmad (Muhammed)." But when he came to them with clear arguments, they said: "This is clear enchantment." One day, an educated person came to Isa and asked him: "What was the most important order from the most gracious Creator?" Isa replied: "To obey the One and Only God the most gracious Creator. And to be good to the neighbors and love them from the heart." More and more people started to follow Jesus, so the bad priests' business became weak. Most of the bad priests became very angry, so they were planning on how to stop Isa. First, they said bad things about Isa to the people, they even said that his birth was not a miracle, and his mother Mary, was a bad woman, which is why he did not have a father. In different places the priests and the bad people tried to stop Isa and his disciples, sometimes they threatened them. But Isa and his strong helpers did not stop. When the priests saw that it was impossible to stop him, they planned to kill him. One of the priests advised not to kill Jesus because much people followed him and would not like that action. One of the priests even said that if they kill Jesus, then the others would think that the priests are even worse. While they were discussing their plan to kill Jesus, one of Isa's 12 disciples, Judas Iscariot, went to them and asked: "What will you give me if I deliver him to you?" Judas bargained with them until they agreed to give him thirty pieces of silver; thus Judas betrayed Isa. So the priests planned a plan and went to the Roman government, He was given the responsibility to control Palestine. The priests convinced the Roman government, that if they could not stop Isa, even the Romans would be affected because they could not make money from synagogues, and would lose their control over Palestine. So the Roman government believed them and became very angry with Isa. Then, the Roman government and the bad priests decided to kill Isa by crucifixion. So the Jews planned and the most gracious Creator planned, He is the Best of planners. When Isa heard about this, he was not worried; he knew that the most gracious Creator will protect him. The most gracious Creator said: "O Jesus, I will cause thee to die and exalt thee in My presence and clear thee of those who disbelieve and make those who follow thee above those who disbelieve to the day of Resurrection. Then to Me is your return, so I shall decide between you concerning that wherein you differ. Then as to those who disbelieve, I shall chastise them with severe chastisement in this world and the Hereafter, and they will have no helpers. And as to those who believe and do good deeds, He will pay them fully their rewards, I do not Love the unjust." These are messages and the Reminder full of wisdom. As planned, the bad Jews on Friday evening carried out their plan, and asked Judas where Isa was. Judas saw Isa and went to the Jews to show them where he was. While leading them to Isa, as a punishment, the most gracious Creator changed the face of Judas to look like Jesus. Then the most gracious Creator resurrected Isa up to the heavens. The bad Jews were confused in the dark, when they saw Judas; they thought he was Jesus because he looked exactly like him. When they seized him, Judas cried out: "I am Judas! I am leading you to Jesus!" But they said: "If you are Judas, how come you look like Jesus." So they took him and crucified him. The bad Jews said in boast, "We killed Isa son of Mary!" But they did not kill him nor crucified him. But the most gracious Creator made it appear to them,

and those who differ therein are full of doubts, with no certain knowledge, but only an assumption to follow, for surely they did not kill him, the most gracious Creator raised him up to Himself; and He is Exalted in Power, Wise.

Chapter Thirty-Four

The story of Prophet Du-l-qarnain

The Heavenly Message

Chapter Thirty-Four
The story of Prophet Du-l-qarnain

Du-l-qarnain was a man gifted by the most gracious Creator with many talents and abilities, including military ability, the ability to rule two kingdoms at a time, he derived the name Du-l-qarnain because he was a king of two kingdoms, and widespread practical knowledge on many aspects of life. He was also a pious and steadfast believer who constantly contemplated over the signs of the most gracious Creator and lived his days traveling from one place to another to establish justice in the land and lessen the suffering of people. Truly, the most gracious Creator established Du-l-qarnain and granted him means of access to everything. So he followed a course to the west. Until, when he reached the setting-place of the sun, he found it going down into a black sea, and found by it a people; a people who were living under oppressed conditions. The most gracious Creator said: "O Du-l-qarnain, either punish them or do them a benefit." Du-l-qarnain said: "As for him who is unjust, we shall chastise him, then he will be returned to his Lord, and He will chastise him with an exemplary chastisement. And as for him who believes and does good, for him is a good reward, and the most gracious Creator shall speak to him an easy word of His command." Having completed his task, Du-l-qarnain and his army followed a course. Until, when he reached the land of the rising sun, he found it rising on a people to whom the most gracious Creator had given no shelter from it. They were backward and ignorant people. So Du-l-qarnain educated the community there on what they needed to do. He shared and imparted his knowledge to them, taught them the skills required such as carpentry and agriculture, and then continued on his journey. The most gracious Creator had full knowledge of what he had. Then Du-l-qarnain followed a course. Until, when he reached a place between two mountains, he found on that side of them a people who could hardly understand a word. They said: "O Dhu-l-qarnain, Gog, and Magog do mischief in the land. May we then pay thee tribute on condition that thou raise a barrier between them and us?" He said: "That wherein my Most Gracious Creator has established me is better, so it only you help me with the strength of men. I will make you a fortified barrier between you and them. Bring me blocks of iron." At length, when he had filled up the space between the two mountain sides, he said, "Blow." Till, when he had made it as fire, he said: "Bring me molten brass to pour over it. So they were not able to scale it, nor could they make a hole in it. He said: "This is a mercy from my Lord, but when the promise of my Lord comes to pass He will crumble it, and the promise of my Lord is ever true. When Gog and Magog are let loose and they sally forth from every elevated place. And the True Promise draws nigh, then lo! The eyes of those who disbelieve will be fixedly open: O woe to us! Surely, we were heedless of this; nay, we were unjust."

Chapter Thirty-Five

The story of the People of the Cave

The Heavenly Message

Chapter Thirty-Five
The story of the People of the Cave

The incident is set against the backdrop of a society that was deeply immersed in idol worshipping and other false beliefs. Departure from the established pagan practices was not tolerated, and anyone caught violating this belief system, faced terrible consequences. There were a small number of youths, who were the sons of rulers and noblemen, and were accustomed to lives of comfort and luxury. Even so, they realized that their townspeople were immersed in wrongful practices by worshipping other than the most gracious Creator as their only Lord. Unlike their elders, they recognized the truth and secretly shunned the false gods and customs that their elders supported. For this, the most gracious Creator increased their faith and guided them. The townspeople, each year, would assemble in a festival, during which time they would prostrate to their idols. During one such event, these youths could no longer bear the situation around them, so they sat in the shade of a tree away from the pagan rituals. Shortly after, more youths joined them. At first, the youths kept their belief in the most gracious Creator concealed for fear of repercussions, but within their secret assembly, they confessed their rejection of idolatry and affirmed their belief in the most gracious Creator. From that day, they met regularly to worship the most gracious Creator in secret. During this time, the most gracious Creator strengthened their faith for the events which would unfold. Eventually, word of their activities reached the king. So they were summoned before the king. When questioned by the king, they refused to submit to him, but instead, tried to invite the king to the Path of the most gracious Creator, and He strengthened their hearts when they stood up and said: "Our Most Gracious Creator is the Lord of the heavens and the earth; we call upon no god beside Him, for then indeed we should utter an enormity. These people have taken gods besides Him. Who is then more unjust than he who forges a lie against the most gracious Creator?" But the king rejected their call to the Path of the most gracious Creator. The youths were stripped of their fine clothing and ornaments; they were giving the night to 'repent' from their ways. With the most gracious Creator's Might, the youths managed to escape captivity during the course of the night. One of them said: "And when you withdraw from them and what they worship besides the most gracious Creator, take refuge in the Cave; your Lord will spread forth for you a profitable course in your affair." The king ordered his men to give chase, but the most gracious Creator concealed the youths from their sight. When the youths sought refuge in the Cave, they said: "Our Lord, the most gracious Creator, grant us mercy from Thyself, and provide for us a right course in our affair." So He prevented them from hearing and He caused them to sleep in the Cave for a number of years, and they remained in their cave three hundred years, and they add nine. But the most gracious Creator knows best how long they remained. The most gracious Creator is the Unseen of the heavens and the earth. How clear His Sight and His Hearing!

There is no guardian for them besides Him, and He associates none in His Judgment. Then He raised them up that He might know which of the two parties was best able to calculate the time for which they remained. Surely, they were youths who believed in their Lord and He increased them in guidance. The most gracious Creator said: "And thou mightest see the sun, when it rose, the decline from their Cave to the right, and when it set, leave them behind on the left, while they were in a wide space thereof. This is of the signs of the most gracious Creator. He whom the most gracious Creator guides, he is on the right way; and whom He leaves in error, thou wilt not find for him a friend to guide aright. And thou mightest think them awake while they were asleep, and He turned them about to the right and to the left, with their dog out-stretching its paws at the entrance." Some say: They (The Youths) were three, the forth of them their dog; and others say: "Five, the sixth of them their dog, making conjectures about the unseen. And others say: "Seven and the eighth of them their dog." Our Most Gracious Creator knows their number – none knows them but a few. So contend not in their matter but with an outward contention, and question not any of them concerning them. If thou didst look at them, thou wouldst turn back from them in flight, and thou wouldst be filled with awe because of them. And thus did He rouse them that they might question each other. A speaker from among them said: "How long have you tarried?" They said: "We have tarried for a day or a part of a day." Others said: "Your Lord knows best how long you have tarried. Now send one of you with this silver coin of yours to the city, then let him see what food is purest, and bring you provision from it, and let him behave with gentleness, and make not your case known to anyone. For if they prevail against you, they would stone you to death or force you back to their religion, and then you would never succeed." And thus did the most gracious Creator make men to get knowledge of them, that they might know that His promise is true and that the Hour – there is no doubt about it. The king and the rest of the unbelievers who had persecuted them had died several generations earlier, but the youth did not know this. As he went into the town cautiously, he did not recognize the place. He tried to buy some food with his coin, but the seller did not recognize the currency or the markings on it. The coins were passed down from person to person, all of whom were baffled and unable to identify their origin. The Youth told the townspeople where he was from and the ruler at that time, and his story was so unlikely that he was brought to face the governor to explain himself. The governor, who believed in the most gracious Creator, listened to the youth's story. The governor and the townspeople where so amazed by what they heard that they asked to meet the rest of the group. By the most gracious Creator's will, the society by then, had embraced monotheistic belief in the most gracious Creator, therefore, the youths safety was no longer under threat. When the rest of the youths came, there was joyfulness in the town, and the people said: "Erect a structure over them. Your Lord knows best about them." Those who prevailed in their

affair said: "We shall certainly build a place of worship over them." And say not of anything: "I will do that tomorrow, unless the most gracious Creator please. And remember thy Lord when thou forget and say: Maybe my Lord will guide me to a nearer course to the right than this."

Chapter Thirty-Six

The Story of Prophet Hammed Nagar

The Heavenly Message

Chapter Thirty-Six
The story of Prophet Hammed Nagar

Prophet Nagar was the forth and the last messenger from the most gracious Creator sent to the dwellers of a Town, where the people of the town spread violence and evildoers everywhere, they were living evil lives; the most gracious Creator at first, had sent two messengers to them preaching the words of the most gracious Creator to them, perhaps they will give up their evilness and return to the straight path, but instead, they turn away from the truth and denied the two messengers, and the third messenger was sent to strengthen those two messengers earlier, in order for the dwellers of the town be admonished. But the people of the town belied the three messengers, they said to the messengers, "You are only human beings like us; the most gracious Creator has revealed nothing, you are only telling lies." The messengers said, "Our Lord the most gracious Creator knows that we have been sent as messengers to you, and our duty is only to convey plainly the message of the most gracious Creator; the people of the town said, "For us we see an evil prophecy in you; and if you cease not, we will surely stone you, and a painful chastisement from us will certainly afflict you." The messengers said, "Your evil prophecy is with you; why do you call our message an evil prophecy, because, you are warned against your transgressions, yet you are a people who have transgressed all bounds by calling the message from the most gracious Creator lies, you are committing all kinds of crimes, sins and disobeying the most gracious Creator." So, here is the fourth man (Prophet Hammed Nagar) running from the farthest part of the town, and said, "O my people! Obey the messengers; obey those who ask no wages of you for themselves, and who are rightly guided, and why should I not worship the most gracious Creator alone, Who has created me and to whom you all shall be returned. Shall I take besides the most gracious Creator other creators or deities? If the most gracious Creator intends me any harm, none of your deities that you call your gods, their intercession will be of any use for me whatsoever, nor can they save me. If I do then verily, that will be for me a plain error. Verily, I have believed in the most gracious Creator is your Lord and my Lord, therefore, listen to me! So, the disbelievers killed him. There the most gracious Creator Almighty said to him, "O 'Hammed Nagar, Enter Paradise, you have been admitted with honor." The prophet Nagar said, "Would that my people knew, that my Lord, Who is the most gracious Creator has granted me forgiveness and has enrolled me among those held in honor! And the most gracious Creator did not send down against a people after him, any host from heaven, nor was it needful for us so to do. It was no more than a single mighty Blast, and Behold! They were like ashes quenched and silent. 'Alas for the servants,' never does a messenger come to them but they mock him. Don't they see how many generations were destroyed before them that they return not to them? And on the Day of Judgment, each of them will be brought before us.

The Heavenly Message

Chapter Thirty-Seven

The stories of the People of the gardens

The Heavenly Message

Chapter Thirty-Seven
The stories of the People of the gardens

There were two companions, one of whom was rich and the other was poor. The rich companion owned two lush gardens of grapevines surrounded them with date-palms, and between them corn-fields. Both these gardens yielded their fruits and failed not in growth thereof, and the most gracious Creator caused a river to gush forth in their midst, and he had fruit. So the rich man said to his companion, while he argued with him: "I have greater wealth than thou have, and am mightier in followers." And he went into his garden, while he was unjust to himself. He said: "I think not that this will ever perish, and I think not the Hour will come; and even if I am returned to my Most Gracious Creator, I will certainly find a returning place better than this." His companion said to him while arguing with him: "Disbelieves thou in Him Who created thee of dust, then of a small life-germ, then He made thee a perfect man? But as for me, He, the most gracious Creator is my Lord, and I associate none with my Lord. And wherefore didst thou not say, when thou enter thy garden: It is as the most gracious Creator pleased – there is no power except in Him? If thou consider me as less than thee in wealth and children – then maybe my Lord will give me better than thy garden, and will send on you a reckoning from heaven so that it is soil without plant: Or its water will sink down into the ground, so thou art unable to find it." These words of wisdom and warning were ignored by the richer companion, and he refused to neither submit himself to the most gracious Creator nor reduce his arrogance. One day, the rich man awoke to find his garden completely ruined. His fruit was destroyed; so he began to wring his hands for what he had spent on it, while it lay waste, its roofs that have fallen down, and he said: "Ah me! Would that I had ascribed no partners to my Most Gracious Creator, the Cherisher!" So he had no host to help him against the most gracious Creator, nor could he defend himself. Thus, protection is only the most gracious Creator's, the True One. He is the Best to reward and the Best in requiting.

Another event occurred, there were brothers having gardens. An old man owned a garden that bore plentiful fruit. Every season, at harvest time, he would give the first cut of his crops to the poor and needy and only used what remained. This practice was so renowned that the poor looked forward to every harvest season. As with the characteristics of pious people, the old man was also extremely generous in giving charity and taking care of the needy. The man had three sons, and when he passed away, they inherited his garden. However, they did not inherit his piety and generosity and resented the idea of having to share their wealth with the poor. They felt a sense of a claim to all the fruits there, overlooking this was the bounty of the most gracious Creator that they should, as believers, share with the less fortunate. Therefore, after some time, the brothers decided to break tradition and bar the poor people from entering the garden during the harvest season. The most gracious Creator tried them when they swore to pluck the fruits in the morning, and would not set aside a portion for the poor. One of the brothers was not comfortable with this plan. He wanted to continue the legacy left by his father, but he did not voice his opinion strongly enough, nor did he prevent his brothers from carrying out their plan. So he followed them. The brothers attributed their abundant harvest to their own skills and abilities, without thanking the most gracious Creator or giving due recognition that the trees only bore fruit because of the power of Him. One night, a visitation from the most gracious Creator came on it; He caused the garden to catch fire, while they slept. So it became as black, barren land, and the brothers were unaware of it. Then they called out to one another in the morning, saying: "Go early to your tilth, if you would pluck the fruit." So they went, having strong intention, while they said one to another in low tones: "No poor man shall enter it today upon you." But when they saw it, they said: "Surely, we are in error; nay, we are made to suffer privation." The best of them said: "Said I not to you, why do you not glorify the most gracious Creator?" They said: "Glory is to our Most Gracious Creator! Surely, we were unjust." Then some of them advanced against others, blaming each other. They said: "O woe to us! Surely, we were inordinate – Maybe, our Lord will give us instead one better than it – surely to our Lord we make a petition." the most gracious Creator accepted their repentance, and in time, their gardens were restored back to their former glory. This time, the brothers, having learned their lesson, were careful to continue acting out as their father wished, and gave in charity generously and never deprived the poor anymore after that.

Chapter Thirty-Eight

The story of the People of Saba

The Heavenly Message

Chapter Thirty-Eight
The story of the People of Saba

Has there not come to you the story of those who disbelieved before, then tasted the evil consequences of their conduct, and they had a painful chastisement? Certainly, there was a sign for Saba` in their abode two gardens on the right and the left. There came to them their messengers with clear arguments, "Eat of the sustenance of your the most gracious Creator and give thanks to Him, A good land, and a Forgiving Lord! But they said: Shall mortals guide us? So they disbelieved and turned away, and the most gracious Creator is above all needs. And He is Self-Sufficient, Praised. So the most gracious Creator sent upon them a violent torrent, and in place of their two gardens, He gave them, two gardens yielding bitter fruit and growing tamarisk and a few lote-trees. With this, He requited them because they were ungrateful; and He punishes none but the ingrate. He made between them and the towns which He had blessed, other towns easy to be seen, and He assigned the journey therein: "Travel through them nights and days, secure." But they said: Our Most Gracious Creator, make longer stages between our journeys. And they wronged themselves; so He made them stories and scattered them a total scattering. Surely, there are signs in this for every patient, grateful one. And the devil indeed found true his conjecture concerning them, so they follow him, except a party of the believers. And he has no authority over them, but that the most gracious Creator may know him who believes in the Hereafter from him who is in doubt concerning it. And thy Most Gracious Creator is the Preserver of all things.

Chapter Thirty-Nine

The story of Prophet Muhammed

The Heavenly Message

Chapter Thirty-Nine
The story of Prophet Muhammed

Prophet Muhammed was of the people of Bakkah-Makkah, he was sent to his people and of its surrounding, he was sent to follow a religion of Al-Islam monotheism, and invite his people to Al- Islam, is the religion of all the prophets from Adam to Noah to Ibrahim, Ismael, Isaac, Jacob, Moses, Isa, Muhammed and the Tribes and all the prophets and messengers from the heaven without any distinction.

The people of Bakkah-Makkah are of the generation of prophet Ibrahim who and his son prophet Ismael was appointed by the most gracious Creator to have built the Ka'aba in Bakkah-Makkah for the commemoration of worship one Creator alone, that we must be aware that our Lord is the most Gracious, the most merciful, the Lord of all the worlds.

Prophet Muhammed said to his people that Ibrahim the prophet was upright, and he was not one of the polytheists. Prophet Muhammed said, to the people of

Bakkah-Makkah and the surrounding to refrain from idolaters, and purify the first House-Ka'aba built for all peoples to worship one Creator, and not to associate any deity with the most gracious Creator, so, it was in the teaching and revelation given to Prophet Ibrahim, that none is worthy of worship except the most gracious Creator.

Prophet Muhammed came to his people with clear signs, saying to his people that their Creator is one, is the most gracious, the most merciful The Most Gracious Creator, who is the master of this day in the present, in the past and is the Lord of the future. And none should be worshiped except the most gracious Creator and non-aid should anyone seek except the aid from the gracious Creator.

Muhammed the prophet recited to his people the Book of guidance without a doubt, that in the place of Ibrahim, there shall be no other deity to be worshiped therein but the most gracious Creator alone is the Lord of all the worlds. And whoever should enter therein with faith in the most gracious Creator is safe, and pilgrimage to the House must not be for the idolaters, and that is the duty which mankind owes to the most gracious Creator.

Prophet Muhammed recited to his people according to the words which came to him from the gracious Creator, that to believe in the unseen, and steadfast in prayer, and spend out of what the gracious Creator has provided for them, that they should believe in the revelation to him given to them, is as the revelation given to prophets and messengers before him to them, that whoever put their trust in the most gracious Creator shall never be perished.

Muhammed the prophet preached only to his people, pointing out the wretched folly of idolatry, saying to his people, your Lord is one there is no other deity but the most gracious Creator, He is the most Beneficent, the most Merciful, the Creator of everything there is. The most gracious Creator is the Lord of the entire worlds. Muhammed the prophet said to his people to remove all the objects they call deities besides the most gracious Creator in the temple of prophet Ibrahim and prophet Ismael, which the temple was built only for the purpose of worshipping the most gracious Creator, the one Creator of everything there is. And do not take for yourselves objects of worship besides the most gracious Creator therein. Ka'bah is a temple for the heavenly Lord and must be sacred only for the worship of one deity, the creator of all the worlds alone.

They rejected him and say shall we shun our gods of ancients which are objects of worship we love dearly. Muhammed said: "You should love the most gracious Creator as those objects you love dearly."

Prophet Muhammed recited to his people, to take heed in the creation of the heavens and the alternation of the night and day, and the ships that run in the sea with that which profits men, and the water that the most gracious Creator sends down from the sky, then gives life therewith to the earth after its death and spreads in the all kinds of animals, and the changing of the winds and the clouds made subservient between heaven and the earth, there is no doubt the guidance of the most gracious Creator is the ultimate guide to those who believe in the most gracious Creator.

That the temple of Ibrahim and Ismael is only to worship therein the unseen Lord, for those who keep their duty to the most gracious Creator alone, keep up their prayer and spend out of what the most gracious Creator has provided for them. And of the hereafter, they are sure. Those are on a right course from their Lord for their success. And your God is one God; the most gracious Creator. There is no God but the most gracious Creator is the most Beneficent the most Merciful.

The most gracious Creator is the Owner and maker of the kingdom of the heavens and the earth. They said: "If the most gracious Creator pleased we would not have set up (aught with Him) nor our fathers, nor would we have made anything unlawful." Prophet Muhammed said, "Those whom you call on besides the most gracious Creator are slaves like yourselves; so call on them, then let them answer you if you are truthful. Have they feet with which they walk, or have they hands with which they hold, or have they eyes with which they see, or have they ears with which they hear? And when Prophet Muhammed recited to them clear messages, they say: "This is naught but a man who desires to turn you away from that which your fathers worshipped." And they said: "This is naught but a forged lie!"

The Prophet Muhammed said, the most gracious Creator, is Who revealed the Book, and He befriends the righteous. And those whom you call upon besides Him are not able to help you, nor can they help themselves. And if you invite them to guidance, they hear not; and thou sees them looking towards thee, yet they see not. Who delivers you from the calamities of the land and the sea? When you call upon Him, in humility and in secret: If He delivers us from this; we will certainly be of the grateful ones. The most gracious Creator delivers you from this and from every distress, yet you set up others with Him. Now surely sincere obedience is due to the most gracious Creator alone."

They said: "We serve them only that they may bring us nearer to the most gracious Creator. Makes He the gods a single God?

Surely, this is a strange thing." And the chiefs among them say: "Go and steadily adhere to your gods, surely, this is a thing intended. We never heard of this in the former faith this is nothing but a forgery." Prophet Muhammed said: "O men, call to mind the favor of the most gracious Creator to you. Is there any Creator besides the most gracious Creator who provides for you from the heaven and the earth? There is no God but He. How are you then turned away? Who created the heavens and the earth?" They said: "the most gracious Creator." Muhammed said: "See you then that those you call upon besides the most gracious Creator, would they, if the most gracious Creator desires to afflict me with harm, remove His harm? Or if He desires to show me mercy, could they withhold His mercy? the most gracious Creator is sufficient for me. On Him do the reliant rely on?" "This is only clear enchantment!" And the most gracious Creator has not given them any Books which they read, nor did He send to them before thee a warner. Prophet Muhammed said: "Show me those whom you join with Him as associates. By no means can you! Nay, He is the most gracious Creator, the Mighty, and the Wise. Have you seen your associates which you call on besides the most gracious Creator? Show me what they have created of the earth! Or, have they any share in the heavens? Or, have the Lord of all the worlds given you any book so that they follow a clear argument thereof? Nay, the wrongdoers hold out promises one to another only to deceive. And whoever invokes, besides the most gracious Creator, another god, he has no proof of this his reckoning is only with his Lord. Surely, the believers will not be successful. So call not upon another god with the most gracious Creator, there is no god but the most gracious Creator, It is only revealed to me that your God is one God: will you then submit?" They said: "Shall we give up our gods for a mad poet?" Prophet Muhammed said: "O my people, if you are in doubt as to my religion, know that I serve not those whom you serve besides the most gracious Creator, but I serve the most gracious Creator, Who causes you to die;

and I am commanded to be of the believers, and that thou set thy purpose towards the Religion uprightly; and be not of the polytheists. And call not beside the most gracious Creator on that which can neither benefit thee nor harm thee; for if thou dost, thou shall then be of the unjust. Do you see if the most gracious Creator were to make the night to continue incessantly on you till the Day of Resurrection, who is the god besides the most gracious Creator who could bring you, light? Will you not then hear? Do you see if the most gracious Creator were to make the day to continue incessantly on you till the Day of Resurrection, who is the god besides the most gracious Creator that could bring you the night in which you take rest? Do you not then see? I say not to you, I have with me the treasures of the most gracious Creator, nor do I know the unseen, nor do I say to you that I am an angel; I follow only that which is revealed to me. Are the blind and the seeing alike? Do you not then reflect? My prayer and my sacrifice and my life and my death are surely for the most gracious

Creator, the Lord of the worlds – No associate has Him. And this I am commanded and I am the first of those who submit. Shall I seek a Lord other than the most gracious Creator, while He is the Lord of all things? And no soul earns evil but against itself. Nor does a bearer of burden bear another's burden. Then to your Lord is your return, so He will inform you of that in which you differed. And He it is Who has made you successors in the land and exalted some of you in rank above others, that He may try you by what He has given you. Surely, thy Lord is quick in requiting evil, and He is surely the Forgiving, the Merciful." They said: "Is this he whom the most gracious Creator has raised to be a messenger? He had well-nigh led us astray from our gods, had we not adhered to them patiently!" Prophet Muhammed said: Praise be to the most gracious Creator and peace on His servants whom He has chosen! Is the most gracious Creator better, or what you associate with Him? Or, Who created the heavens and the earth, and sends down for you water from the cloud? Then He caused to grow thereby beautiful gardens— is it not possible for you to make the trees thereof to grow. Is there a god with the most gracious Creator? Nay, you are a people who deviate! Or, Who made the earth a resting-place, and made in it rivers, and rose on it mountains, and placed between the two seas a barrier? Is there a god with the most gracious Creator? Nay, most of you know not! Or, Who answers the distressed one when he calls upon Him and removes the evil, and will make you successors in the earth? Is there a god with the most gracious Creator? Little it is that you mind! Or, Who guides you in the darkness of the land and the sea, and Who sends the wind as good news before His mercy? Is there a god with the most gracious Creator? Exalted be the most gracious Creator above what you associate with Him. Or, Who originates the creation, then reproduces it, and Who gives you sustenance from the heaven and the earth? Is there a god with the most gracious Creator? Bring your proof, if you are truthful. See if the chastisement of the most gracious Creator overtake you or the hour come upon you, will you call on others than the most gracious Creator, if you are truthful? Nay, Him you call upon, so He removes that for which you pray if He pleases, and you forget what you set up with Him. O people, a parable is set forth, so listen to it. Surely, those whom you call upon besides the most gracious Creator cannot create a fly, though they should gather for it. And if the fly carries off aught from them, they cannot take it back from it. Weak are both the invoker and the invoked. They estimate not the most gracious Creator with his due estimation. Surely, the most gracious Creator is Strong, Mighty." They said: "Is this he who speaks of your gods? And they deny when the Beneficent God is mentioned." Muhammed said: "What! Even though your gods control naught, nor do they understand. Call upon your associate-gods then plot against me and give me no respite. Surely, my Friend is the most gracious Creator's is the intercession altogether. His is the kingdom of the heavens and the earth. Then to Him, you will be returned. And those who eschew the worship of the idols and turn to the most gracious Creator, for them is good news. Or, have you gods who can defend you against the most gracious Creator? They cannot help you, nor can you be defended from the most gracious Creator. Or, have you gods besides the most gracious Creator, the Lord of the worlds? Bring your proof. This is the reminder of those with me. Nay, most of you know not the Truth so you turn away. Or, have you taken gods from the earth who gives life? If there were in them gods besides the most gracious Creator, they would both have been in disorder. And whoever of you should say, I am a god besides Him, such a one He will recompense with hell. Thus, We reward the unjust. So Glory be to the most gracious Creator, the Lord of the Throne, being above what you describe! That is because the most gracious Creator is the Truth, and that which you call upon besides Him – that is the falsehood, and because the most gracious Creator – He is the High, the Great. Being upright for the most gracious Creator and not associating aught with Him. And whoever associates aught with the most gracious Creator, it is as if he had fallen from on high, then the birds had snatched him away, or the wind had carried him off to a distant place. And you serve besides the most gracious Creator that for which He has not sent any authority, and of which you have no knowledge. And for the unjust, there is no helper. Praise be to the most gracious Creator, Who created the heavens and the earth, and made darkness and light. Yet those who disbelieve set up equals to their Lord. And call not with the most gracious Creator any other god. There is no god but He. Everything will perish but He. His is the judgment, and to Him, you will be brought back. The parable of those who take guardians besides the most gracious Creator is as the parable of the spider that makes for itself a house; surely the frailest of the houses is the spider's house – if they but knew! Surely, the most gracious Creator knows whatever they call upon besides Him. And He is the Mighty, the Wise. Or, have you taken protectors besides Him? the most gracious Creator is the Protector, and He gives life to the dead, and He is Possessor of power over all things. O disbelievers, I serve not what you serve, nor do you serve Him Whom I serve, nor shall I serve that which you serve, nor do you serve Him Whom I serve. For you is your recompense and for me my recompense. Is the most gracious Creator sufficient for His servant? And you seek to frighten me with those besides Him. And whomsoever the most gracious Creator leaves in error, there is no guide for him. And those that eschew the worship of idols and turn to the most gracious Creator, for them is good news. O people, the most gracious Creator sets forth a parable: a man belonging to partners differing with one another, and a man devoted wholly to one man. Are the two alike in condition? Praise be to the most gracious Creator? Nay, most of you know not. And you have taken gods besides the most gracious Creator that they should be to them a source of strength − By no means! They will soon deny your worshipping them, and be their adversaries. Your idols create naught, while they are themselves created, and they control for themselves neither harm nor profit, nor can they control death nor life nor rising to life. Shall we be turned back on our heels after the most gracious Creator has guided us? Like one whom the devils cause to follow his low desires, in bewilderment in the earth — he has companions who call him to the right way (saying), come to us. Surely, the guidance of the most gracious Creator is the true guidance. And we are commanded to submit to the Lord of the worlds Who created the heavens and the earth in six periods, and He is established on the Throne of Power regulating the Affair. There is no intercessor except after His permission. This is the most gracious Creator, your Lord, therefore serve Him. Will you not mind? Would you inform the most gracious Creator of what He knows not in the heavens and the earth? Glory be to Him, and supremely exalted is He above what you set up with Him! Now, surely, whatever is in the heavens and whatever is in the earth is the most gracious Creator's. And what do you follow those who call on associates besides the most gracious Creator? They follow naught but conjecture, and you only lie. If there were with Him gods, as you say, then certainly they would have been able to seek a way to the Lord of the Throne; Glory to Him! And He is highly exalted above what you say! Call on those whom you assert besides Him; they have no power to remove distress from you or to change. Those whom they call upon, themselves seek the means of access to their Lord – whoever of them is nearest – and they hope for His mercy and fear His chastisement. Surely, the chastisement of thy Lord is a thing to be cautious. Shall I take for a friend other than the most gracious Creator, the Originator of the heavens and the earth, and He feeds and is not fed? I am commanded to be the first of those who submit. And be thou not of the polytheists. I am forbidden to serve those whom you call upon besides the most gracious Creator. I follow not your low desires, for then indeed, I should go astray and should not be of the guided ones. Surely, I have manifest proof from my Lord and you call it a lie. I have not with me that which you would hasten. The judgment is only the most gracious Creator's. He relates the truth and He is the Best of deciders. If that which you hasten were with me, the matter would have certainly been decided between you and me. And the most gracious Creator knows best the wrongdoers. He is the most gracious Creator, besides Whom there is no god; The King, The Holy, The Author of Peace, The Granter of Security, Guardian over all, The Mighty, The Supreme, The Possessor of Greatness. Glory be to the most gracious Creator from that which you set up with Him! They said: He has forged what he says from his God. Muhammed said: Nay, you have no faith. If so, then bring a saying like it, if you are truthful. Or were you created without a creative agency? Or were you the creators? Or did you create the heavens and the earth? Nay, you are sure of nothing. Or have you the treasures of thy Lord with you? Or have you an absolute authority? Or have you the means by which you listen? If so, then let your listener bring a clear authority. Or has He daughters and you have sons? Or have I asked from you a reward for the Truth? Nay, I am only a plain warner to you from the most gracious

Creator. Or possess you the unseen, so you write it down? Or do you intend a plot? But those who disbelieve will be the ensnared ones in the plot. Or have you a god other than the most gracious Creator? Glory be to the most gracious Creator from what you set up with Him! And He it is Who takes your souls at night, and He knows what you earn by day, then He raises you up therein that an appointed term may be fulfilled. Then to Him is your return, then He will inform you of what you did. He causes the night to enter in upon the day and causes the day to enter in upon the night, and He has made subservient the sun and the moon, each one moves to an appointed time. This is the most gracious Creator, your Lord; the kingdom is His. And those whom you call upon besides Him own not a straw. If you call on them, they hear not your call; and if they heard, they could not answer you. Or lest you should say: Only our fathers ascribed partners to the most gracious Creator before us, and we were their descendants after them. There is no God but He; He gives life and causes death – your Lord and the Lord of fathers of yore. Surely, the most gracious Creator forgives not setting up partners with Him, and He forgives all besides this to whom He pleases. And whoever sets up a partner with the most gracious Creator, he indeed goes far astray. Besides Him, you call on nothing but female divinities and you call on nothing but a rebellious devil, whom the most gracious Creator has cursed. And your God is one God; there is no God but He! He is the Beneficent the Merciful. Also, the most gracious Creator bears witness that there is no God but He, and so do the angels and those possessed of knowledge, maintaining justice. There is no god but Him, the Mighty, the Wise. The most gracious Creator sets forth a parable relating to you. Have you among those whom your right hands possess partners in that which the most gracious Creator have provided you with so that with respect to it you are alike – you fear them as you fear each other? Thus do We make the messages clear for a people to understand. Call upon those whom you assert besides the most gracious Creator; they control not the weight of an atom in the heavens or in the earth, nor have they any partnership in either, nor has the most gracious Creator a helper among them. And intercession avails naught with the most gracious Creator, except him whom the most gracious Creator permits. Until when fear is removed from their hearts, they say: What is it that your Lord said? They say: The Truth. And He is the Highest, the Great. The most gracious Creator is He Who created you, then He sustains you, then He causes you to die, then brings you to life. Is there any of your associate-gods who does aught of it? Glory be to Him, and exalted be He above what they associate with Him! And of His signs are the night and the day and the sun and the moon. Adore neither the sun nor the moon, but adore the most gracious Creator Who created them, if He is that you serve. Seest thou him who takes his desire for his god, and the most gracious Creator leaves him in error knowingly, and seals his hearing and his heart and puts a covering on his sight? Who can then guide him after the most gracious Creator? Will you not mind? Is there anyone among your associate-gods who produces the first creation, then reproduces it? the most gracious Creator produces the first creation, then He reproduces it. How are you then turned away! Is there any of your associate-gods who guides to the Truth? the most gracious Creator guides to the Truth. Is He then Who guides to the Truth more worthy to be followed or he who finds not the way unless he is guided? What is the matter with you? How do you judge? And most of you follow naught but conjecture. Surely, conjecture will not avail aught against the Truth. Truly, the most gracious Creator is Knower of what you do. And the most gracious Creator has said: Take not two gods. He is only one God: So the most gracious Creator alone should you fear. And whatever is in the heavens and the earth is His, and to Him is obedience due always. Will you then fear other than the most gracious Creator? And whatever good you have, it is from the most gracious Creator; when evil afflicts you, to Him do you cry for aid; then, when He removes the evil from you, lo! Some of you associate others with their Lord, to deny what the most gracious Creator has given you. Then enjoy yourselves, for soon you shall know. On the Day when you will be raised up, you will see your associate-gods and say: Our Lord, these are our associate-gods on whom we called besides Thee. But they will throw back at you the word: Surely you are liars; it was not us that you served. So the most gracious Creator suffices as a witness between us and you that we were quite unaware of your serving us. And you will tender submission to the most gracious Creator on that Day, and what you used to forge will fail you. The most gracious Creator will say: Call on those whom you considered to be My partners. So you will call on them, but they will not answer you, and the most gracious Creator shall cause a separation between you. It will be said: Gather those who did wrong and their associates, and what they worshipped besides the most gracious Creator, and then lead them to the way of hell. And you set up equals with the most gracious Creator to lead astray from His path. And O that the wrongdoers had seen when you see the chastisement, that power is wholly the most gracious Creator's, and that the most gracious Creator is Severe in chastising! the most gracious Creator will cast terror into your hearts because you set up with the most gracious Creator that for which He has sent down no authority and your abode is the Fire. And evil is the abode of the wrongdoers. Enjoy yourselves, for surely your return is to the Fire. All Praises be to the most gracious Creator who created the heavens and the earth and made darkness and light. Yet you who disbelieve set up equals to your Lord. And you set apart a portion for the most gracious Creator out of what He has created of tilth and cattle, and say: This is for the most gracious Creator – so you assert – and this for our associate-gods. Then that which is for your associate-gods reaches not the most gracious Creator, and that which is for the most gracious Creator reaches your associate-gods. Evil is what you judge. They said: Such and such cattle and crops are prohibited none shall eat them except as we please. In the wombs of such and such cattle is reserved for our males, and forbidden to our wives, and if it is stillborn, we are partners in it. Muhammed said: Eight in pairs – of the sheep two and of the goats two. Has the most gracious Creator forbidden the two males or the two males or the two females or that which the wombs of the two females contain? Inform me with knowledge, if you are truthful; and of the camels two and of the cows two. Has the most gracious Creator forbidden the two males or the two females contain? Or were you witnesses when the most gracious Creator enjoined you this? Who is then more unjust than he who forges a lie against the most gracious Creator to lead men astray without knowledge? Surely, the most gracious Creator guides not the iniquitous people. The most gracious Creator has not ordained a bahirah or a saibah or a wasilah or a hami, but you who disbelieve fabricate a lie against the most gracious Creator. And most of you understand not. And when it is said to you, come to that which the most gracious Creator has revealed and to the Messenger, you say: Sufficient for us is that wherein we found our fathers. What! Even though your fathers knew nothing and had no guidance! And your associate-gods have made fair-seeming to many polytheists, the killing of your children, that they may cause you to perish and obscure for them your religion. Or has the most gracious Creator taken daughters to Himself of what He creates and chosen you to have sons? And when one of you is given news of that of which he sets up a likeness for the Beneficent, his face becomes black and he is full of rage. He hides himself from the people because of the evil of what is announced to him. Shall he keep it with disgrace or bury it alive in the dust? Now surely evil is what you judge! Have you considered Lat and Uzza, and another, the third Manat? Are the males for you and for Him the females? This is surely an unjust division! They are naught but names which you have named, - you and your fathers – the most gracious Creator has sent no authority for you. You follow naught but conjecture and what your souls desire. And certainly, the guidance has come to you from your Lord. Or shall man have what he wishes? But for the most gracious Creator is the Hereafter and the former life. Is one decked with ornaments and unable to make plain speech in disputes (a partner with the Merciful Creator)? And you make the angels, who are the servants of the Beneficent, females. Did you witness their creation? Your evidence will be recorded and you will be questioned. Surely, you utter a grievous saying. Has the most gracious Creator preferred daughters to sons? What is the matter with you? How you judge! Will you not then mind? Or have you a clear authority? Then bring your book, if you are truthful. And you assert a relationship between the most gracious Creator and the jinn. And certainly, the jinn know that they will be brought up for judgment – Glory be to the most gracious Creator from what you describe! O People of the Book, exceed not the limits in your religion nor speak anything about the most gracious Creator but the truth. The Messiah, Jesus, son of Mary, is only a messenger of the most gracious Creator and His word which He communicated to Mary and a mercy from

Him. So believe in the most gracious Creator and His messengers. And say not, Trinity. Desist, it is better for you. The most gracious Creator is only one God. Far be it from His glory to have a son. To Him belongs whatever is in the heavens and whatever is in the earth. And sufficient is the most gracious Creator as having charge of affairs. And you say: Surely, the most gracious Creator -- He is the Messiah, son of Mary. Who then can control anything as against the most gracious Creator when He wishes to destroy the Messiah, son of Mary, and his mother and all those on the earth? And the most gracious Creator is the Possessor of Power over all things. And the Jews and the Christians say: We are sons of the most gracious Creator and His beloved ones. Muhammed said: Why does He then chastise you for your sins? Nay, you are mortals from among those whom He has created. He forgives whom He pleases and chastises whom He pleases. And the most gracious Creator's is the kingdom of the heavens and the earth and what is between them and to Him is the eventual coming.

And the Messiah said: O Children of Israel serve the most gracious Creator, my Lord and your Lord. Surely, whoever associates others with the most gracious Creator, the most gracious Creator has forbidden him the Garden and his abode is the Fire. And for the wrongdoers there will be no helpers. Certainly, you disbelieve when you say: the most gracious Creator is the third of the three. And there is no God but One God. Will you not then turn to the most gracious Creator and ask His forgiveness? And the most gracious Creator is Forgiving, Merciful. The Messiah, son of Mary, was only a messenger; messengers before him had indeed passed away. And his mother was a truthful woman. They both used to eat food. See how the most gracious Creator makes the messages clear to you! Then behold how you are turned away! It is not meet for a mortal that the most gracious Creator should give him the Book and the judgment and the prophethood, then he should say to men: Be my servants besides the most gracious Creator's; but (he would say): Be worshippers of the Lord because you teach the Book and because you study it; Nor would he enjoin you to take the angels and the prophets for lords. Would He enjoin you to disbelieve after you submit? the most gracious Creator, The Wonderful Originator of the heavens and the earth! And you say: the most gracious Creator has taken to Himself a son – Glory be to Him! Certainly, you make an abominable assertion! The heavens may almost be rent thereat, and the earth cleaves asunder, and the mountains fall down in pieces, that they ascribe a son to the Beneficent! And it is not worthy of the Beneficent! And it is not worthy of the Beneficent that He should take to Himself a son. Rather, whatever is in the heavens and the earth is His. All are obedient to Him. The Beneficent has no son; so I am the foremost of those who serve God. Glory be to the Lord of the heavens and the earth, the Lord of the Throne of Power from what they describe! How could He have a son when He has no consort? And He created everything, and He is the Knower of all things. That is the most gracious Creator, your Lord. There is no God but He; the Creator of all things therefore worship Him, for He has charge over all things. And the Jews say: Ezra is the son of the most gracious Creator; and the Christians say: The Messiah is the son of the most gracious Creator. These are the words of your mouths. You imitate the saying of those who disbelieved before. The most gracious Creator's curse be on you! How you are turned away! You take your doctors of law and your monks for lords besides the most gracious Creator, and the Messiah, son of Mary. And they were enjoined that you should serve one God only – there is no god but He. Be is He glorified from what they set up with Him! the most gracious Creator is the Self-Sufficient. His is what is in the heavens and what is in the earth. You have no authority for this. Say you against the most gracious Creator what you know not of? On the Day of Judgment when the most gracious Creator will say O Jesus, son of Mary, didst thou say to men: Take my mother and me for two gods besides the most gracious Creator? He will say: Glory is to Thee! It was not for me to say what I had no right to say. If I had said it, Thou would indeed have known it. Thou know what is in my mind, and I know not what is in Thy mind. Surely, Thou art the great Knower of the unseen. I said to them naught except as Thou didst command me: Serve the most gracious Creator, my Lord and your Lord; and I was a witness of them so long as I was among them, but when Thou didst cause me to die Thou wast the Watcher over them. And Thou art Witness of all things. Those who disbelieve from among the People of the Book and the idolaters will be in the Fire of hell, abiding therein. They are the worst of creatures. Those who believe and do goodness, they are the best of creatures. Praise be to the most gracious Creator! Who has not taken to Himself a son, and Who has not a partner in the kingdom, and Who has not a helper because of weakness; and proclaim His greatness, magnifying Him. He, the most gracious Creator, is One. The most gracious Creator is He whom all depends. He begets not, nor is He begotten; and none is like Him.

Revelation to Mankind

The Heavenly Message

Praise is to the most gracious Creator, the Cherisher and Sustainer of the worlds; Most Gracious, Most Merciful; Master of the Day of Judgment. You do us worship, and Your aid we seek. Show us the right way. The way of those on whom You have bestowed Your Grace, those whose portion is not wrath, and who do not go astray.

Say: I seek refuge with the Lord and Cherisher of Mankind; The King, Ruler of Mankind; The God, Judge of Mankind, from the mischief of the whisperer of evil who withdraws after his whisper, and whispers into the hearts of Mankind; among jinn and among men.

These are the messages of the most gracious Creator – We recite them to thee with truth; and surely, thou art of the Messengers.

Say: I seek refuge with the Lord of the Dawn, from the mischief of created things, from the mischief of darkness as it overspreads, from the mischief of those who practice witchcraft, and from the mischief of the envious one as he practices envy.

When comes the Help of the most gracious Creator, and Victory, and you see the People enter the most gracious Creator's Religion in crowds, celebrate the Praises of your Lord, and pray for His Forgiveness, for He is Often-Returning in Grace and Mercy.

This Quran is not such as could be forged by those besides the most gracious Creator, but it is a verification of that which is before it and a clear explanation of the Book, there is no doubt in it, from the Lord of the worlds. Or say they: He has forged it? Say: Then bring a chapter like it, and invite who you can besides the most gracious Creator, if you are truthful.

Say: I am forbidden to serve those whom you call upon besides the most gracious Creator when clear arguments have come to me from my Lord, and I am commanded to submit to the Lord of the worlds.

Say: I only call upon my Lord and associate naught with Him. Say: I do not control evil or good for you. Say: None can protect me against the most gracious Creator, nor can I find any refuge besides Him.

To you We have granted the Fountain of

Abundance, therefore to your Lord turn in prayer and sacrifice; For he who hates you will be cut off.

Do you see one who denies the Judgment to come? That is the one who treats the orphan with harshness and does not encourage the feeding of the poor. So woe to the worshippers that are neglectful of their prayers, who do good deeds only to be seen by others and refuse to supply simple assistance.

For the covenants of security and safeguard enjoyed by the Quraysh, their covenants covering their winter and summer journeys, let them adore the Lord of this Temple, Who provides them with food against hunger, and with security against the fear of danger.

Read! In the Name of thy Lord the Cherisher who created, created Mankind out of a clot of congealed blood. Proclaim! For thy Lord is Most Bountiful. It is He who taught the writing by the pen. He has taught man that which he knew not. Nay! Verily, man does transgress because he considers himself self-sufficient. Surely, unto your Lord is the return. Do you see one who forbids a votary when he turns to pray? Do you see if he is on the road of Guidance? Or enjoins Righteousness? Do you see if he denies Truth and turns away? Doesn't he know the most gracious Creator sees? Let him Beware! If he desists not, We will drag him by the forelock, a lying sinful forelock! Then, let him call his council. We will call on the angels of punishment to deal with him! Nay, heed him not. But bow down in adoration, and bring thyself closer to the most gracious Creator!

By the Fig and the Olive, and the Mount of Sinai, and this City of security, We have indeed created man in the best of molds, then do We abase him the lowest of the low, except such as believe and do righteous deeds, for they shall have a reward unfailing. Then what can, after this, contradict you as to the Judgment? Is not the most gracious Creator the Greatest of Judges?

Have We not expanded you your breast? And removed from you your burden which did gall your back? And raised high the esteem in which you are held? So, verily, with every difficulty, there is a relief, verily,

with every difficulty, there is a relief. Therefore, when you are free, still labor hard, and to your Lord turn your attention.
By the Glorious Morning Light, and by the Night when it is still, your Guardian-Lord has not forsaken you, nor is He displeased. And verily the Hereafter will be better for you than the present. And soon will your Guardian-Lord give you that you shall be well-pleased. Did He not find you an orphan and give you shelter and care? And He found you wandering, and He gave you guidance. And He found you in need and made you independent. Therefore, do not treat the orphan with harshness, nor repulse the petitioner. But the Bounty of the Lord – rehearses and proclaims it!
Whatever is in the heavens and whatever is in the earth glorifies the most gracious Creator, the King, the Holy, the Mighty, the Wise. The most gracious Creator is Who raised among the illiterates a Messenger from among themselves, who recites to them His messages and purifies them, and teaches them the Book and the Wisdom – although they were before certainly in

manifest error – And others from among them who have not yet joined them. And He is the Mighty, the Wise. That is the most gracious Creator's grace; He grants it to whom He pleases. And the most gracious Creator is the Lord of Mighty Grace. The likeness of those who were charged with the Torah, then they observed it not, is as the likeness of the ass carrying books. Evil is the likeness of the people who reject the Messages of the most gracious Creator. And He guides not the iniquitous people. Say: O you, who are Jews, if you think that you are the favorites of the most gracious Creator to the exclusion of other people, then invoke death, if you are truthful. But they will never invoke it because of what their hands have sent before. And the most gracious Creator is Knower of the wrongdoers. Say: The death from which you flee, will surely overtake you; then you will be sent back to the Knower of the unseen and the seen, so He will inform you of that which you did. And when they see merchandise or sport, they break away to it and leave thee standing. Say: What is with the most gracious Creator is better than sport and merchandise. And the most gracious Creator is the best of Providers.

He frowned and turned away because the blind man came to him. And what would make thee know that he might purify himself, or be mindful, so the Reminder should profit him? As for him who considers himself free from a need to him, thou dost attend. And no blame is on thee if he purifies himself not. And as to him who comes to thee striving hard and he fears – To him, thou pay no regard. Nay, surely it is a Reminder. So let him, who will mind it. In honored Books, Exalted, purified, in the hands of scribes, Noble, virtuous. Woe to man! What has made him reject the most gracious Creator? From what substance has He created him? From a sperm-drop He has created him, and then molded him in due proportion; then He makes his path smooth for him; then He causes him to die, and puts him in his grave; then, when it is His Will, He will raise him up. By no means has he fulfilled what the most gracious Creator has commanded him. Then let man look at his food, for that We pour forth water in abundance, and We split the earth in fragments, and produce therein corn, and grapes and nutritious plants, and olives and dates, and enclosed gardens, dense with lofty trees, and fruits and fodder, for use and convenience to you and your cattle.

And certainly, We gave Moses the Book after We had destroyed the former generations – clear arguments for men and guidance and mercy, that they may be mindful. And thou wast not on the western side when We revealed to Moses the commandment, nor wast thou among those present, but We rose up generations, then life became prolonged to them. And thou wast not dwelling among the people of Midian, reciting to them Our Messages, but We are the Sender of messengers. And thou wast not at the side of the mountain when We called, but a mercy from thy Lord that thou mayest warn a people to whom no warner came before thee, that they may be mindful.

When the hypocrites come to thee, they say: We bear witness that thou art indeed the most gracious Creator's Messenger. And the most gracious Creator knows thou art indeed His Messenger. And the most gracious Creator bears witness that the hypocrites are surely liars. They take shelter under their oaths, thus turning men from the most gracious Creator's way. Surely evil is that which they do. That is because they believed, then disbelieved; thus their hearts are sealed, so they understand not. And when thou see them, their persons please thee; and if they speak, thou listen to their speech. They are like pieces of wood, clad with garments. They think every cry to be against them. They are the enemy, so beware of them. May the most gracious Creator destroy them! How they are turned back! And when it is said to them: Come, the Messenger of the most gracious Creator will ask forgiveness for you, they turn away their heads and thou see them hindering others, and they are big with pride. It is alike to them whether thou ask forgiveness for them or asks not forgiveness for them – the most gracious Creator will never forgive them. Surely, the most gracious Creator guides not the transgressing people. They are those who say: Spend not on those who are with the Messenger of the most gracious Creator that they may disperse. And the most gracious Creator is the treasures of the heavens and the earth, but the hypocrites understand not. They say: If we return to Madinah, the mightier will surely drive the meaner therefrom. And might belongs to the most gracious Creator and His Messenger and the believers, but the hypocrites know not.

O you who believe, call to mind the favor of the most gracious Creator to you when there came against you hosts, so We sent against them a strong wind and hosts that you saw not. And the most gracious Creator is ever Seer of what you do. When they came upon you from above you and from below you, and when the eyes turned dull and the hearts rose up to the throats, and you began to think diverse thoughts about the most gracious Creator. There were believers tried and they were shaken with a severe shaking. And when the hypocrites and those in whose hearts was a disease began to say: the most gracious Creator and His Messenger did not promise us victory but only to deceive. And when a party of them said: O people of Yathrib, you cannot make a stand, so go back. And a party of them asked permission of the Prophet, saying, our houses are exposed. And they were not exposed. They only desired to run away. And if entries were made upon them from the outlying parts of it, then they were asked to wage war against the Muslims, they would certainly have done it, and they would not have stayed in it but a little while. And they had indeed made a covenant with the most gracious Creator before that they would turn their backs. And a covenant with the most gracious Creator must be answered for. Say: Flight will not profit you if you flee from death or slaughter, and then you will not be allowed to enjoy yourselves but a little. Say: Who is it that can protect you from the most gracious Creator, if He intends harm for you, or intends to show you mercy? And they will not find for themselves a guardian or a helper besides the most gracious Creator. The most gracious Creator indeed knows those among you who hinder others and those who say to their brethren: Come to us. And they come not to the fight but a little being ungenerous with respect to you. But when fear comes, thou wilt see them looking to thee their eyes rolling like one swooning because of death. But when fear is gone they smite you with sharp tongues, being covetous of wealth. These have not believed, so the most gracious Creator makes their deeds naught. And that is easy for the most gracious Creator. They think the allies are not gone, and if the allies should come again, they would fain be in the deserts with the Arabs, asking for news about you. And if they were among you, they would not fight except a little. Certainly, you have in the Messenger of the most gracious Creator an excellent exemplar for him who hopes in the most gracious Creator and the Latter-Day and remembers the most gracious Creator much. And when the believers saw the allies, they said: This is what the most gracious Creator and His Messenger promised us, and the most gracious Creator and His Messenger spoke the truth. And it is only added to their faith and submission. Of the

believers are men who are true to the covenant they made with the most gracious Creator; so of them is he who has accomplished his vow, and of them is he who yet waits, and they have not yet changed in the least – That the most gracious Creator may reward the truthful for their truth, and chastise the hypocrites, if He please, or turn to them mercifully. Surely, the most gracious Creator is ever Forgiving, Merciful. And the most gracious Creator turned back the disbelievers in their rage – they gained no advantage. And the most gracious Creator sufficed the believers in fighting. And the most gracious Creator is Ever Strong, Mighty. And He drove down those of the People of the Book who backed them from their fortresses and He cast awe into their hearts; some you killed and you took captive some. And He made you heirs to their land and their dwellings and their property, and to a land which you have not yet trodden. And the most gracious Creator is ever Possessor of power over all things.
Hast thou not seen the hypocrites? They say to their brethren who disbelieve from

among the People of the Book: If you are expelled, we certainly will go forth with you, and we will never obey anyone concerning you; and if you are fought against, we will certainly help you. And the most gracious Creator bears witness that they are certainly liars. If they are expelled, they will not go forth with them, and if they are fought against, they will not help them; and even if they help them, they will certainly turn their backs; then they shall not be helped. Your fear in their hearts is indeed greater than the most gracious Creator's. That is because they are a people who understand not. They will not fight against you in a body save in fortified towns or from behind walls. Their fighting between them is severe. Thou would think them united, but their hearts are divided. That is because they are a people who have no sense, like those before them: they tasted the evil consequences of their conduct, and for them is a painful chastisement. Like the devil when he says to man: Disbelieve. But when he disbelieves, he says: I am free of thee: surely I fear the most gracious Creator, the Lord of the worlds. So the end of both of them is that they are both in the Fire to abide therein. And that is the reward of the wrongdoers.

Surely We have granted thee a clear victory, that the most gracious Creator may cover for thee thy alleged shortcomings in the past and those to come, and complete His favor to thee and guide thee on a right path, and that the most gracious Creator might help thee with a mighty help. He is Who sent down tranquility into the hearts of the believers that they might add faith to their faith. And the most gracious Creator's are the hosts of the heavens and the earth, and the most gracious Creator is ever Knowing, Wise – That He may cause the believing men and the believing women to enter Gardens wherein rivers flow to abide therein and remove from them their evil. And that is a grand achievement with the most gracious Creator, and that He may chastise the hypocritical men and the hypocritical women, and the polytheistic men and polytheistic women, the entertainers of evil thoughts about the most gracious Creator. On them is the evil turn, and the most gracious Creator is wroth with them and has cursed them and prepared hell for them; evil is the resort. And the most gracious Creator is the hosts of the heavens and the earth; the most gracious Creator is ever Mighty Wise. Surely, We have sent thee as a witness and as a bearer of good news and as a warner, That you may believe in the most gracious Creator and His Messenger and may aid him and revere him. And that you may declare His glory, morning and evening. Those who swear allegiance to the most gracious Creator, the Hand of the most gracious Creator is above their hands. So whoever breaks his faith, he breaks it only to his soul's injury. And whoever fulfills his covenant with the most gracious Creator, He will grant him a mighty reward. Those of the Arabs who lagged behinds will say to thee: Our property and our families kept us busy so ask forgiveness for us. They say with their tongues what is not in their hearts. Say: Then who can control aught for you from the most gracious Creator, if He intends to do you harm or if He intends to do you good. Nay, the most gracious Creator is ever aware of what you do. Nay, you thought that the Messenger and the believers would never return to their families, and that was made clear fair-seeming in your hearts, and you thought an evil thought, and you are a people doomed to perish. And whoever believes not in the most gracious Creator and His Messenger – then surely, We have prepared burning Fire for the disbelievers. And the most gracious Creator's is the kingdom of the heavens and the earth. He forgives whom he pleases and chastises whom He pleases. And the most gracious Creator is ever Forgiving, Merciful. Those who lagged behind will say when you set forth to acquire gains: Allow us to follow you. They desire to change the word of the most gracious Creator. Say: You shall not follow us. Thus, did the most gracious Creator say before? But they will say: Nay, you are jealous of us. Nay, they understand not but a little. Say to those of the Arabs who lagged behind: You will soon be called against a people of mighty prowess to fight against them until they submit. Then if you obey, the most gracious Creator will grant you a good reward; but, if you turn back as you turned back before, He will chastise you with a painful chastisement. There is no blame on the blind, nor is there blame on the lame, nor is there blame on the sick. And whoever obeys the most gracious Creator and His Messenger, He will cause him to enter gardens wherein rivers flow. And whoever turns back, He will chastise with a painful chastisement. The most gracious Creator indeed was well pleased with the believers, when they swore allegiance to thee under the tree, and He knew what was in their hearts, so He sent down tranquility on them and rewarded them with a near victory, and many gains which they will acquire. And the most gracious Creator is ever Mighty, Wise. The most gracious Creator promised you many gains which you will acquire, then He hastened this on for you, and held back the hands of men from you; and that it may be a sign for the believers and that He may guide you on a right path, and others which you have not yet been able to achieve – the most gracious Creator has surely encompassed them. And the most gracious Creator is ever Powerful over all things. And if those who disbelieve fight with you, they will certainly turn their backs, and then they will find neither protector nor helper. Such has been the course of the most gracious Creator that has run before, and thou wilt not find a change in the most gracious Creator's course. And He it is who held back their hands from you and your hands from them in the valley of Makkah after He had given you victory over them. And the most gracious Creator is Seer of what you do. It is they, who disbelieved and debarred you from the Sacred Mosque — and the offering withheld from reaching its goal. And were it not for the believing men and the believing women, whom, not having known, you might have trodden down and thus something hateful might have afflicted you on an account without knowledge — so that the most gracious Creator may admit to His mercy whom He pleases. Had they been apart, we would surely have chastised those who disbelieved from among them with a painful chastisement. When those who disbelieved harbored disdain into their hearts, the disdain of ignorance, but the most gracious Creator sent down His tranquility on His Messenger and on the believers and made them keep the word of observance of duty, and they were entitled to it and worthy of it. And the most gracious Creator is ever Knower of all things. The most gracious Creator indeed fulfilled the vision for His Messenger with truth. You shall certainly enter the Sacred Mosque, if the most gracious Creator please, insecurity, your heads shaved and hair cut short, not fearing. But He knows what you know not, so He has ordained a near victory before that. He it is Who sent His Messenger with the guidance and the Religion of Truth that He may make it prevail over all religions. And the most gracious Creator is enough for a witness. Muhammed is the Messenger of the most gracious Creator and those with him are firm of heart against the disbelievers, compassionate among themselves. Thou sees them bowing down, prostrating themselves, seeking the most gracious Creator's grace and pleasure.

Their marks are on their faces in

consequence of prostration. That is their description in the Torah – and their description in the Gospel – like seed-produce that puts forth its sprout, then strengthens it, so it stands firmly on its stem, delighting the sowers that He may enrage the disbelievers because of them. The most gracious Creator has promised such of them who believe and do good. Such of them the most gracious Creator will promise them, forgiveness, and a great reward.

And We tried them with blessings and misfortunes that they might turn. Then after them came an evil posterity who inherited the Book, taking the frail goods of this low life and saying: It will be forgiven us. And if the like good came to them, they would take it too. Was not a promise taken from them in the Book that they would not speak anything about the most gracious Creator but the truth? And they study what is in it. And the abode of the Hereafter is better for those who keep their duty. Do you not then understand? And as for those who hold fast by the Book and keep up the prayer – surely We waste not the reward of the reformers.

Hast thou not seen how your Lord dealt with the possessors of the elephant? Did He not cause their war to end in confusion? And send against them birds in flocks? Casting at them decreed stones – He rendered them like straw eaten up?

These are they on whom the most gracious Creator bestowed favors, from among the prophets, of the seed of Adam, and of those whom We carried with Noah, and of the seed of Abraham and Israel, and of those whom We guided and chose. When the messages of the Beneficent were recited to them, they fell down in submission, weeping.

And We indeed gave Moses the Book and We sent messengers after him one after another; and We gave Jesus, son of Mary, clear arguments and strengthened him with the Holy Spirit. Is it then that whenever there come to you a messenger with what your souls desired not, you were arrogant? And some you gave the lie to and others you would slay. And they say: Our hearts are repositories. Nay, the most gracious Creator has cursed them because of their unbelief;

so little it is that they believe. And when there come to them a Book from the most gracious Creator verifying that which they have, and aforetime they used to pray for victory against those who disbelieved – but when there came to them that which they recognized, they disbelieved in it; so the most gracious Creator's curse is on the disbelievers. Evil is that for which they sell their souls – that they should deny that which the most gracious Creator revealed, out of envy that the most gracious Creator should send down of His grace on whomsoever of His servants He pleases; so they incur wrath upon wrath. And there is an abasing chastisement for the disbelievers. And when it is said to them: Believe in that which the most gracious Creator has revealed, they say: We believe in that which was revealed to us. And they deny what is besides that, while it is the truth verifying which they have. Say: Why then did you kill the most gracious Creator's prophets before this if you were believers? And Moses indeed came to you with clear arguments, and you took the calf for a god in his absence and you were wrongdoers. And when We made a covenant with you and raised the mountain above you: Take hold of that which We have given you with firmness and obey. They said: We hear and disobey. And they were made to imbibe the love of the calf into their hearts because of their disbelief. Say: Evil is that which your faith bids you if you are believers. Say: If the abode of the Hereafter with the most gracious Creator is especially for you to the exclusion of the people, then invoke death if you are truthful. And they will never invoke it because of what their hands have sent on before, and the most gracious Creator knows the wrongdoers. And thou wilt certainly finds them the greediest of men for life, greedier even than those who set up gods with the most gracious Creator. One of them loves to be granted a life of a thousand years, and his being granted a long life will in no way remove him further off from the chastisement. And the most gracious Creator is Seer of what they do. Thou wilt certainly find the most violent of people in enmity against the believers to be the Jews and the idolaters, and thou wilt finds the nearest in friendship to the believers to be those who say, We are Christians. That is because there are priests and monks among them and because they are not proud.

Follow that which is revealed to thee from thy Lord—there is no god but He; turn away from the polytheists. And if the most gracious Creator had pleased, they would not have set up others with Him. And We have not appointed thee a keeper over them, and thou art not placed in charge of them. And abuse not those whom they call upon besides the most gracious Creator, lest, exceeding the limits, they abuse the most gracious Creator through ignorance. Thus to every people have We made their deeds fair-seeming; then to their Lord is their return so He will inform them of what they did.

These are they on whom the most gracious Creator bestowed favors, from among the Prophets, of the seed of Adam, and of those whom We guided and chose. When the messages of the Beneficent were recited to them, they fell down in submission, weeping.

And the most gracious Creator indeed gave Moses the Book – so doubt not the meeting with Him – and We made it a guide for the Children of Israel. And We made from among them leaders to guide by Our command when they were patient. And they were certain of Our Messages. Surely thy Lord will judge between them on the Day of Resurrection concerning that wherein they differed.

And when Moses said to his servant: I will not cease until I reach the junction of the two rivers, otherwise I will go on for years. So when they reached the junction of the two (rivers), they forgot their fish, and it took its way into the river, being free. But when they had gone further, he said to this servant: Bring to us our morning meal, certainly we have found fatigue in this our journey. He said: Sawest thou when we took refuge on the rock, I forgot the fish, and none but the devil made me forget to speak of it, and it took its way into the river; what a wonder! He said: This is what we sought. So they returned retracing their footsteps.

Then they found one of Our servants whom We had granted mercy from Us and whom We had taught knowledge from Ourselves. Moses said to him: May I follow thee that thou mayest teach me of the good thou hast been taught? He said: Thou canst not have patience with me. And how canst thou have patience in that whereof thou hast not a comprehensive knowledge? He said: If the most gracious Creator please, thou wilt find me patient, nor shall I disobey thee in aught. He said: If thou wouldst follow me, question me not about aught until I myself speak to thee about it. So they set out until, when they embarked in a boat, he made a hole in it. Moses said: Hast thou made a hole in it to drown its occupants? Thou hast surely done a grievous thing. He said: Did I not say that thou couldst not have patience with me? He said: Blame me not for what I forgot and be not hard upon me for what I did. So they went on, until, when they met a boy, he slew him. (Moses) said: Hast thou slain an innocent person, not guilty of slaying another? Thou hast indeed done a horrible thing. He said: Did I not say to thee that thou couldst not have patience with me? He said: If I ask thee about anything after this, keep not company with me. Thou wilt then indeed have found an excuse in my case. So they went on, until, when they came to the people of a town, they asked its people for food, but they refused to entertain them as guests. Then they found in it a wall which was on the point of falling, so he put it into a right state. Moses said: If thou hadst wished, thou couldst have taken a recompense for it. He said: This is the parting between me and thee. Now I will inform thee of the significance of that with which thou couldst not have patience. As for the boat, it belonged to poor people working on the river, and I intended to damage it, for there was behind them a king who seized every boat by force. And as for the boy, his parents were believers and we feared lest he should involve them in wrongdoing and disbelief. So we intended that their Lord might give them in his place one better in purity and nearer to mercy. And as for the wall, it belonged to two orphan boys in the city, and there was beneath it a treasure belonging to them, and their father had been a righteous man. So thy Lord intended that they should attain their maturity and take out their treasure — a mercy from thy Lord — and I did not do it of my own accord. This is the significance of that with which thou couldst not have patience.

And warn with it those who fear that they will be gathered to their Lord—there is no protector for them, nor any intercessor besides Him – so that they may keep their duty.

And who is more unjust than he who forges a lie against the most gracious Creator or gives the lie to His messages? Surely the wrongdoers will not be successful. And on the day We gather them all together, then We shall say to those who set up gods with the most gracious Creator: Where are your associate-gods whom you asserted? Then their excuse would be nothing but that they would say: By the most gracious Creator, our Lord! We were not polytheists. See how they lie against their own souls, and that which they forged shall fail them! And of the is he who hearkens to thee and We cast veils over their hearts so that they understand it not and a deafness into their ears. And even if they see every sign they will not believe in it. So much so that when they come to thee they only dispute with thee --- those who disbelieve say: This is naught but stories of the ancients. And they forbid others from it, and they keep away from it; they ruin none but their own souls while they perceive not.

And those whom they call upon besides Him control not intercession, but he who bears witness to the Truth and they know Him. And if thou were to ask them who created them, they would say the most gracious Creator. How are they then turned back?

And to warn those who say: the most gracious Creator has taken to Himself a son. They have no knowledge of it, nor had their fathers. Grievous is the word that comes out of their mouths. They speak nothing but a lie.

Alif, Lam, Mim. (I, the most gracious Creator, Am the Best Knower). The Romans are vanquished in a near land, and they, after their defeat, will gain victory within nine years. The most gracious Creator's is the command before and after. And on that day the believers will rejoice in the most gracious Creator's help. He helps whom he pleases, and He is the Mighty, the Merciful – It is the most gracious Creator's promise! the most gracious Creator will not fail in His promise, but most people know not. They know the outward of this world's life, but of the Hereafter, they are heedless. Do they not reflect within themselves? the most gracious Creator did not create the heavens and the earth and what is between them but with truth, and for an appointed term. And surely, most of the people are deniers of the meeting with their Lord. Have they not traveled in the earth and seen what was the end of those before them? They were stronger than those in prowess were, and dug up the earth, and built on it more than these built. And their messengers came to them with clear arguments. So it was not the most gracious Creator who wronged them, but they wronged themselves. Then evil was the end of those who did evil because they rejected the messages of the most gracious Creator and mocked at them.

Verily, We have sent this Quran down in the Night of Power. And what will make you know what the Night of Power is? The Night of Power is better than a thousand months. Therein come down the Angels and the Spirit by the most gracious Creator's permission; on every errand. Peace! Until the rise of the morning!

And they serve beside the most gracious Creator that which can neither harm nor profit them, and they say: These are our intercessors with the most gracious Creator. Say: Would you inform the most gracious Creator of what He knows not in the heavens and the earth? Glory be to Him, and supremely exalted is He above what they set up beside Him!

Glorify the name of your Guardian-Lord Most High, Who has created, and further, given order and proportion; Who has ordained laws, and granted guidance; and Who brings out the pasture, and then makes it swarthy stubble. By degrees shall We teach you to declare, so you shall not forget, except as the most gracious Creator wills, for He knows what is manifest and what is hidden. And We will make it easy for the simple. Therefore give admonition in case the admonition benefits. The admonition will be received by those who fear the most gracious Creator, but it will be avoided by those most unfortunate ones, who will enter the Great Fire, in which they will then neither die nor live. But those will prosper who purify themselves, and glorify the Name of their Guardian-Lord, and in Prayer. Nay, you prefer the life of this world; but the Hereafter is better and more enduring. And this is in the Books of the earliest, the Books of Abraham and Moses.

By the Sky and the Night-Visitant; and what will explain to you what the Night-Visitant is? The Star of piercing brightness. There is no soul but has a protector over it. Now let man but think from what he is created! He is created from a drop emitted, proceeding from between the backbone and the ribs. Surely the most gracious Creator is able to bring him back. The Day that hidden things shall be made manifest, will have no power, and no helper. By the Firmament which returns. And by the Earth which opens out.

Behold this is the Word that distinguishes. It is not a thing for amusement. As for them, they are but plotting a plan, and I am plotting a plan. Therefore grant a delay to the unbelievers. Give respite to them gently for a while.

Has the story of Moses reached you? Behold, your Lord called him in the sacred valley of Tuwa, "Go to Pharaoh, for he has transgressed all bounds. And say to him, 'Would you like that you should be purified? And that I guide you to your Lord, so you should fear Him?'" Then Moses showed him the Great Sign. But Pharaoh rejected it and disobeyed; further, he turned his back striving hard. Then he collected his men and made a proclamation, saying, "I am your Lord Most High." But the most gracious Creator did punish him, and made an example of him, in the hereafter, as in this life. Verily in this is an instructive warning for whosoever fears the most gracious Creator. What! Are you the more difficult to create, or the heaven? the most gracious Creator has constructed it. On high has He raised its canopy, and He has given it order and perfection. He endows its night with darkness, and He brings out its splendor. And the earth, moreover, He has extended; He draws out there from its moisture and its pasture; and the mountains He has firmly fixed; for use and convenience to you and your cattle.

Surely We have revealed the Qur'an to thee, in portions. So wait patiently for the judgment of thy Lord, and obey not a sinner or an ungrateful one among them. And glorify the name of thy Lord morning and evening. And during part of the night adore Him, and glorify Him throughout a long night. Surely these love the transitory life and neglect a grievous day before them. We created them and made firm their make, and, when We will, We can bring in their place the like of them by change. Surely this is a Reminder; so whoever will, let him take a way to his Lord, and you will not, unless the most gracious Creator pleases. Surely the most gracious Creator is Ever-Knowing, Wise – He admits whom He pleases to His Mercy, and the wrongdoers – He has prepared for them a painful chastisement.

O thou who wrap thyself up, arise and warn, and thy Lord do magnify, and thy garments do purify, and uncleanness do shun and do no favor seeking gain, and for the sake of thy Lord, be patient. For when the trumpet is sounded, that will be – that Day – a difficult Day, for the disbelievers, anything but easy. Leave Me alone with him whom I created, and give him vast riches, and sons dwelling in his presence, and made matters easy for him, and yet he desires that I should give more! By no means! Surely he is inimical to Our Messages. I will make a distressing punishment overtake him. Surely he reflected and determined, But may he be destroyed how he determined! Then he looked, then frowned and scowled, then turned back and was big with pride, then said: This is naught bet magic from old! This is naught but the word of a mortal! I will cast him into Hell. And what will make thee realize what Hell is? It leaves naught and spares not. It scorches the mortal. Over it are nineteen. And We have made none but angels wardens of the Fire, and We have not made their number but as a trial for those who disbelieve, that those who have been given the Book may be certain and those who believe may increase in faith, and those who have been given the Book and the believers may not doubt; and that those in whose hearts is a disease and the disbelievers may say: What does the most gracious Creator mean by this parable? Thus the most gracious Creator leaves in error who He pleases, and guides whom He pleases. And none know the hosts of thy Lord but He. And this is naught but a Reminder to mortals.

O thou who is covering thyself up! Rise to pray by night except a little, half of it, or lessen it a little, or add to it, and recite the Qur'an in a leisurely manner. Surely We shall charge thee with a weighty word. The rising by night is surely the firmest way to tread and most effective in speech. Truly thou hast by day prolonged occupation. And remember the Name of thy Lord and devote thyself to Him with devotion. The Lord of the East and the West — there is no God but He — so take Him for Protector. Thy Lord knows indeed that thou pass in prayer nearly two-thirds of the night, and half of it, and a third of it, as for a party of those with thee. And the most gracious Creator measures the night and the day. He knows that you are not able to do it, so He has turned to you mercifully; so read the Qur'an that which is easy for you. He knows that there are sick among you, and others who travel in the land seeking of the most gracious Creator's bounty, and others who fight in the most gracious Creator's way. So read as much of it as is easy, and keep up prayer and pay the poor-rate and offer to the most gracious Creator a goodly gift. And whatever of good you send on beforehand for yourselves, you will find it with the most gracious Creator – that is best and greatest in reward. And ask forgiveness of the most gracious Creator. Surely the most gracious Creator is Forgiving, Merciful.

The sure Truth! What is the sure Truth? And what would make thee realize what the sure truth is? Thamud and Ad called the calamity a lie. Then as for Thamud, they were destroyed by the severe punishment. And as for Ad, they were destroyed by a roaring,

violent wind, which He made to prevail against them for seven nights and eight days continuously so that thou mightest have seen the people therein prostrate as if they were trunks of hollow palm-trees. So canst thou see a remnant of them? And Pharaoh and those before him and the overthrown cities wrought evil. And they disobeyed the Messenger of their Lord, so He punished them with a vehement punishment. Surely We carried you in the ship when the water rose high, that We might make it a reminder for you, and that the retaining ear might retain it.
But nay! I swear by that which you see, and that which you see not! Surely, it is the word of an honorable Messenger, and it is not the word of a poet; little is it that you believe! Nor a word of a soothsayer; little is it that you mind! It is a revelation from the worlds. And if he had fabricated against Us certain sayings, We would certainly have seized him by the right hand, then cut off his heart's vein. And not one of you could have withheld Us from him. And surely it is a Reminder for the dutiful. And We certainly

The Heavenly Message

know that some of you are rejecters. And it is indeed a grief to the disbelievers. And surely it is the certain Truth. So glorify the name of thy Lord, the incomparably Great.

The inkstand and the pen and that which thy write! By the Grace of thy Lord thou art not mad. And surely for you is a reward never to be cut off. And surely thou hast sublime morals. So thou wilt see, and they will see, which of you is mad, surely thy Lord knows best who is erring from His Way, and He knows best those who go aright. So obey not the rejecters. They wish that thou should be pliant. And obey not any spiteful swearer, defamer going about with slander, hinderer of good, outstepping the limits, sinful, ignoble, besides all that, notoriously mischievous – because he possesses wealth and sons. When Our Messages are recited to him, he says: "Stories of those of yore!" We shall brand him on the snout. We shall try them as We tried the owners of the garden, when they swore to pluck the fruits in the morning, and would not set aside a portion for the poor. But a visitation from thy Lord came on it, while they slept. So it became as black, barren land – Then they called out to one another in the morning, saying: Go early to your tilth, if you would pluck the fruit. So they went, while they said one to another in low tones: "No poor man shall enter it today upon you." And in the morning they went, having the power to prevent. But when they saw it, they said: Surely, we are in error; nay, we are made to suffer privation. The best of them said: "Said I not to you, why do you not glorify the most gracious Creator?" They said: "Glory be to our Lord! Surely, we were unjust." Then some of them advanced against others, blaming each other. They said: "O woe to us! Surely, we were inordinate – Maybe, our Lord will give us instead one better than it – surely to our Lord we make a petition." Such is the chastisement. And certainly, the chastisement of the Hereafter is greater, did they but know! Surely the dutiful have with their Lord Gardens of Bliss. Shall We then make those who submit as the guilty? What is the matter with you? How do you judge? Or have you a book wherein you read that you shall surely have therein what you choose? Or have you covenants from Us on oath, extending to the Day of Resurrection, that yours is surely what you judge? Ask them which of them will vouch for that. Or have they associate–gods? Then let them bring their associates if they are truthful. On the Day when there is a severe affliction, and they are called upon to prostrate themselves, but they are not able – their looks cast down, abasement will cover them. And they were indeed called upon to prostrate themselves, while yet they were safe. So leave me alone with him who rejects this announcement. We shall overtake them by degrees, from whence they know not. And I bear with them, surely My Plan is firm. Or dost thou ask from them a reward so that they are burdened with debt? Or is the unseen with them so that they write down? So wait patiently for the Judgment of thy Lord, and be not like the Companion of the fish, when he cried while he was in distress. Had not favor from his Lord reached him, he would certainly have been cast down on naked ground while he was blamed. Then his Lord chose him, and He made him of the

righteous. And those who disbelieve would almost smite thee with their eyes when they hear the Reminder, and they say: "Surely he is mad!" And it is naught but a Reminder for the nations.
Blessed is He in Whose hand is the Kingdom, and He is Possessor of Power over all things, Who created death and life that He might try you – which if you are best in deeds. And He is the Mighty, the Forgiving, Who created the seven heavens alike. Thou seest no incongruity in the creation of the Beneficent. Then turn the eye again and again – thy look will return to thee confused, while it is fatigued.
O Prophet, why dost thou forbid that which the most gracious Creator has made lawful for thee? Seekest thou to please thy wives? the most gracious Creator is Forgiving, Merciful. The most gracious Creator indeed has sanctioned for you the expiration of your oaths; the most gracious Creator is your Patron, and He is the Knowing, the Wise. And when the Prophet confided information to one of his wives – but when she informed others of it, he made known

part of it and passed over part. So when he told her of it, she said: "Who informed thee of this?" He said: "The Knowing, the One Aware, informed me." If you both turn to the most gracious Creator, then indeed your hearts are inclined to this; and if you back up one another against him, then surely the most gracious Creator is his Patron, and Gabriel and the righteous believers, and the angels after that are the aiders. Maybe, his Lord, if he divorces you, will give him in your place wives better than you, submissive, faithful, obedient, penitent, adorers, fasters, widows, and virgins.

O Prophet, strive against the disbelievers and the hypocrites and remain firm against them, and their abode is Hell; and evil is the resort. The most gracious Creator sets forth an example for those who disbelieve – the wife of Noah and the wife of Lot. They were both under two of Our righteous servants, but they acted treacherously towards them, so they availed them naught against the most gracious Creator, and it was said: "Enter the Fire with those who enter."

O Prophet, when you divorce women,

divorce them for their prescribed period and calculate the period; and keep your duty to the most gracious Creator, your Lord; turn them not out of their houses – nor should they themselves go forth – unless they commit an open indecency. And these are the limits of the most gracious Creator. And whoever goes beyond the limits of the most gracious Creator, he indeed wrongs his own soul. Thou knowest not that the most gracious Creator may after that, bring about an event. So when they have reached their prescribed time, retain them with kindness or dismiss them with kindness, and call to witness two just ones from among you, and give upright testimony for the most gracious Creator. With that is admonished he who believes in the most gracious Creator and the Last Day. And whoever keeps his duty to the most gracious Creator, he ordains a way out for him and gives him sustenance from whence he imagines not. And whoever trusts in the most gracious Creator, He is sufficient for him. Surely the most gracious Creator attains His purpose. The most gracious Creator indeed has appointed a measure for everything. And those of your women who despair of menstruation, if you have a doubt, there prescribed time is three months, and of those, too, who have not had their courses. And the pregnant woman, their prescribed time is that they lay down their burden. And whoever keeps his duty to the most gracious Creator, He makes his affair easy for him. That is the command of the most gracious Creator, which He has revealed to you. And whoever keeps his duty to the most gracious Creator, He will remove from him his evils and give him a great reward. Lodge them where you live according to your means, and injure them not to straighten them. And if they are pregnant, spend on them until they lay down their burden. Then if they suckle for you, give them their recompense, and enjoin one another to do good; and if you disagree, another will suckle for him. Let him who has abundance spend out of his abundance, and whoever has his means of subsistence straightened to him, let him spend out of that which the most gracious Creator has given him. The most gracious Creator lays

not on any soul a burden beyond that which He has given it. The most gracious Creator brings about ease after difficulty.
the most gracious Creator is he Who created seven heavens, and of the like thereof. The Command descends among them, that you might know that the most gracious Creator has Power over all things and that the most gracious Creator encompasses everything in His Knowledge.
O Prophet, when believing women come to thee giving thee a pledge that they will not associate aught with the most gracious Creator, and will not steal, not commit adultery; nor kill their children, nor bring a calumny which they have forged of themselves, nor disobey thee in what is good, accept their pledge, and ask forgiveness for them from the most gracious Creator. Surely the most gracious Creator is Forgiving, Merciful.
Had We sent down this Quran on a mountain, thou would certainly have seen it falling down, splitting asunder because of the fear of the most gracious Creator. And We set forth these parables to men that they

may reflect. He is the most gracious Creator besides Whom there is no God: The Knower of the unseen and the seen; He is the Beneficent, the Merciful. He is the most gracious Creator, besides Whom there is no God; the King, the Holy, the Author of Peace, the granter of Security, Guardian over all, the Mighty, the Supreme, the Possessor of greatness. Glory be to the most gracious Creator from that which they set up with Him! He is the most gracious Creator; the Creator, the Maker, the Fashioner; His are the Most Beautiful Names. Whatever is in the heavens and the earth declares his Glory; and He is the Mighty, the Wise.

Seest thou not that the most gracious Creator knows whatever is in the heavens and whatever is in the earth? There is no secret counsel between three but He is the fourth of them, nor between five but He is the sixth of them, nor between less than that nor more than He is with them wheresoever they are; then He will inform them of what they did on the Day of Resurrection. Surely the most gracious Creator is Knower of all things. Seest thou not those who are forbidden secret counsels, then they return to that which they are forbidden and hold secret counsels for sin and revolt and disobedience to the Messenger. And when they come to thee with a greeting with which the most gracious Creator greets thee not, and say within themselves: "Why does not the most gracious Creator punish us for what we say?" Hell is enough for them; they will burn in it, and evil is the resort!

Hast thou not seen those who take for friends a people with whom have the Wrath of the most gracious Creator upon them? They are neither of you nor of them, and they swear falsely, while they know. The most gracious Creator has prepared for them a severe chastisement. Evil indeed is that which they do! They take shelter under their oaths, so they turn from the most gracious Creator's Way; for them is an abasing chastisement. Of no avail against Him, will be to them their wealth of their children. They are the companions of the Fire; therein they will abide. On the Day when the most gracious Creator will raise them all up, they will swear to Him as they swear to you, and they think that they have some excuse. Now surely they are the liars. The devil has gained the mastery over them, so he has made them forget the remembrance of the most gracious Creator. They are the devil's party. Now surely the devil's party are the losers. The most gracious Creator has written down: I shall certainly prevail, I and My Messengers. Surely the most gracious Creator is Strong, Mighty. Thou wilt not find a people who believe in the most gracious Creator and the Latter Day loving those who oppose the most gracious Creator and His Messenger, even though they are their fathers, or their sons, or their brother, or their kinsfolk. These are they into whose hearts he has impressed faith, and strengthened them with a Spirit from Himself, and he will cause them to enter Gardens wherein flow rivers, abiding therein. The most gracious Creator is well-pleased with them and they are well-pleased with Him. These are the most gracious Creator's party. Now surely it is the most gracious Creator's party who are successful!

The Heavenly Message

Have they associates who have prescribed for them any religion that the most gracious Creator does not sanction? And were it not for the word of judgment, it would have been decided between them. And surely for the wrongdoers is a painful chastisement.

By the star when it sets! Your companion errs not, nor does he deviate. Nor does he speak out of desire. It is naught but revelation that is revealed – One Mighty in Power has taught him, the Lord of Strength. Endued with Wisdom, for he appeared in stately form, and he is in the highest part of the horizon. Then he drew near, drew nearer yet, so he was the measure of two bows or closer still. So He revealed to His servant what He revealed. The heart was not untrue in seeing what he saw. Do you then dispute with him as to what he saw? And certainly, he saw him in another descent, at the farthest lote-tree. Near it is the Garden of Abode. When that which covers covered the lote-tree; the eye turned not aside, nor did it exceed the limit. Certainly, he saw the greatest signs of his Lord.

And how many angels are in the heavens,

whose intercession avails naught except after the most gracious Creator gives permission to whom He pleases and chooses. Surely those who believe not in the Hereafter name the angels with female names. And they have no knowledge of it. They follow but conjecture and surely conjecture avails naught against Truth. So shun him who turns his back upon Our Reminder, and desires nothing but this world's life. That is their goal of knowledge. Surely thy Lord knows best him who strays from His Path and He knows best him who goes aright. And the most gracious Creator's is whatever is in the heavens and whatever is in the earth, that He may reward those who do evil for that which they do and reward those who do good with goodness. Those who avoid the great sins and the indecencies, but the passing idea – surely thy Lord is Liberal in Forgiving. He knows you best when He brings you forth from the earth and when you are embryos in the wombs of your mothers; so ascribe not purity to yourselves. He knows him best who guards against evil.

Seest thou him who turns back, and give a little, then withholds? Has he the knowledge of the unseen so that he can see? Or has he not been informed of what is in the scriptures of Moses, and Abraham who fulfilled Commandments? That is no bearer of burden bears another burden: And that man can have nothing but what he strives for: and that his striving will soon be seen. Then he will be rewarded for it with the fullest reward: and that to thy Lord is the goal: And that He it is Who makes men laugh and makes them weep: And that is Who causes death and gives life: and that He creates pairs, the male and the female; from the small life-germ when it is adapted: And that He has ordained the second bringing forth: And that He it is Who gives wealth and contentment: and that he is the Lord of Sirius: and that he destroyed the first 'Ad: and Thamud, so he spared not: and the people of Noah before. Surely they were most iniquitous and inordinate. And the overthrown cities, He hurled down: So there covered them that which covered. Which, then, of thy Lord's benefits wilt thou dispute?

The Heavenly Message

This is a warner of the warners of old. The near Event draws nigh. There is none besides the most gracious Creator to remove it. Wonder you then at this announcement? And do you laugh and not weep, while you sport? So bow down in prostration before the most gracious Creator and serve Him.

So remind for, by the grace of thy Lord, thou art no soothsayer, nor madman. Or say they: A poet – we wait for him the evil accidents of time. Say: Wait, I too wait along with you. Or do their understandings bid them this? Or are they an inordinate people? Or say they: He has forged it. Nay, they have no faith. Then let them bring a saying like it if they are truthful. Or were they created without a creative agency? Or were they the creators? Or did they create the heavens and the earth? Nay, they are sure of nothing. Or have they the treasures of thy Lord with them? Or have they absolute authority? Or have they the means by which they listen? Then let their listener bring a clear authority. Or has He daughters and you have sons? Or have thou ask from them so that they are overburdened by a debt? Or possess they the unseen, so they write it down. Or do they intend a plot? But those who disbelieve will be the ensnared ones in the plot. Or have they a god other than the most gracious Creator? Glory be to the most gracious Creator from what they set up with Him! And if they were to see a portion of the heaven coming down, they would say: Piled up clouds! Leave them then till they meet that Day of theirs wherein they are smitten with punishment: The day when their struggle will avail them naught, nor will they be helped. And surely for those who do wrong, there is a chastisement besides that; but most of them know not. And wait patiently for the judgment of thy Lord, for surely thou art before Our Eyes, and celebrate the praise of thy Lord, when thou rise, and in the night, give Him glory, too, and at the setting of the stars.

By those scattering broadcast! And those bearing the load! And those running easily! And those distributing the Affair! – What you are promised is surely true, and the Judgment will surely come to pass. By the heaven full of paths! Surely you are of varying opinion – He is turned away from it who would be turned away. Cursed be the falsehood mongers! They ask: When is the Day of Judgment? It is the Day when they are tried at the Fire. Taste your persecution! This is what you would hasten on. Surely the dutiful are amid Gardens and fountains, taking that which their Lord gives them. Surely they were before that the doers of good. They used to sleep but little at night. And in the morning they asked for Divine protection. And in their wealth, there was a due share for the beggar and for one who is denied. And in the earth are signs for those who are sure, and in yourselves – do you not see? And in the heavens is your sustenance and that which you are promised. So by the Lord of the heavens and the earth! It is surely the truth, just as you speak. Has the story of Abraham's guests reached thee? When they came to him, they said: Peace! Peace! Said he: Strangers! Then he turned aside to his family and brought a fat calf. So he placed it before them. He said: Will you not eat? So he conceived a fear of them. They said: Fear not. And they gave him the good news of a boy possessing knowledge. Then his wife came up in grief, and she smote her face and said: A barren old woman! They said: Thus says thy Lord. Surely He is the Wise, the Knowing. He said: What is your errand, O Messengers! They said: We have been sent to a guilty people that we may send upon them stones of clay, marked from thy Lord for the prodigal. Then We brought forth such believers as were there. And we found there but a house of Muslims. And We left therein a sign for those who fear the painful chastisement. And in Moses, when We sent him to Pharaoh with clear authority. But he turned away on account of his might and said: An enchanter or a madman! So We seized him and his hosts and hurled them into the sea, and he was blamable. And in Ad, when We sent upon them the destructive wind. It spared naught that it came against, but made it like ashes. And in Thamud, when it was said to them: Enjoy yourselves for a while. But they revolted against the commandment of their Lord, so the punishment overtook them, while they saw. So they were unable to rise up, nor could they defend themselves; and the people of Noah before. Surely they were a transgressing people. And the heaven, We raised it high with power, and We are Makers of the vast extent. And the earth, We have spread it out. How well We prepared it! And of everything We have created pairs that you may be mindful. So flee to the most gracious Creator. Surely I am a plain warner to you from Him. And do not set up with the most gracious Creator another god. Surely I am a plain warner to you from Him. Thus there came not a messenger to those before them but they said: An enchanter or a madman! Have they charged each other with this? Nay, they are an inordinate people. So turn away from them, for thou art not to blame; and remind, for reminding profits the believers. And I have not created the jinn and the men except that they should serve Me. I desire no sustenance from them, nor do I desire that they should feed me. Surely the most gracious Creator is the Bestower of sustenance, the Lord of Power, the Strong. Surely the lot of the wrongdoers is as was the lot of their companions, so let

them not ask Me to hasten on. Woe, then, to those who disbelieve because of that day of theirs which they are promised!
And inform them of the guests of Abraham. When they entered upon him, they said, Peace! He said: We are afraid of you. They said: Be not afraid, we give thee good news of a boy, possessing knowledge. He said: Do you give me good news when old age has come upon me? Of what then do you give me good news? They said: We give thee good news with truth, so be not thou of the despairing ones. He said: And who despairs of the mercy of his Lord but the erring ones? He said: What is your business, then, O Messengers? They said: We have been sent to a guilty people, except Lot's followers. We shall deliver them all, except his wife: We ordained that she shall surely be of those who remain behind. So when the Messengers came to Lot's followers, he said: Surely you are an unknown people. They said: Nay, we have come to thee with that about which they disputed. And we have come to thee with the truth, and we are surely truthful. So travel with thy followers

The Heavenly Message

for a part of the night and thyself follow their rear and let not any one of you turn round, and go whither you are commanded. And We made known to him this decree, that the roots of these should be cut off in the morning. And the people of the town came rejoicing. He said: These are my guests, so disgrace me not, and keep your duty to the most gracious Creator and shame me not. They said: Did we not forbid thee from entertaining people? He said: These are my daughters if you will do aught. By thy life! They blindly wandered on in their frenzy. So the cry overtook them at sunrise; thus We turned it upside down and rained upon them hard stones. Surely in this are signs for those who take a lesson. And it is on a road that still abides. Verily therein is a sign for the believers. And the dwellers of the grove were indeed iniquitous: So We inflicted retribution on them. And they are both on an open high road. And the dwellers of the Rock indeed rejected the Messengers, and We gave them Our Messages, but they turned away from them; and they hewed houses in the mountains, in security. So the cry overtook them in the morning; what they earned availed them not. And We created not the heavens and the earth and what is between them but with the truth. And the Hour is surely coming, so turn away with kindly forgiveness. Surely thy Lord — He is the Creator, the Knower.

Tell My servants who believe to keep up prayer and spend out of what We have given them, secretly and openly, before the coming of the day in which there is no bartering, nor befriending. The most gracious Creator is He Who created the heavens and the earth and sent down water from the clouds, then brought forth with it fruits as a sustenance for you, and He has made the ships subservient to you to run their course in the sea by His command, and He has made the rivers subservient to you. And He has made subservient to you the sun and the moon, pursuing their courses; and He has made subservient to you the night and the day. And He gives you of all you ask of Him. And if you count the most gracious Creator's favors, you will not be able to number them. Surely man is very unjust, very ungrateful. And when Abraham said: My Lord, make this city secure, and save me and my sons from worshipping idols. My Lord, surely they have led many men astray. So whoever follows me, he is surely of me; and whoever disobeys me, Thou surely art Forgiving, Merciful. Our Lord, I have settled a part of my offspring in a valley unproductive of fruit near Thy Sacred House, our Lord, that they may keep up prayer; so make the hearts of some people yearn towards them, and provide them with fruits; haply they may be grateful. Our Lord, surely Thou knowest what we hide and what we proclaim. And nothing is hidden from the most gracious Creator, either in the earth or in the heaven. Praise be to the most gracious Creator, Who has given me, in old age, Ishmael and Isaac! Surely my Lord is the Hearer of prayer. My Lord, make me keep up prayer and from my offspring too, our Lord, and accept my prayer. Our Lord, grant me protection and my parents and the believers on the day when the reckoning comes to pass.

Qaf! (Almighty God!) By the Glorious Qur'an!

Nay, they wonder that a warner has come to them from among themselves; so the disbelievers say: This is a wonderful thing! When we die and become dust – that is a far return. We know indeed what the earth diminishes of them and with Us is a book that preserves. Nay, they reject the Truth when it comes to them, so they are in a state of confusion. Do they not look at the sky above them? – how We made it and adorned it has no gaps. And the earth, We have spread it out and cast therein mountains, and We made to grow therein of every beautiful kind – to give sight and as a reminder to every servant who turns to the most gracious Creator. And We send down from the clouds water abounding in good, then We cause to grow thereby gardens and the grain that is reaped, and the tall palm-trees having flower spikes piled one above another – A sustenance for the servants, and We give thereby to a dead land. This is the rising. Before them, the people of Noah rejected the Truth and the dwellers of the Wood and Thamud and Ad and Pharaoh and Lot's brethren, and the dwellers of the grove and the people of Tubba. They all rejected the Messengers, so My threat came to pass. Were We then fatigued with the first creation? Yet they are in doubt about a new creation.

And how many a generation We destroyed before them who were mightier in prowess than they! So they went about in the lands. Is there a place of refuge? Surely there is a reminder in this for him who has a heart or he gives ear and is a witness. And certainly We created the heavens and the earth and what is between them in six periods, and no fatigue touched Us. So bear with what they say, and celebrate the praise of thy Lord before the rising of the sun and before the setting. And glorify Him in the night and after prostration. And listen on the Day when the crier cries from a near place – The day when they hear the cry in truth. That is the Day of coming forth. Surely We give life and cause to die, and to Us is the eventual coming – The Day when the earth cleaves asunder from them, hasting forth. That is a gathering easy for Us. We know best what they say, and thou art not one to compel them. So remind by means of the Qur'an him who fears My threat.

Those who call out to thee from behind the private apartments, most of them have no sense. And if they had patience till thou come out to them, it would be better for them. And the most gracious Creator is Forgiving, Merciful.

And how many a town, more powerful than thy town which has driven thee out — We destroyed them, so there was no helper for them. Is then he who has a clear argument from his Lord like him to whom his evil conduct is made fair-seeming, and they follow their low desires.

And there are those of them who seek to listen to thee, till, when they go forth from thee, they say to those who have been given knowledge: What was it that he said just now? These are they whose hearts the most gracious Creator has sealed and they follow their low desires. And those who follow guidance, He increases them in guidance and grants them their observance of duty. Wait they for aught but the Hour that it should come upon them of a sudden? Now tokens thereof have already come. But how will they have their reminder, when it comes on them? So know that there is no god but the most gracious Creator and ask protection for thy sin and for the believing men and the believing women. And the most gracious Creator knows your moving about and your staying. And those who believe say: Why is not a chapter revealed? But when a decisive chapter is revealed, and fighting is mentioned therein, thou see those in whose hearts is a disease look to thee with the look of one fainting at death. So woe to them! Obedience and a gentle word were proper. Then when the affair is settled, it is better for them if they remain true to the most gracious Creator. But if you turn away, you are sure to make mischief in the land and cut off the ties of kinship! Those it is whom the most gracious Creator has cursed, so He has made them deaf and blinded their eyes. Do they not reflect on the Qur'an? Or, are there locks on their hearts? Surely those who turn back after guidance is manifest to them, the devil embellishes it for them; and lengthens false hopes for them. That is because they say to those who hate what the most gracious Creator has revealed: We will obey you in some matters. And the most gracious Creator knows their secrets. But how will it be when the angels cause them to die, smiting their faces and their backs? That is because they follow that which displeases the most gracious Creator and are averse to His Pleasure, so He makes their deeds fruitless. Or do those in whose hearts is a disease thinks that the most gracious Creator will not bring forth their spite? And if We please, We could show them to thee so that thou should know them by their marks. And certainly, thou can recognize them by the tone of speech. And the most gracious Creator knows your deeds. And certainly, We shall try you, till We know those among you who strive hard and the steadfast, and manifest your news. Surely those who disbelieve and hinder from the most gracious Creator's way and oppose the Messenger after guidance is quite clear to them, cannot harm the most gracious Creator in any way, and He will make their deeds fruitless.

And certainly We destroyed the towns round about you, and We repeat the messages that they may turn. Then why did those whom they took for gods besides the most gracious Creator to draw nigh not help them? Nay, they failed them. And this was their lie and what they forged. And when We turned towards thee a party of the jinn, who listened to the Quran; so when they were in its presence, they said: Be silent. Then when it is finished, they turned back to their people warning. They said: O our people, we have heard a Book revealed after Moses, verifying that which is before it, guiding to the truth and to a right path. O our people, accept the Inviter to the most gracious Creator and believe in Him. He will forgive you some of your sins and protect you from a painful chastisement. And whoever accepts not the Inviter to the most gracious Creator, he cannot escape in the earth, nor has he protectors besides Him. These are in manifest error. See they not that the most gracious Creator, who created the heavens and the earth and was not tired by their creation, is able to give life to the dead? Aye,

He is surely Possessor of power over all things.

Ha Mim (Beneficent God!) The revelation of the Book is from the most gracious Creator, the Mighty, the Wise. Surely in the heavens and the earth are signs for believers. And in your creation and in the creatures He spreads abroad are signs for people with certainty. And the variation of the night and the day and the sustenance which the most gracious Creator sends down from the heaven then gives life thereby to the earth after its death, and the changing of the winds, are signs for a people who understand. These are the messages of the most gracious Creator, which We recite to thee with the truth. In what announcement will they then believe after the most gracious Creator and His Signs?

the most gracious Creator is He Who made subservient to you the sea that the ships may glide therein by His Command, and that you may seek of His Grace, and that you may give thanks. And He has made subservient to you whatsoever is in the heavens and whatsoever is in the earth, all, from Himself.

Surely there are signs in this for a people who reflect. Tell those who believe to forgive those who fear not the days of the most gracious Creator that He may reward a people for what they earn. Whoever does good it is for himself, and whoever does evil, it is against himself; then to your Lord, you will be brought back. And certainly, We gave the Children of Israel the Book and judgment and prophethood and provided them with good things, and made them excel the nations. And We gave them clear arguments in the Affair. So they differed not until after knowledge had come to them, out of envy among themselves. Surely thy Lord will judge between them on the Day of Resurrection concerning that wherein they differed. Then We made thee follow a course in the Affair, so follow it, and follow not the low desires of those who know not. Surely they can avail thee naught against the most gracious Creator. And surely the wrongdoers are friends of each other, and the most gracious Creator is the Friend of the dutiful. These are clear proofs for men, and a guidance and a mercy for a people who are sure. Or do those who do evil deeds think that We shall make them as those who believe and do good – their life and their death being equal? Evil is what they judge! And the most gracious Creator created the heavens and the earth with truth, and that every soul may be rewarded for what has earned, and they will not be wronged. Seest thou him who takes his desire for his god, and the most gracious Creator leaves him in error knowingly, and seals his hearing and his heart and puts a covering on his sight? Who can then guide him after the most gracious Creator? Will you not mind? And they say: There is naught but our life of the world; we die and we live and nothing destroys us but time, and they have no knowledge of that; they only conjecture. And when Our clear messages are recited to them, their only argument is that they say: Bring our fathers, if you are truthful. Say: the most gracious Creator gives you life, then makes you die, then will He gather you to the Day of Resurrection, wherein is no doubt, but most people know not.

Ha Mim (Beneficent God!) By the Book that

makes manifest! We revealed it on a blessed night truly We are ever warning. Therein is made clear every affair full of wisdom – A command from Us – truly We are ever sending Messengers – A mercy from thy Lord – truly He is the Hearing, the Knowing, the Lord of the heavens and the earth and what is between them if you would be sure. There is no God but He; He gives life and causes death – your Lord and the Lord of your fathers of yore. Nay, in doubt they sport. So wait for the day when the heaven brings a clear drought, enveloping men. This is a painful chastisement. Our Lord, remove from us the chastisement – surely we are believers. When will they be reminded? And a Messenger has indeed come, making clear; yet they turned away from him and said: One taught, a madman! We shall remove the chastisement a little, you will surely return. On the Day when We seize them with the most violent seizing; surely We shall exact retribution. And certainly, We tried before them Pharaoh's people and a noble messenger came to them, Saying: Deliver to me the servants of the most gracious Creator. Surely I am a faithful messenger to you. And exalt not yourselves against the most gracious Creator. Surely I bring to you a clear authority. And I take refuge with my Lord and your Lord, lest you stone me to death. And if you believe not in me, leave me alone. Then he called upon his Lord: These are a guilty people. So go forth with My servants by night; surely you will be pursued. And leave the sea behind calm. Surely they are a host to be drowned. How many of the gardens and springs they left behind! And cornfields and noble places! And goodly things wherein they rejoiced! Thus it was. And We made other people inherit them. So the heaven and the earth wept not for them, nor were they respited. And We indeed delivered the Children of Israel from the abasing chastisement, from Pharaoh. Surely he was haughty, prodigal. And certainly, We have chosen them above the nations, having knowledge. And We gave them signs wherein was a clear blessing. These do indeed say: There is naught but our first death and we shall not be raised again. So bring our back, if you are truthful.

And they better or the people of Tubba, and those before them? We destroyed them, for surely they were guilty. And We did not create the heavens and the earth and that which is between them in a sport. We created them not but with truth, but most of them know not. Surely the Day of Decision is the term for them all, the Day when a friend will avail friend in naught, nor will they be helped – except those on whom the most gracious Creator has mercy. Surely He is the Mighty, the Merciful.

Say: It has been revealed to me that a party of the jinn listened, so they said: Surely we have heard a wonderful Qur'an, guiding to the right way – so we believe in it and we shall not set up anyone with our Lord: And He – exalted be the Majesty of our Lord! – has not taken a consort, nor a son: And the foolish among us used to forge extravagant lies against the most gracious Creator: And we thought that men and jinn did not utter a lie against the most gracious Creator: And persons from among men used to seek refuge with persons from among the jinn, so they increased them in evil doing: And they thought, as you think, that the most gracious Creator would not raise anyone: And we sought to reach heaven, but we found it filled with strong guards and flames: And we used to sit in some of the sitting-places thereof to steal a hearing, but he who tries to listen now finds a flame lying in wait for him: And we know not whether evil is meant for those on earth or whether their Lord means to direct them aright: And some of us are good and others of us are blow that – we are sects following different ways: And we know that we cannot escape the most gracious Creator in the earth, nor can we escape him by flight: And when we heard the guidance, we believed in it. So whoever believes in his Lord, he fears neither loss nor injustice: And some of us are those who submit, and some of us are deviators, they are fuel of hell: And if they keep to the right way, We would certainly give them to drink of abundant water, so that We may try them thereby. And the mosques are the most gracious Creator's, so call not upon anyone with Him: And when the Servant of the most gracious Creator stood up praying to Him, they well-nigh crowded him. Say: I only call upon my Lord, and associate none with Him. Say: I control not evil not good for you. Say: None can protect me against the most gracious Creator, nor can I find any refuge besides Him: Mine is naught but to deliver the Commands of the most gracious Creator and His Messages; and whoever disobeys the most gracious Creator and His Messenger, surely for him is the Fire of Hell, to abide therein for ages, till when they see that which they are promised, they will know who is weaker in helpers and less in numbers. Say: I know not whether that which you are promised is nigh or it my Lord will appoint for it a distant term. The Knower of the unseen, so He makes His secrets known to none, except a messenger who He chooses. For surely he makes a guard to go before him and after him, that he may know that they have truly delivered the Messages of their Lord; and He encompasses what is with them, and He keeps account of all things.

He it is Who made the earth subservient to you, so go about in the spacious sides thereof, and eat of His sustenance. And to Him is the rising. Do you feel secure that He Who is in the heaven will not make the earth to swallow you up? Then lo! It will shake. Or do you feel secure that He Who is in the heaven will not send on you a violent wind? Then shall you know how truthful was My warning! And certainly, those before them denied, then how terrible was My disapproval! Do they not see the birds above them spreading and contracting their wings? Naught upholds them except the Beneficent. Surely He is Seer of all things Or who is it that will be a host for you to help you against the Beneficent? The disbelievers are in naught but delusion. Or who is it that will give you sustenance, if He should withhold His sustenance? Nay, they persist in disdain and aversion. Is, then, he who goes prone upon his face better guided or he who walks upright on a straight path? Say: He it is Who brought you into being and made for you, ears and eyes and hearts. Little thanks it is you give! Say: He it is Who multiplies you in the earth and to Him you will be gathered.

Say: Have you considered if the most

gracious Creator should destroy me and those with me – rather He will have mercy on us – yet who will protect the disbelievers from a painful chastisement? Say: He is the Beneficent – we believe in Him and on Him do we rely upon. So you will come to know who it is that is in clear error. Say: Have you considered if you water should subside, who is it then that will bring you flowing water?
Ha Mim (Beneficent God!) By the Book that makes manifest! Surely We have made it an Arabic Quran that you may understand. And it is in the Original of the Book with Us, truly elevated, full of wisdom. Shall We then turn away the Reminder from you altogether because you are a prodigal people? And how many a prophet did We send among the ancients! And no prophet came to them but they mocked him. Then We destroyed those stronger than these in prowess, and the example of the ancients has gone before. And if thou ask them, Who created the heavens and the earth? They would say: The Mighty, the Knowing One, has created them, Who made the earth a resting-place for you, and made in it ways for you that you might

go aright. And Who sends down water from the cloud according to a measure, then We raise to life thereby a dead land; even so will you be brought forth. And Who created pairs of all things, and made for you ships and cattle on which you ride, that you may sit firmly on their backs, then remember the favor of your Lord, when you are firmly seated thereon, and say: Glory be to Him Who made this subservient to us and we were not able to do it, and surely to our Lord we must return. And they assign to Him a part of His servants. Man, to be sure, is clearly ungrateful.

And they say: If the Beneficent had pleased, we should not have worshipped them. They have no knowledge of this; they only lie. Or have We given them a Book before it so that they hold fast to it? Nay, they say: We found our fathers on a course, and surely we are guided by their footsteps. And thus, We sent not before thee a warner in a town, but its wealthy ones said: Surely we found our fathers following a religion, and we follow their footsteps. The warner said: And even if I bring to you a better guide than that which you found your fathers following? They said: We surely disbelieve in that with which you are sent. So We exacted retribution from them, then see what was the end of the rejecters! And when Abraham said to his sire and his people: I am clear of what you worship, except Him Who created me, for surely He will guide me. And he made it a word to continue in his posterity that they might return. Nay! I let these and their fathers enjoy till there came to them the Truth and a Messenger making manifest. And when the Truth came to them they said: This is an enchantment, and surely we are disbelievers in it. And they say: Why was not this Quran revealed to a man of importance in the two towns? Do they apportion the mercy of thy Lord? We portion out among them their livelihood in the life of this world, and We exalt some of them above others in rank, that some of them may take others in service. And the mercy of thy Lord is better than that which they amass. And were it not that all people would become one disbelieving community, We would provide for those who disbelieve in the Beneficent, roofs of silver for their houses and stairs by which they ascend, and the doors of their houses and the couches on which they recline, and of gold. And all this is naught but a provision of this world's life; and the Hereafter is with thy Lord only for the dutiful. And whoever turns himself away from the remembrance of the Beneficent, We appoint for him a devil, so he is his associate. And surely they hinder them from the right path, and they think that they are guided aright. Until when he comes to Us, he says: O would that between me and thee were the distance of the East and the West! So evil is the associate! And as you did wrong, it will profit you naught this day that you are sharers in the chastisement. Canst thou then make the deaf to hear or guide the blind and him who is in clear error? So if We take thee away, still We shall exact retribution from them, or shall We shall show thee that which We promise them – surely We are Possessors of power over them. So hold fast to that which has been revealed to thee; surely thou art on the right path. And surely it is a reminder for thee and thy people, and you will be questioned. And ask those of Our Messengers whom We sent before thee: Did We ever appoint gods to be worshipped besides the Beneficent? And surely We sent Moses with Our Messages to Pharaoh and his chiefs, so he said: I am the messenger of the Lord of the worlds. But when he brought them Our Signs, lo! They laughed at them. And We showed them not a sign but it was greater than its fellow, and We seized them with chastisement that they might turn. And they said: O enchanter, call on thy Lord for us, as He made the covenant with thee; we shall surely follow guidance. But when We removed from them the chastisement, lo! They broke the pledge. And Pharaoh proclaimed among his people, saying: O my people, is not the kingdom of Egypt mine and these rivers flowing beneath me? Do you not see? Rather I am better than this fellow who is contemptible and can hardly express himself clearly. Why, then, have bracelets of gold not been bestowed on him, or angels come along with him in procession? So he incited his people to levity and they obeyed him. Surely they were a transgressing people. Then when they displeased Us, We exacted retribution from them, so We drowned them all together. And We made them a thing past and an example for later generations. And when the son of Mary is mentioned as an example, lo! Thy people raise a clamor thereat. And they say: Are our gods better, or is he? They set it forth to thee only by way of disputation. Nay, they are a contentious people. He was naught but a servant on whom We bestowed favor and We made him an example for the Children of Israel; And if We pleased, We could make among you angels to be Our vicegerents in the land. And this revelation is surely knowledge of the Hour, so have no doubt about it and follow me. This is the right path. And let not the devil hinder you; surely he is your open enemy. And when Jesus came with clear arguments, he said: I have come to you indeed with wisdom, and to make clear to you some of that about which you differ. So keep your duty to the most gracious Creator and obey me. Surely the most gracious Creator is my Lord and your Lord, so serve Him. This is the right path. But parties among them differed, so woe to those who did wrong for the chastisement of a painful day! Wait they for aught but the Hour, that it should come on them all of a sudden, while they perceive not?

Or have they settled an affair? But it is We Who settle affairs. Or do they think that We bear not their secrets and their private counsels? Aye, and Our Messengers with them write down. Say: The Beneficent has no son; so I am the foremost of those who serve The Beneficent. Glory be to the Lord of the heavens and the earth, the Lord of the Throne of Power, from what they describe! So let them talk and sport until they meet their Day which they are promised. And He it is Who is God of the heavens and the God of the earth. And He is the Wise, the Knowing. And blessed is He Whose is the kingdom of the heavens and the earth and all between them, and with Him is the knowledge of the Hour, and to Him, you will be returned. And those whom they call on besides Him control not intercession, but he who bears witness to the Truth and they know. And if thou were to ask them, they would say the most gracious Creator. How are they then turned back? And his cry – O my Lord, these are a people who believe not! So turn away from them and say Peace! They will soon come to know.

Ha Mim (Beneficent God!) Ain Sin Sad (Knowing, Hearing, Powerful God!) Thus does the most gracious Creator, the Mighty, the Wise, reveal to thee, and to those before thee. To Him belongs whatever is in the heavens and whatever is in the earth; and He is the High, the Great. The heavens may almost be rent asunder above them, while the angels celebrate the praise of thy Lord and ask forgiveness for those on earth. Now surely the most gracious Creator is the Forgiving, the Merciful. And those who take protectors besides Him – He watches over them; and thou hast not charge over them. And thus have We revealed to thee an Arabic Qur'an, that thou may warn the mother-town and those around it, and give warning of the Day of Gathering wherein is no doubt. A party will be in the Garden and another party in the burning Fire. And if the most gracious Creator had pleased, He would surely have made them a single nation, but He admits whom He pleases to His Mercy. And the wrongdoers have no protector or helper. Or have they taken protectors besides Him? But the most gracious Creator is the Possessor of power over all things.

He has made plain to you the religion which He enjoined upon Noah and which We have revealed to thee, and which We enjoined on Abraham and Moses and Jesus – to establish religion and not to be divided therein. Hard for the polytheists is that to which thou call them. The most gracious Creator chooses for Himself whom He pleases, and guides to Himself him who turns to Him. And they were not divided until after knowledge had come to them, out of envy among themselves. And had not a word gone forth from thy Lord for an appointed term, the matter would surely have been judged between them. And those who were made to inherit the Book after them are surely in a disquieting doubt about it. To this then go on inviting, and be steadfast as thou art commanded, and follow not their low desires, and say: I believe in what the most gracious Creator has revealed of the Book, and I am commanded to do justice between you. The most gracious Creator is our Lord and your Lord. For us are our deeds and for you, your deeds. There is no contention between us and you. The most gracious Creator will gather us together, and to Him is the eventual coming. And those who dispute about the most gracious Creator after obedience has been rendered to Him, their plea is null with their Lord, and upon them is wrath, and for them is severe chastisement. The most gracious Creator is He Who revealed the Book with truth, and the Balance; and what will make thee know that perhaps the Hour is nigh. Those who believe not in it would hasten it on, and those who believe are in fear from it, and they know that it is the Truth. Now surely those who dispute concerning the Hour are far astray. The most gracious Creator is Benignant to His servants; He gives sustenance to whom He pleases; He is Strong the Mighty. Whoso desires the tilth of the Hereafter, We give him increase in his tilth; whoso desires the tilth of this world, We give him thereof, and he has no portion in the Hereafter. Or have they associates who have prescribed for them any religion that the most gracious Creator does not sanction? And were it not for the word of judgment, it would have been decided between them. And surely for the wrongdoers is a painful chastisement. Thou seest the unjust fearing on account of what they have earned, and it must befall them. Or say they: He has forged a lie against the most gracious Creator? So, if He please, He would seal thy heart against them. And the most gracious Creator blots out the falsehood and confirms the Truth with His words. Surely He is Knower of what is in the breasts. And he whom the most gracious Creator leaves in error has no friend after Him. And thou wilt see them brought before it, humbling themselves because of abasement, looking with a faint glance. And those who believe will say: Surely the losers are they who lose themselves and their followers on the Resurrection Day. Now surely the iniquitous are in lasting chastisement. And they will have no friends to help them besides the most gracious Creator. And he whom the most gracious Creator leaves in error cannot find a way. Hearken to your Lord before there comes from Him the Day which there is no averting. You will have no refuge on that Day, nor will it be yours to make a denial. But if they turn away, We have not sent thee as a watcher over them, thy duty is only to deliver the message. And surely when We make man taste mercy from Us, he rejoices thereat; and if an evil afflicts them on account of what their hands have sent before, then surely man is ungrateful. The most gracious Creator's is the kingdom of the heavens and the earth. He creates what He pleases. He grants females to whom He pleases and grants males to whom He pleases, or He grants them both males and females, and He makes them whom He pleases, barren. Surely he is Knower, Powerful. And it is not vouchsafed to a mortal that the most gracious Creator should speak to him, except by revelation or from behind a veil, or by sending a messenger and revealing by His permission what He pleases. Surely He is High, Wise. And thus did We reveal to thee an inspired Book by Our Command. Thou know not what the Book was, nor what Faith was, but We made it a light, guiding thereby whom We please of Our Servants. And surely thou guidest to the right path – The path of the most gracious Creator, to Whom belongs whatsoever is in the heavens and whatsoever is in the earth. Now surely to the most gracious Creator do all affairs eventually come.

And who is better in speech than one who calls to the most gracious Creator and does good, and says: I am surely of those who submit? And not alike are the good and the evil. Repel evil with what is best, when lo! He between whom and there is enmity would be as if he were a warm friend. And none is granted it but those who are patient, and none is granted it but the owner of a mighty good fortune. And if a false imputation from the devil afflicts thee, seek refuge in the most gracious Creator. Surely He is the Hearing, the Knowing. And of His signs are the night and the day and the sun and the moon. Adore not the sun nor the moon, but adore the most gracious Creator Who created them, if He it is that you serve. But if they are proud, yet those with thy Lord glorify Him night and day, and they tire not. And of His signs is this, that thou see the earth still, but when We send down water thereon, it stirs and swells. He Who gives it life is surely the Giver of life to the dead. Surely He is Possessor of power over all things. Those who distort Our Messages are not hidden from Us. Is he then who is cast into the Fire better or he who comes safe on the Day of Resurrection? Do what you like, surely He is Seer of what you do. Those who disbelieve in the Reminder when it comes to them, and surely it is an Invincible Book: Falsehood cannot come at it from before or behind it: a revelation from the Wise, the Praised One. Naught is said to thee but what was said to Messengers before thee. Surely thy Lord is the Lord of Forgiveness and the Lord of painful

Retribution. And if We had made it a Quran in a foreign tongue, they would have said: Why have not its messages been made clear? What! A foreign tongue and an Arab! Say: It is to those who believe a guidance and a healing, and those who believe not, there is a deafness in their ears and it is obscure to them. These are called to from a place afar. And indeed We gave Moses the Book, but differences arose therein. And had not a word already gone forth from thy Lord, a judgment would have been given between them. And surely they are in a disquieting doubt about it. Whoever does good, it is for his own soul; and whoever does evil, it is against it. And thy Lord is not in the least unjust to the servants. To Him is referred the knowledge of the Hour. And no fruit comes forth from its coverings, nor does a female bear or bring forth but with His knowledge.

Ha Mim (Beneficent God)! The revelation of the Book is from the most gracious Creator, the Mighty, the Knowing, Forgiver of sin and Acceptor of repentance, Severe to punish, Lord of bounty. There is no God but He; to

Him is the eventual coming. None dispute concerning the messages of the most gracious Creator but those who disbelieve, so let not their control in the land deceive thee. Before them the people of Noah and the parties after them rejected, and every nation purposed against its Messenger to destroy him, and disputed by means of falsehood to render null thereby the truth, so I seized them: how terrible was then My retribution! And thus did the word of thy Lord proved true against those who disbelieve that they are the companions of the Fire. Those who bear the Throne of Power and those around it celebrate the praise of their Lord and believe in Him and ask protection for those who believe: Our Lord, Thou embrace all things in mercy and knowledge, to protect those who turn to Thee and follow Thy way, and save them from the chastisement of hell. Our Lord, make them enter the Gardens of perpetuity, which Thou hast promised them and such of their fathers and their wives and their offspring as are good. Surely Thou art the Mighty, the Wise: And guard them against evil, and whom Thou guard against evil this day, Thou hast indeed mercy on him. And that is the mighty achievement. Those who disbelieve are told: Certainly, the most gracious Creator's hatred of you, when you were called upon to the faith and you rejected, was much greater than your hatred now of yourselves. They say Our Lord, twice hast Thou made us die, and twice hast Thou has given us life; so we confess our sins. Is there then a way of escape? That is because when the most gracious Creator alone was called upon, you disbelieved, and when associates were given to Him, you believed. This judgment belongs to the most gracious Creator, the High, the Great. He it is Who shows you His signs and sends down for you sustenance from heaven, and none minds but he who turns to Him. So call upon the most gracious Creator, being sincere to Him in obedience, though the disbelievers are averse – Exalter of degrees, Lord of the Throne of Power, He makes the spirit to light by His command upon whom He pleases of His servants, that he may warn men of the Day of Meeting – The Day when they come forth. Nothing concerning them remains hidden from the most gracious Creator. To whom belongs the kingdom this Day? It is to the most gracious Creator, the One, the Subduer of all. This Day every soul is rewarded with what it has earned. No injustice this Day! Surely the most gracious Creator is Swift in Reckoning. And warn them of the Day that draws near, when hearts, grieving inwardly, rise up to the throats. The iniquitous will have no friend, nor any intercessor who should be obeyed. He knows the dishonest of eyes and that which the breasts conceal. And the most gracious Creator judges with the truth. And those whom they call upon besides Him judge naught! Surely the most gracious Creator is the Hearing, the Seeing. Have they not traveled in the land and seen what was the end of those who were before them? Mightier than these were they in strength and in fortifications in the land, but the most gracious Creator destroyed them for their sins. And they had none to protect them from the most gracious Creator. That was because there came to them their

Messengers with clear arguments, but they disbelieved, so the most gracious Creator destroyed them. Surely He is Strong, Severe in Retribution. And certainly We sent Moses with Our Messages and clear authority, to Pharaoh and Haman and Korah, but they said: A lying enchanter! So when he brought to them the Truth from Us, they said: Slay the sons of those who believe with him and keep their women alive. And the plot of the disbelievers is bound to fail. And Pharaoh said: Leave me to slay Moses and let him call upon his Lord. Surely I fear that he will make mischief to appear in the land. And Moses said: Truly I seek refuge in my Lord and your Lord from every proud one who believes not in the Day of Reckoning. And a believing man of Pharaoh's people, who hid his faith, said: Will you slay a man because it says, My Lord is the most gracious Creator, and indeed he has brought you clear arguments from your Lord? And if he is a liar, on him will be his lie, and if he is truthful, there will befall you some of that which he threatens you with. Surely the most gracious Creator guides not one who is a prodigal, a liar. O, my people, yours is the kingdom this day, being masters in the land, but who will help us against the punishment of the most gracious Creator, if it comes to us? Pharaoh said: I only show you which I see and I guide you only to the right way. And he who believed said: O my people, surely I fear for you the like of what befell the parties, the like of what befell the people of Noah and Ad and Thamud and those after them. And the most gracious Creator wishes no injustice for His servants. And, O my people, I fear for you the Day of Calling Out – The Day on which you will turn back retreating, having none to save you from the most gracious Creator; and whomsoever the most gracious Creator leaves in error there is no guide for him. And Joseph indeed came to you before with clear arguments, but you ever remained in doubt as to what he brought you; until, when he died, you said: the most gracious Creator will never raise a Messenger after thee. Thus does the most gracious Creator leave him in error who is a prodigal, a doubter –Those who dispute concerning the messages of the most gracious Creator without any authority that has come to them. Greatly hated is it by the most gracious Creator and by those who believe. Thus does the most gracious Creator seal every heart, of a proud, haughty one. And Pharaoh said: O Haman, build for me a tower that I may attain means of access – the means of access to the heavens, then reach the God of Moses, and I surely think him to be a liar. And thus the evil of his deed was made fair-seeming to Pharaoh, and he was turned aside from the way. And the plot of Pharaoh ended in naught but ruin. And he who believed said: O my people, follow me I will guide you to the right way. O my people, this life of the world is but a passing enjoyment, and the Hereafter, that is the abode to settle. Whoever does evil, he is requited with only with the like of it; and whoever does good, whether male or female, and he is a believer, these shall enter the Garden, to be given therein sustenance without measure. And O my people, how is it that I call you to salvation and you call me to the Fire? You call me to disbelieve in the most gracious Creator and to associate with

Him that of which I have no knowledge, and I call you to the Mighty, the Forgiving. Without a doubt that which you call me to has no title to be called to in this world, or in the Hereafter, and our return is to the most gracious Creator, and the prodigals are companions of the Fire. So you will remember what I say to you, and I entrust my affair to the most gracious Creator. Surely He is Seer of the servants. So the most gracious Creator protected him from the evil that they planned.

Say: Praise be to the most gracious Creator and peace on His servants whom He has chosen! Is the most gracious Creator better, or what they associate with Him? Or, Who created the heavens and the earth, and sends down for you water from the cloud? Then We cause to grow thereby beautiful gardens — it is not possible for you to make the trees thereof to grow. Is there a god with the most gracious Creator? Nay, they are a people who deviate! Or, Who made the earth a resting-place, and made in it rivers, and raised on it mountains, and placed between the two seas a barrier? Is there a god with the most gracious Creator? Nay, most of them know not! Or, Who answers the distressed one when he calls upon Him and removes the evil, and will make you successors in the earth? Is there a god with the most gracious Creator? Little is it that you mind! Or, Who guides you in the darkness of the land and the sea, and Who sends the winds as good news before His mercy? Is there a god with the most gracious Creator? Exalted be the most gracious Creator above what they associate with Him! Or, Who originates the creation, then reproduces it, and Who gives you sustenance from the heaven and the earth? Is there a god with the most gracious Creator? Say: Bring your proof, if you are truthful. Say: No one in the heavens and the earth knows the unseen but the most gracious Creator; they know not when they will be raised. Nay, their knowledge reaches not the Hereafter. Nay, they are in doubt about it. Nay, they are blind to it. And those who disbelieve say: When we have become dust and our fathers too, shall we indeed be brought forth? We have certainly been

promised this — we and our fathers before; these are naught but stories of the ancients! Say: Travel in the earth, then see what was the end of the guilty! And grieve not for them, nor be distressed because of what they plan. And they say: When will this promise come to pass if you are truthful?
Know that this world's life is only sport and play and gaiety and boasting among yourselves and a vying in the multiplication of wealth and children. It is as rain, whose causing the vegetation to grow pleases the husbandmen, then it withers away so that thou see it turning yellow, then it becomes dry and crumbles away. And in the Hereafter is a severe chastisement and forgiveness from the most gracious Creator and pleasure. And this world's life is naught but a source of vanity. No disaster befalls in the earth, or in yourselves, but is in a book before We bring it into existence – surely that is easy to the most gracious Creator – So that you grieve not for what has escaped you, nor exult in that which He has given you. And the most gracious Creator loves not any arrogant boaster: Such as are

niggardly and enjoin niggardliness on men. And whoever turns back, then surely the most gracious Creator is the Self-Sufficient, the Praised. Certainly, We sent Our Messengers with clear arguments, and sent down with them the Book and the measure, that men may conduct themselves with equity. And We sent down iron, wherein is great violence and advantages to men, and that the most gracious Creator may know who helps Him and His messengers, unseen. Surely the most gracious Creator is Strong, Mighty. And certainly We sent Noah and Abraham, and We gave prophethood and the Book to their offspring; so among them is he who goes aright, but most of them are transgressors. Then We made Our Messengers to follow in their footsteps, and We made Jesus son of Mary to follow, and We gave Him the Gospel. And We put compassion and mercy in the hearts of those who followed him. And monasticism, they innovated it – We did not prescribe it to them – only to seek the most gracious Creator's pleasure, but they did not observe it with its due observance. So We gave those of them who believed their reward, but most of them are transgressors.

And we indeed gave Moses the guidance, and We made the Children of Israel inherit the Book – a guidance and a reminder for men of understanding. So be patient; surely the promise of the most gracious Creator is true; ask protection for thy sin and celebrate the praise of thy Lord in the evening and the morning. Those who dispute about the Messages of the most gracious Creator without any authority having come to them, there is naught in their breasts but a desire to become great, which they will never attain. So seek refuge in the most gracious Creator. Surely He is the Hearing, the Seeing. Assuredly the creation of the heavens and the earth is greater than the creation of men, but most people know not, and the blind and the seeing are not alike, nor those who believe and do good and the evildoers. Little do you mind! The Hour is surely coming – there is no doubt therein – but most people believe not. And your Lord says: Pray to Me, I will answer you. Those who disdain My service will surely enter hell, abased. The most gracious Creator is He Who made for you the night for resting in and the day for seeing. Surely the most gracious Creator is Full of Grace to men, but most men give not thanks. The most gracious Creator is the most gracious Creator, your Lord, the Creator of all things. There is no God but He. Whence are you then turned away? Thus are turned away those who deny the Messages of the most gracious Creator. The most gracious Creator is He Who made the earth a resting-place for you and the heaven a structure, and He formed you, and then made goodly your forms, and He provided you with goodly things. That is the most gracious Creator, your Lord – so blessed is He, the Lord of the worlds. He is the Living; there is no God but He; so call on Him, being sincere to Him in obedience. Praise be to the most gracious Creator, the Lord of the worlds! Say: I am forbidden to serve those whom you call upon besides the most gracious Creator when clear arguments have come to me from my Lord; I am commanded to submit to the Lord of the worlds. He it is Who created you from dust, then from a small life-germ, then from a clot, then He brings you forth as a child, then that you may attain your maturity, then that you may be old; and of you are some who die before and that you may reach an appointed term, and that you may understand He it is Who gives life and causes death, so when He decrees an affair, He only says to it, Be, and it is. Seest thou not those who dispute concerning the Messages of the most gracious Creator? How are they turned away?

And certainly, We sent Messengers before thee – of them are those We have mentioned to thee and of them are those We have not mentioned to thee. Nor was it possible for a Messenger to bring a sign except with the most gracious Creator's Permission; so when the most gracious Creator's Command comes, judgment is given with truth, and those who treat it as a lie are lost.

The revelation of the Book is from the most gracious Creator, the Mighty, the Wise. Surely We have revealed to thee the Book with truth, so serve the most gracious Creator, being sincere obedience is due to the most gracious Creator alone. And those who choose protectors besides Him say: We serve them only that they may bring us nearer to the most gracious Creator. Surely He will judge between them in that which they differ. Surely the most gracious Creator guides not him who is a liar, ungrateful.

And those who eschew the worship of the idols and turn to the most gracious Creator, for them is good news. So give good news to My servants, Who listen to the Word, then follow the best of it. Such are they whom the most gracious Creator has guided, and such are the men of understanding. He against whom the sentence of chastisement is due – can thou save him who is in the Fire? But those who keep their duty to their Lord, for them are high places, above them, higher places, built in for them, wherein rivers flow. It is the Promise of the most gracious Creator. He fails not in His Promise. Seest thou not that the most gracious Creator sends down water from the clouds, then makes it go down into the earth in springs, then brings forth therewith herbage of various hues; then it withers so that thou seest it turn yellow, then He makes it chaff? Surely there is a reminder in this for men of understanding. Is he whose breast the most gracious Creator has opened to Islam so that he follows a light from his Lord--? So woe to those whose hearts are hardened against the remembrance of the most gracious Creator! Such are the in clear error. The most gracious Creator has revealed the best announcement, a Book consistent, repeating its injunctions, whereat do shudder the skins of those who fear their Lord, then their skins and their hearts soften to the most gracious Creator's remembrance. This is the most gracious Creator's guidance—He guides with it whom He pleases. And he whom the most gracious Creator leaves in error, there is no guide for him. Is then he who has to guard himself with his own person against the evil chastisement of the Resurrection Day --? And it will be to the iniquitous: Taste what you earned. Those before them denied, so the chastisement came to them from whence they perceived not. So the most gracious Creator made them taste disgrace in this world's life, and certainly, the chastisement of the Hereafter is greater. Did they but know! And certainly, We have set forth for men in this Qur'an, similitudes of every sort that they may mind. An Arabic Qur'an without any crookedness that they may guard against evil. The most gracious Creator sets forth a parable: A man belonging to partners differing with one another, and a man devoted wholly to one man. Are the two alike in condition? Praise be to the most gracious Creator! Nay, most of them know not. Surely thou will die and they too will die; then surely on the Day of Resurrection, you will contend one with another before your Lord. Who is then more unjust than he who utters a lie against the most gracious Creator and denies the truth, when it comes to him? Is there not in hell an abode for the disbelievers? And he who brings the truth and accepts the truth – such are dutiful. They shall have with their Lord what they please. Such is the reward of the doers of good – That the most gracious Creator may ward off from them the worst of what they did, and give them their reward for the best of what they did. Is not the most gracious Creator sufficient for His servant? And they seek to frighten thee with those besides Him. And whomsoever the most gracious Creator leaves in error, there is no guide for him. And whom the most gracious Creator guides, there is none that can lead him astray. Is not the most gracious Creator Mighty, the Lord of retribution? And if thou ask them, Who created the heavens and the earth? They would say the most gracious Creator. Say: See you then that those you call upon besides the most gracious Creator, would they if the most gracious Creator desire to afflict me from harm, remove His harm? Or if He desires to show me mercy, could they withhold His Mercy? Say: the most gracious Creator is sufficient for me. On Him do the reliant rely. Say: O people, work in your place. Surely I am a worker, so you will come to know, who it is to whom there comes a chastisement abasing him, and on whom falls a lasting chastisement. Surely We have revealed to thee the Book with truth for the good of men. So whoever follows the right way, it is for his own soul, and whoever errs, he errs only to its

detriment. And thou art not a custodian over them. The most gracious Creator takes men's soul at the time of their death, and those that die not, during their sleep. Then He withholds those on whom He has passed the decree of death and sends the others back till an appointed term. Surely there are signs in this for a people who reflect. Or, take they intercessors besides the most gracious Creator? Say: What! Even though they control naught, nor do they understand. Say: the most gracious Creator's is the intercession altogether. His is the kingdom of the heavens and the earth. Then to Him, you will be returned. And when the most gracious Creator alone is mentioned, the hearts of those who believe not in the Hereafter shrink, and when those besides Him are mentioned, lo! They are joyful. Say: O most gracious Creator, Originator of the heavens and the earth, Knower of the unseen and the seen, Thou judges between Thy servants as to that wherein they differ.
Sad! (Truthful God!) By the Qur'an, possessing eminence! Nay, those who disbelieve are in self-exaltation and

opposition. How many a generation We destroyed before them, then they cried when there was no longer time to escape! And they wonder that a warner from among themselves has come to them, and the disbelievers say: This is an enchanter, a liar. Makes he the gods a single God? Surely this is a strange thing. And the chiefs among them say: Go and steadily adhere to your gods: surely this is a thing intended. We never heard of this in the former faith: this is nothing but a forgery. Has the Reminder been revealed to him from among us? Nay, they are in doubt as to My Reminder. Nay, they have not yet tasted My chastisement. Or, have they the treasures of the Mercy of thy Lord, the Mighty, the Great Giver? Or is the kingdom of the heavens and the earth and what is between them theirs? Then let them rise higher in means. What an army of the allies is here put to flight! The people of Noah, and Ad, and Pharaoh, the lord of hosts, rejected prophets before them, and Thamud and the people of Lot and the dwellers of the grove. These were the parties opposing Truth). Not one of them but rejected the messengers, so just was My retribution. And these waits but for one cry, wherein there is no delay. And they say: Our Lord, hasten on for us our portion before the Day of Reckoning. Bear patiently what they say, and remember Our servant David, the possessor of power. He ever turned to the most gracious Creator. Truly We made the mountains subject to him, glorifying the most gracious Creator at nightfall and sunrise, and the birds gathered together. All were obedient to him. And We strengthened his kingdom and We gave him wisdom and a clear judgment. And has the story of the adversaries reached thee? When they made an entry into the private chamber by climbing the wall – When they came upon David so he was afraid of them. They said: Fear not; two litigants, of whom one has wronged the other, so decide between us with justice, and act not unjustly, and guide us to the right way. This is my brother. He has ninety-nine ewes and I have a single ewe. Then he said, Make it over to me, and he has prevailed against me in dispute. He said: Surely he has wronged thee in demanding thy ewe to add to his own ewes. And surely many partners wrong one another save those who believe and do good, and very few are they And David knew that We had tried him, so he asked his Lord for protection, and he fell down bowing and turned to God. So We gave him this protection, and surely he had a nearness to Us and an excellent resort. O David, surely We have made thee a ruler in the land; so judge between men justly and follow not desire, lest it leads thee astray from the path of the most gracious Creator. Those who go astray from the path of the most gracious Creator, for them is surely a severe chastisement because they forgot the Day of Reckoning. And We created not the heaven and the earth and what is between them in vain. That is the opinion of those who disbelieve. So woe to those who disbelieve on account of the Fire! Shall We treat those who believe and do good like the mischief-makers in the earth? Or shall We make the dutiful like the wicked? This is a Book that We have revealed to thee abounding in good, that they may ponder over its verses, and that the man of understanding may mind. And We gave to David, Solomon. Most excellent the servant! Surely he ever turned to the most gracious Creator. When well-bred, swift horses were brought to him at evening – so he said, I love the good things on account of the remembrance of my Lord – until they were hidden behind the veil. He said: Bring them back to me. So he began to stroke their legs and necks. And certainly We trained Solomon, and We put on his throne a mere body, so he turned to the most gracious Creator. He said: My Lord, forgive me and grant me a kingdom which is not fit for anyone after me; surely Thou art the Great Giver. So We made the wind subservient to him, running gently by the most gracious Creator's command wherever he desired, and the devils, every builder and diver, and others fettered in chains. This is Our free gift, so five freely or withhold, without reckoning. And surely he had a nearness to Us and an excellent resort. And remember Our servant Joab. When he cried out to his Lord: The devil has afflicted me with toil and torment. Urge with thy foot; here is a cool washing-place and a drink. And We gave him his people and the like of them with them, a mercy from Us, and a reminder for men of understanding. And take in thy hand few worldly goods and earn goodness therewith and incline not to falsehood. Surely We found him patient; most excellent the servant! Surely he ever turned to Us. And remember Our servants Abraham and Isaac and Jacob, men of power and insight. We indeed purified them by a pure quality, the keeping in mind of the final abode. And surely they were with Us, of the elect, the best. And remember Ishmael and Elisha and Dhu-l-Kifl; they were all of the best. This is a reminder.

By those ranging in ranks, and those who restrain holding in restraint, and those who recite the Reminder, surely your God is One. The Lord of the heavens and the earth and what is between them, and the Lord of the eastern lands. Surely We have adorned the lower heaven with an adornment, the stars, and there is a safeguard against every rebellious devil. They cannot listen to the exalted assembly and they are reproached from every side, driven off; and for them is a perpetual chastisement, except him who snatches away but once, then there follows him a brightly shining flame. So ask them whether they are stronger in creation or those others whom We have created. Surely We created them of firm clay. Nay, thou wonder, while they mock, and when they are reminded, they mind not, and when they see a sign, they seek to scoff and say: This is nothing but a clear chastisement. When we are dead and have become dust and bones, shall we then be raised, or our fathers of yore? Say Yea, and you will be humiliated.

And Noah certainly called upon Us, and excellent Answerer of prayers are We! And We delivered him and his people from the great distress; and made his offspring the survivors, and left for him praise among the later generations. Peace be to Noah among the nations! Thus indeed do We reward the doers of good. Surely he was of Our believing servants. Then We drowned the others. And surely of his party was Abraham; when he came to his Lord with a secure heart. When he said to his sire and his people: What is it that you worship? A lie – gods besides the most gracious Creator do you desire? What is then your idea about the Lord of the worlds? Then he glanced a glance at the stars and said: Surely I am sick of your deities. So they turned their backs on him, going away. Then he turned to their gods and said: Do you not eat? What is the matter with you that you speak not? So he turned upon them, smiting with the right hand. Then they came to him, hastening. He said: Do you worship that which you hue out? And the most gracious Creator has created you and what you make. They said: Build for him a building, then cast him into the flaming fire. And they designed a plan against him, but We brought them low. And he said: Surely I flee to my Lord – He will guide me. My Lord, grant me a doer of good deeds. So We gave him the good news of a forbearing son. But when he became of age to work with him, he said: O my son, I have seen in a dream that I should sacrifice thee: so consider what thou seest. He said: O my father, do as thou art commanded: if the most gracious Creator please, thou wilt find me patient. So when they both submitted and he had thrown him down upon his forehead, And We called out to him saying, O Abraham, thou hast indeed fulfilled the vision. Thus do We reward the doers of good. Surely this is a manifest trial. And We ransomed him with a great sacrifice. And We granted him among the later generations the salutation, Peace be to Abraham! Thus do We reward the doers of good. Surely he was one of Our believing servants. And We gave him the good news of Isaac. And of their offspring, some are doers of good, but some are clearly unjust to themselves. And certainly, We conferred a favor on Moses and Aaron. And We delivered them, and their people from the mighty distress. And We helped them, so they were the vanquishers. And We gave them both the clear Book. And We guided them on the right way. And We granted them among the later generations the salutation, Peace be to Moses and Aaron! Thus do We reward the doers of good. Surely they were both of Our believing servants. And Elias was surely of those sent.

When he said to his people: Will you not guard against evil? Do you call upon Baal and forsake the Best of the creators, the most gracious Creator, your Lord and the Lord of your fathers of yore? But they rejected him, so they shall be brought up, But not the servants of the most gracious Creator, the purified ones. And We granted him among the later generations the salutation, Peace be to Elias! Even thus We reward the doers of good. Surely he was one of Our believing servants. And Lot was surely of those sent. When We delivered him and his people, all – except an old woman among those who remained behind. Then We destroyed the others. And surely you pass by them in the morning, and at night. Do you not then understand? And Jonah was surely of those sent; when he fled to the laden ship, so he shared with others but was of those cast away. So the fish took him into its mouth while he was blamable. But had he not been of those who glorify Us, He would have tarried in its belly till the Day when they are raised. Then We cast him on the naked shore, while he was sick. And We caused a gourd to grow up for him. And We sent him to a hundred thousand or more. And they believed, so We gave them provision till a time. Now ask them whether thy Lord has daughters and they have sons? Or did We create the angels females, while they witnessed? Now surely it is of their own lie that they say: the most gracious Creator has begotten. And truly they are liars. Has He preferred daughters to sons? What is the matter with you? How you judge! Will you not then mind? Or have you a clear authority? Then bring your Book, if you are truthful. And they assert a relationship between Him and the jinn. And certainly the jinn know that they will be brought up for judgment – Glory be to the most gracious Creator from what they describe! – But not so the servants of the most gracious Creator, the purified ones. So surely you and that which you serve, not against the Him can you cause any to fall into a trial, except him who will burn in the flaming Fire. And there is none of us but has an assigned place, and verily we are ranged in ranks, and we truly glorify Him. And certainly they used to say:

Had we a reminder from those of yore, we would have been sincere servants of the most gracious Creator. But they disbelieve in it, so they will come to know. And certainly, Our word has already gone forth to Our servants, to those sent, that they, surely they, will be helped, and Our hosts, surely they, will be triumphant. So turn away from them till a time, and watch them, they too will see. Would they hasten on Our chastisement? So when it descends in their court, evil will be the morning of the warned ones. And turn away from them till a time, and watch, for they too will see. Glory be to thy Lord, the Lord of Might, above what they describe! And peace be to those sent! And Praise be to the most gracious Creator, the Lord of the worlds!

Ya Sin (O man), By the Qur'an, full of wisdom! Surely thou art one of the Messengers, on a right way. A Revelation of the Mighty, the Merciful, that thou may warn a people whose fathers were not warned, so they are heedless. The word has indeed proved true of most of them, so they believe not. Surely We have placed on their necks chains reaching up to the chins, so they have their heads raised aloft. And We have set a barrier before them and a barrier behind them, thus We have covered them so that they see not. And it is alike to them whether thou warn them or warn them not—they believe not. Thou can warn him only who follows the Reminder and fears the Beneficent in secret; so give him the good news of forgiveness and a generous reward. Surely We give life to the dead, and We write down that which they send before and their footprints, and We record everything in a clear writing. And set out to them a parable of the people of the town, when apostles came to it. When We sent to them two, they rejected them both; then We strengthened them with a third, so they said: Surely we are sent to you. They said: You are only mortals like ourselves, nor has the Beneficent revealed anything – you only lie. They said: Our Lord knows that we are surely sent to you. And our duty is only a clear deliverance of the message. They said: Surely we augur evil from you. If you desist not, we will surely stone you, and a painful chastisement from us will certainly afflict you. They said: Your evil fortune is with you. What! If you are reminded! Nay, you are an extravagant people. And from the remote part of the city, there came a man running. He said: O my people, follow the apostles. Follow him who asks of you no reward and they are on the right course. And what reason have I that I should not serve Him Who created me and to Whom you will be brought back? Shall I take besides Him gods whose intercession, if the Beneficent should desire to afflict me with harm will avail me naught, nor can they deliver me? Then I shall surely be in clear error. Surely I believe in your Lord, so hear me. It was said: Enter the Garden. He said: Would that my people knew, how my Lord has forgiven me and made me of the honored ones! And We sent not down upon his people after him any host from heaven, nor do We ever send. It was naught but a single cry, and lo! They were still. Alas for the servants! Never does a Messenger come to them but they mock him. See they not how many generations We destroyed before them, that they return not to them? And all – surely all – will be brought before Us. And a sign to them is the dead earth: We give life to it and bring forth from it grain so they eat of it. And We make therein gardens of date-palms and grapes and We make springs to flow forth therein, that they may eat of the fruit thereof, and their hands made it not. Will they not then give thanks? Glory be to Him Who created pairs of all things, of what the earth grows, and of their kind and of what they know not! And a sign to them is the night: We draw forth from it the day, then lo! They are in darkness, and the sun moves on to its destination. That is the ordinance of the Mighty, the Knower. And the moon, We have ordained it for its stages till it becomes again as an old dry palm-branch. Neither is it for the sun to overtake the moon nor can the night outstrip the day. And all float on in an orbit. And a sign to them is that We bear their offspring in the laden ship, and We have created for the like thereof, whereon they ride. And if We please, We may drown them, then there is no succor for them, nor can they be rescued – but by mercy from Us and for enjoyment till a time. And when it is said to them: Guard against that which is before you and that which is behind you, that mercy may be shown to you. And there comes to them no message of the messages of their Lord but they turn away from it. And when it is said to them: Spend out of that which the most gracious Creator has given you, those who disbelieve say to those who believe: Shall we feed him whom, if the most gracious Creator please, He could feed? You are in naught but clear error.

And whomsoever We cause to live long, We reduce to an abject state in creation. Do they not understand? And We have not taught him poetry, nor is it meet for him. This is naught a Reminder and a plain Qur'an, to warn him who would have life and that the word may prove true against the disbelievers. See they not that We have created cattle for them, out of what Our hands have wrought, so they are their masters? And We have subjected them to them, so some of them they ride, and some they eat. And therein they have advantages and drinks. Will they not then give thanks?

And they take gods besides the most gracious Creator that they may be helped. They are not able to help them, and they are a host brought up before them. Do let not their speech grieve thee. Surely We know what they do in secret and what they do openly. Does not man see that We have created him from the small life-germ? Then lo! He is an open disputant. And he strikes out a likeness for Us and forgets his own creation. Says he: Who will give life to the bones, when they are rotten? Say: He will give life to them, Who brought them into existence at first, and He is Knower of all creation, Who produced fire for you out of the green tree so that with it you kindle. Is not He Who created the heavens and the earth able to create the like of them? Yea! And He is the Creator of all, the Knower. His command, when He intends anything, is only to say to it, Be, and it is. So Glory be to Him in Whose Hand is the kingdom of all things! And to Him, you will be returned.

Praise be to the most gracious Creator, the Originator of the heavens and the earth, the Maker of the Angels, messengers flying on wings, two, and three, and four. He increases in creation what He pleases. Surely the most gracious Creator is Possessor of power over all things. Whatever He grants to men of His Mercy, there is none to withhold it, and what He withholds, none can grant thereafter. And He is the Mighty, the Wise. O men, call to mind the favor of the most gracious Creator to you. Is there any Creator besides the most gracious Creator who provides for you from the heaven and the earth? There is no God but He. How are you then turned away? And if they reject thee – truly Messengers before thee were rejected. And to the most gracious Creator are all affairs returned.

O men, surely the promise of the most gracious Creator is true, so let not the life of this world deceive you. And let not the arch-deceiver deceive you about the most gracious Creator. Surely the devil is your enemy, so take him for an enemy. He only invites his party to be companions of the burning Fire. Those who disbelieve, for them is a severe chastisement. And those who believe and do good, for them is forgiveness and a great reward. Is he whose evil deed is made fair-seeming to him so that he considers it good? – Now surely the most gracious Creator leaves in error whom He pleases and guides aright whom He pleases, so let not thy soul waste in grief for them. Surely the most gracious Creator is Knower of what they do. And the most gracious Creator is He Who sends the winds, so they raise a cloud, then We drive it on to a dead land, and therewith give life to the earth after its death. Even so is the quickening. Whoever desires might, then to the most gracious Creator belongs the might wholly. To Him do ascend the goodly words, and the goodly deed – He exalts it. And those who plan evil – for them is a severe chastisement. And their plan will perish. And the most gracious Creator created you from dust, then from the life-germ, then He made you pairs. And no female bears, nor brings forth, except with His knowledge. And no one living long is granted a long life, nor is aught diminished of one's life, but it is all in a book. Surely this is easy to the most gracious Creator. And the two seas are not alike: the one sweet, very sweet, pleasant to drink; and the other salt, bitter. Yet from both, you eat fresh flesh and bring forth ornaments which you wear. And thou see the ships cleave through it, that you may seek of His bounty and that you may give thanks. He causes the night to enter in upon the day and causes the day to enter in upon the night, and He has made subservient the sun and the moon, each one moves to an appointed time. This is the most gracious Creator, your Lord; His is the kingdom. And those whom you call upon besides Him own not a straw. If you call on them, they hear not your call; and if they heard, they could not answer you. And on the Day of Resurrection, they will deny your associating them with the most gracious Creator. And none can inform thee like the All-Aware One. O men, it is you that have need of the most gracious Creator, and He is the Self-Sufficient, the Praised One. If He pleases, He will remove you and bring a new creation. And this is not hard to the most gracious Creator. And no burdened soul can bear another's burden. And if one weighed down by a burden calls another to carry his load, naught of it will be carried, even though he be near to kin. Thou warn only those who fear their Lord in secret and keep up prayer. And whoever purifies himself, purifies only for his own good. And to the most gracious Creator is the eventual coming. And the blind and the seeing are not alike, nor the darkness and the light, nor the shade and the heat; neither are the living and the dead alike. Surely the most gracious Creator makes whom He pleases hear, and thou canst not make those hear who are in the graves. Thou art naught but a warner. Surely We have sent thee with the Truth as a bearer of good news and a warner. And there are not a people but a warner has gone among them. And if they reject thee, those before them also rejected – their Messengers came to them with clear arguments, and with scriptures, and with the illuminating Book. Then I seized those who disbelieved, so how terrible was My Disapproval! Seest thou not that the most gracious Creator sends down water from the clouds, then We bring forth therewith fruits of various hues? And in the mountains are streaks of white and red, of various hues and others intensely black. And of men and beasts and cattle there are various colors likewise. Those of His servants only who are possessed of knowledge fear the most gracious Creator. Surely He is Mighty, Forgiving. Surely those who recite the Book of the most gracious Creator and keep up prayer and spend out of what We have given them, secretly and openly, hope for a gain which perishes not – That He may pay them back fully their rewards and give them more out of His grace. Surely He is Forgiving, Multiplier of rewards. And that which We have revealed to thee of the Book, that is the truth, verifying that which is before it. Surely the most gracious Creator is Aware, Seer of His servants. Then We have given the Book as an inheritance to those whom We have chosen from among Our servants: so of them is he who wrongs himself, and of them is he who takes a middle course, and of them is he who is foremost in deeds of goodness by the most gracious Creator's permission. That is a great grace.

Surely the most gracious Creator is the

knower of the unseen in the heavens and the earth. Surely He is Knower of what is in the hearts. He it is Who made you successors in the earth. So whoever disbelieves, his disbelief is against himself. And their disbelief increases the disbelievers with their Lord in naught but hatred; their disbelief increases the disbelievers in naught but loss. Say: Have you seen your associates which you call upon besides the most gracious Creator? Show me what they have created of the earth! Or have they any share in the heavens? Or, have We given them a Book so that they follow a clear argument thereof? Nay, the wrongdoers hold out promises one to another only to deceive. Surely the most gracious Creator upholds the heavens and the earth lest they come to naught. And if they come to naught, none can uphold them after Him. Surely the most gracious Creator upholds the heavens and the earth lest they come to naught. And if they come to naught, none can uphold them after Him. Surely he is ever Forbearing, Forgiving. And they swore by the most gracious Creator, their strongest oaths, that, if a warner came to them, they would be better guided than any of the nations. But when a warner came to them, it increased them in naught but aversion, behaving proudly in the land and planning evil. And the evil plan besets none save the authors of it. So they wait for naught but the way of the ancients. But thou wilt find no alteration in the course of the most gracious Creator; thou wilt find no change in the course of the most gracious Creator. Have they not traveled in the land and seen what was the end of those before them – and they were stronger than those in power? And the most gracious Creator is not such that anything in the heavens or the earth can escape Him. Surely He is ever Knowing, Powerful. And were the most gracious Creator to punish men for what they earn, He would not leave on the back of it any creature, but He respites them till an appointed term; so when their doom comes, then surely the most gracious Creator is ever Seer of His servants.

The Arabs say: We believe. Say: You believe not, but say: We submit; faith has not yet entered into your hearts. And if you obey the most gracious Creator and His Messenger, He will not diminish aught of your deeds. Surely the most gracious Creator is Forgiving, Merciful. The believers are those only who believe in the most gracious Creator and His Messenger, then they doubt not, and struggle hard with their wealth and their lives in the way of the most gracious Creator. Such are the truthful ones. Say: Would you instruct the most gracious Creator of your religion? And the most gracious Creator knows what is in the heavens and what is in the earth. And He is Knower of all things. They presume to lay thee under an obligation by becoming Muslims. Say: Lay me not under an obligation by your Islam; rather the most gracious Creator lays you under an obligation by guiding you to the faith, if you are truthful. Surely the most gracious Creator knows the unseen of the heavens and the earth. And the most gracious Creator is Seer of what you do.

Ha Mim. (Beneficent God!) The revelation of the Book is from the most gracious Creator, the Mighty, the Wise. We created not the heavens and the earth and all between them except with truth and for an appointed term. And those who disbelieve turn away from that whereof they are warned. Say: Have you considered that which you invoke besides the most gracious Creator? Show me what they have created of the earth, or have they a share in the heavens? Bring me a Book before this or any relics of knowledge, if you are truthful. And who is in greater error than he who invokes besides the most gracious Creator such as answer him not till the Day of Resurrection, and they are heedless of their call? And when men are gathered together, they will be their enemies and will deny their worshipping them. And when Our clear messages are recited to them, those who disbelieve say of the Truth when it comes to them: This is a clear enchantment. Nay, they say: He has forged it. Say: If I have forged it, you control naught for me from the most gracious Creator. He knows best what you utter concerning it. He is enough as a witness between me and you. And He is the Forgiving, the Merciful. Say: I am not the first of the Messengers, and I know not what will be done with me or with you. I follow naught but that which is revealed to me, and I am but a plain warner. Say: See you if it is from the most gracious Creator, and you disbelieve in it, and a witness from among the Children of Israel has borne witness of one like him, so he believed, while you are big with pride. Surely the most gracious Creator guides not the iniquitous people. And those who disbelieve say of those who believe: If it had been good, they would not have attained it before us. And as they are not guided thereby, they say: It is an old lie. And before it was the Book of Moses, a guide, and a mercy. And this is a Book verifying in the Arabic language, that it may warn those who do wrong, and as good news for the doers of good. Surely those who say, Our Lord is the most gracious Creator, then continue on the right way, on them is no fear, nor shall they grieve. These are the owners of the Garden, abiding therein – a reward for what they did. And We enjoined on man the doing of good to his parents. His mother bears him with trouble and she brings him forth in pain. And the bearing of him and the weaning of him is thirty months. Till, when he attains his maturity and reaches forty years, he says: My Lord, grant me that I may give thanks for Thy favor, which Thou hast bestowed on me and on my parents, and that I may do good which pleases Thee; and be good to me in respect of my offspring. Truly I turn to Thee, and truly I am of those who submit. These are they from whom We accept the best of what they do and pass by their evil deeds – among the owners of the Garden. A promise of truth, which they were promised. And he who says to his parents: Fie on you! Do not threaten me that I shall be brought forth when generations have passed away before me? And they both call for the most gracious Creator's aid: Woe to thee! Believe; surely the promise of the most gracious Creator is true. But he says: This is nothing but stories of the ancients. These are they against whom the word proves true, among nations of the jinn and the men that have passed away before them. Surely they are losers. And for all are degrees according to what they do, and that He may pay them for their deeds and they will not be wronged.

Ha Mim (Beneficent God!) A revelation from the Beneficent, the Merciful; a Book of which the verses are made plain, an Arabic Qur'an for a people who know – Good news and a warning. But most of them turn away, so they hear not. And they say: Our hearts are under coverings from that to which thou call us, and there is a deafness in our ears, and there is a veil between us and thee, so act we too are acting. Say: I am only a mortal like you. It is revealed to me that your God is One God, so keep on the straight path to Him, and ask His protection. And woe to the polytheists! Who give not the poor-rate, and who are disbelievers in the Hereafter. Those who believe and do good, for them is surely a reward never to be cut off. Say: Do you indeed disbelieve in Him Who created the earth in two days, and do you set up equals with Him? That is the Lord of all the worlds. And He made in it mountains above its surface, and He blessed therein and ordained therein its foods, in four days; alike for all seekers. Then He directed

Himself to the heaven and it was a vapor, so He said to it and the earth: Come both, willingly or unwillingly. They both said: We come willingly. So He ordained them seven heavens in two days and revealed in every heaven its affair. And We ordained the lower heaven with lights and made it guard. That is the decree of the Mighty, the Knowing.

Man tires not of praying for good, but, if evil touch him, he is despairing, hopeless. And if We make him taste mercy from Us after distress has touched him, he says: This is due to me, and I think not that the Hour will come to pass; and if I am sent back to my Lord, I shall have sure good with Him. So We shall certainly inform those who disbelieve of what they do, and We shall make them taste of hard chastisement. And when We show favor to man, he turns away and withdraws himself; but when evil touches him, he is full of lengthy supplications. Say: See you, if it is from the most gracious Creator, then you disbelieve in it, who is in greater error than he who is in opposition far away? We will soon show them Our signs in farthest regions and among their own people until it is quite clear to them that it is the Truth. Is it not enough that thy Lord is a Witness over all things? Now surely they are in doubt as to the meeting with their Lord. Lo! He surely encompasses all things.

Praise be to the most gracious Creator! Whose is whatsoever is in the heavens and whatsoever is in the earth, and to Him be praise in the Hereafter! And He is the Wise, the Aware. He knows that which goes down into the earth and that which comes down from heaven and that which goes up to it. And He is the Merciful, the Forgiving. And those who disbelieve say: The Hour will never come to us. Say Yea, by my Lord, the Knower of the unseen! It will certainly come to you. Not an atom's weight escapes Him in the heavens or in the earth, nor it there less than nor greater, but all is in a clear book, that He may reward those who believe and do good. For them are forgiveness and an honorable sustenance. And those who strive hard in opposing Our Messages, for them is a painful chastisement of an evil kind. And those who have been given knowledge see that what is revealed to thee from thy Lord, is the Truth and it guides into the path of the Mighty, the Praised. And those who disbelieve say: Shall we show to you a man who informs you that, when you are scattered the utmost scattering, you will then be in a new creation? Has he forged a lie against the most gracious Creator or is there madness in him? Nay, those who believe not in the Hereafter are in torment and in far error. See they not what is before them and what is behind them of the heavens and the earth? If We please, We can make them low in the land or bring them down upon them a portion of heaven. Surely there is a sign in this for every servant turning to the most gracious Creator. And certainly We gave David abundance from Us: O mountains, repeat praises with him, and the birds and We made the iron pliant to him, saying: Make ample coats of mail, and assign a time to the making of coats of mail and do ye good. Surely I am Seer of what you do. And We made the wind subservient to Solomon; it made a month's journey in the morning and a month's journey in the evening; We made a fountain of molten brass to flow for him. And of the jinn, there were those who worked before him by the command of his Lord. And whoever turned aside from Our command from among them, We made him taste of the chastisement of burning. They made for him what he pleased, of synagogues and images, and bowls as large as watering-troughs and fixed cooking-pots. Give thanks, O people of David! And very few of My servants are grateful. But when We decreed death for him, naught showed them his death but a creature of the earth that ate away his staff. So when it fell down, the jinn saw clearly that, if they had known the unseen, they would not have tarried in humiliating torment. Certainly, there was a sign for Saba' in their abode – two gardens on the right and the left; eat of the sustenance of your Lord and give thanks to Him. A good land and a Forgiving Lord! But they turned aside, so We sent upon them a violent torrent, and in place of their two gardens, We gave them two gardens yielding bitter fruit and growing tamarisk and a few lote-trees. With this We requited them because they were ungrateful; We punish none but the ingrate. And We made between them and the towns which We had blessed, other towns easy to be seen, and We apportioned the journey therein: Travel through them nights and days, secure. But they said: Our Lord, make longer stages between our journeys. And they wronged themselves; so We made them stories and scattered them a total scattering. Surely there are signs in this for every patient, grateful one. And the devil indeed found true his conjecture concerning them, so they follow him, except a party of the believers. And he has no authority over them, but that We may know him who believes in the Hereafter from him who is in doubt concerning it. And thy Lord is the Preserver of all things. Say: Call upon those who you assert besides the most gracious Creator; they control not the weight of an atom in the heavens or in the earth, nor have they any partnership in either, nor has He a helper among them. And intercession avails naught with Him, save of him whom He permits.

Until when fear is removed from their hearts, they say: What is it that your Lord said? They say The Truth. And He is the Highest, the Great. And intercession avails naught with Him, save of him whom He permits. Until when fear is removed from their hearts, they say: What is it that your Lord said? They say The Truth. And He is the Highest, the Great. Say: Who gives you sustenance from the heavens and the earth? Say the most gracious Creator. And surely we or you are on a right way or in manifest error. Say: You will not be asked of what we are guilty, nor shall we be asked of what you do. Say: Our Lord will gather us together, then He will judge between us with the truth. And He is the Best Judge, the Knower. Say: Show me those whom you join with Him as associates. By no means can you! Nay, He is the most gracious Creator, the Mighty, the Wise. And We have not sent thee but as a bearer of good news and as a warner to all mankind, but most men know not. And they say: When will this promise be fulfilled if you are truthful? Say: You have the appointment of a day which you cannot postpone by an hour, nor hasten on. And those who disbelieve say: We believe not in this Quran, nor in that which is before it. And if thou couldst see when the wrongdoers are made to stand before their Lord, throwing back the blame one to another! Those who were reckoned weak say to those who were proud: Had it not been for you, we would have been believers. Those who were proud say to those who were deemed weak: Did we turn you away from the guidance after it had come to you? Nay, you yourselves were guilty. And those who were deemed weak say to those who were proud: Nay, it was your planning by night and day when you told us to disbelieve in the most gracious Creator and to set up likes with Him. And they will manifest regret when they see the chastisement. And We put shackles on the necks of those who disbelieve. They will not be requited but for what they did. And We never sent a warner to a town but those who led easy lives in it said: We are disbelievers in that with which you are sent. And they say: We have more wealth and children, and we cannot be punished. Say: Surely my Lord amplifies and straitens provision for whom He pleases, but most men know not. And it is not your wealth, nor your children, that bring you near to Us in rank; but whoever believes and does good, for such is a double reward for what they do, and they are secure in the highest places. And those who strive in opposing Our Messages, they will be brought to the chastisement. Say: Surely my Lord amplifies provision for whom He pleases of His servants and straitens it for him. And whatsoever you spend, He increases it in reward, and He is the Best of Providers.

And when Our clear messages are recited to them, they say: This is naught but a man who desires to turn you away from that which your fathers worshipped. And they say: This is naught but a forged lie! And those who disbelieve say of the Truth when it comes to them: This is only clear enchantment! And We have not given them any Books which they read, nor did We send to them before thee a warner. And those before them rejected the truth, and these have not yet attained a tenth of that which We gave them, but they gave the lie to My messengers. How terrible was then My disapproval! Say: I exhort you only to one thing, that you rise up for the most gracious Creator's sake by twos and singly; then ponder! There is no madness in your companion. He is only a warner to you before a severe chastisement. Say: Whatever reward I ask of you, that is only for yourselves. My reward is only with the most gracious Creator, and He is a Witness over all things. Say: Surely my Lord casts the Truth, the great Knower of the unseen. Say: The Truth has come, and falsehood neither originates nor reproduces. Say: If I err, I err only to my own loss; and if I go aright, it is because of what my Lord reveals to me. Surely He is Hearing, Nigh. And couldst thou see when they become terrified, but then there will be no escape and they will be seized from a near place; And they will say: We believe in it. And how can they attain to faith from a distant place? And they indeed disbelieved in it before, and they utter conjectures with regard to the unseen from a distant place. And a barrier is placed between them and that which they desire, as was done with their partisans before. Surely they are in a disquieting doubt.

O Prophet, keep thy duty to the most gracious Creator and obey not the disbelievers and the hypocrites. Surely the most gracious Creator is ever Knowing, Wise; And follow that which is revealed to thee from thy Lord. Surely the most gracious Creator is ever Aware of what you do; trust in the most gracious Creator. And the most gracious Creator is enough as having charge of affairs.

And when We took a covenant from the prophets and from thee, and from Noah and Abraham and Moses and Jesus, son of Mary, and We took from them a solemn covenant, that He may question the truthful of their truth, and He has prepared for the disbelievers a painful chastisement.

O Prophet, say to thy wives: If you desire this world's life and its adornment, come, I will give you a provision and allow you to depart a goodly departing. And if you desire the most gracious Creator and His

Messenger and the abode of the Hereafter, then surely the most gracious Creator has prepared for the doers of good among you a mighty reward.

And when thou said to him to whom the most gracious Creator had shown favor and to whom thou had shown a favor: Keep thy wife to thyself and keep thy duty to the most gracious Creator; thou concealed in thy heart what the most gracious Creator would bring to light, and thou fearest men and the most gracious Creator has a greater right that thou shouldst fear Him. So when Zaid dissolved her marriage-tie, We gave her to thee as a wife, so that there should be no difficulty for the believers about the wives of their adopted sons, when they have dissolved their marriage-tie. And the most gracious Creator's command is ever performed.

O Prophet, We have made lawful to thee thy wives whom thou hast given their dowries, and those whom thy right hand possesses, out of those whom the most gracious Creator has given thee as prisoners of war, and the daughters of thy paternal uncle and the daughters of thy paternal aunts, and the daughters of thy maternal uncle and the daughters of thy maternal aunts who fled with thee; and a believing woman, if she gives herself to the Prophet, if the Prophet desires to marry her. (It is) especially for thee, not for the believers — We know what We have ordained for them concerning their wives and those whom their right hands possess in order that no blame may attach to thee. And the most gracious Creator is ever Forgiving, Merciful. Thou may put off whom thou pleases of them, and take to thee whom thou pleasest. And whom thou desire of those whom thou hadst separated provisionally, no blame attaches to thee. This is most proper so that their eyes may be cool and they may not grieve, and that they should be pleased, all of them, with what thou givest them. And the most gracious Creator knows what is in your hearts. And the most gracious Creator is ever Knowing, Forbearing. It is not allowed to thee to take wives after this, nor to change them for other wives, though their beauty is pleasing to thee, except those whom thy right hand possesses. And the most gracious Creator is ever Watchful over all things.

O Prophet, tell thy wives and thy daughters and the women of believers to let down upon them their over-garments. This is more proper, so that they may be known, and not be given trouble. And the most gracious Creator is ever Forgiving, Merciful. If the hypocrites and those in whose hearts is a disease and the agitators in Madinah desist not, We shall certainly urge thee on against them, then they shall not be thy neighbors in it but for a little while — Accursed, wherever they are found they will be seized and slain. That was the way of the most gracious Creator concerning those who have gone before; thou wilt find no change in the way of the most gracious Creator. Men ask thee about the Hour. Say: The knowledge of it is only with the most gracious Creator. And what will make thee comprehend that the Hour may be nigh?

Alif, Lam, Mim. (I, the most gracious Creator, Am the Best Knower). The revelation of the Book, there is no doubt in it, is from the Lord of the worlds. Or do they say: He has forged it? Nay, it is the Truth from thy Lord that thou may warn a people to whom no warner has come before thee that they may walk aright. The most gracious Creator is He Who created the heavens and the earth and what is between them in six periods, and He is established on the Throne of Power. You have not besides Him a guardian or an intercessor. Will you not then mind? He orders the Affair from the heaven to the earth; then it will ascend to Him in a day the measure of which is a thousand years as you count. Such is the Knower of the unseen and the seen, the Mighty, the Merciful, Who made beautiful everything that He created, and He began the creation of man from dust. Then He made his progeny of an extract, of worthless water. Then He made him complete and breathed into him of His Spirit, and gave you ears and eyes and hearts; little it is that you give thanks! And they say: When we are lost in the earth, shall we then be in a new creation? Nay, they are disbelievers in the meeting with their Lord. Say: The angel of death, who is given charge of you, will cause you to die, then to your Lord, you will be returned. And couldst thou but see when the guilty hang their heads before their Lord: Our Lord, we have seen and heard, so send us back, we will do good; we are now certain. And if We had pleased, We could have given every soul its guidance, but the word from Me was just: I will certainly fill hell with the jinn and men together. So taste, because you forgot the meeting of this Day of yours; surely We forsake you; taste the abiding chastisement for what you did. Only they believe in Our Messages who, when they are reminded of them, fall down prostrate and celebrate the praise of their Lord, and they are not proud. They forsake (their) beds, calling upon their Lord in fear and in hope, and spend out of what We have given them. So no soul knows what refreshment of the eyes is hidden for them: a reward for what they did. Is he then, who is a believer, like him who is a transgressor? They are not equal.

And We indeed gave Moses the Book — so doubt not the meeting with Him — and We made it a guide for the Children of Israel.

And We made from among them leaders to guide by Our command when they were patient. And they were certain of Our Messages. Surely thy Lord will judge between them on the Day of Resurrection concerning that wherein they differed. Is it not clear to them, how many of the generations, in whose abodes they go about, We destroyed before them? Surely there are signs in this. Will they not then hear? See they not that We drive the water to a land having no herbage, then We bring forth thereby seed-produce, of which their cattle and they themselves eat. Will they not then see? And they say: When will this victory come if you are truthful? Say: On the day of victory the faith of those who (now) disbelieve will not profit them, nor will they be respited. So turn away from them and wait, surely they too are waiting.

And when it is said to them: Follow that which the most gracious Creator has revealed, they say: Nay, we follow that wherein we found our fathers. What! Though the devil calls them to the chastisement of the burning Fire! And whoever submits himself to the most gracious Creator and does good to others, he indeed takes hold of the firmest handle. And the most gracious Creator's is the end of affairs. And whoever disbelieves let not his disbelief grieve thee. To Us is their return, then We shall inform them of what they did. Surely the most gracious Creator is Knower of what they did. Surely the most gracious Creator is Knower of what is in the breasts. We give them to enjoy a little, then We shall drive them to a severe chastisement. And if thou ask them who created the heavens and the earth? They will say the most gracious Creator. Say: Praise be to the most gracious Creator! Nay, most of them know not. To the most gracious Creator belongs whatever is in the heavens and the earth. Surely the most gracious Creator is the Self-Sufficient, the Praised. And if all the trees in the earth were pens, and the sea with seven more seas added to it (were ink), the words of the most gracious Creator would not be exhausted. Surely the most gracious Creator is Mighty, Wise. Your creation or your raising is only like a single soul. Surely the most gracious

Creator is Hearing, Seeing. Seest thou not that the most gracious Creator makes the night to enter into the day, and He makes the day to enter into the night, and He has made the sun and the moon subservient (to you) — each pursues its course till an appointed time — and that the most gracious Creator is Aware of what you do? This is because the most gracious Creator is the Truth, and that which they call upon besides Him is falsehood and that the most gracious Creator is the High, the Great. Seest thou not that the ships glide on the sea by the most gracious Creator's grace, that He may show you of His signs? Surely there are signs in this for every patient endurer, grateful one. And when a wave like awnings covers them, they call upon the most gracious Creator, being sincere to Him in obedience. But when He brings them safe to land, some of them follow the middle course. And none denies Our signs but every perfidious, ungrateful one.

Corruption has appeared in the land and the sea on account of that which men's hands have wrought, that He may make them taste a part of that which they have done, so that they may return. Say: Travel in the land, then see what was the end of those before! Most of them were polytheists. Then set thyself, being upright, to the right religion before there come from the most gracious Creator the day which cannot be averted: on that day they will be separated. Whoever disbelieves will be responsible for his disbelief; and whoever does good, such prepare good for their own souls, that He may reward out of His grace those who believe and do good. Surely He loves not the disbelievers. And of His signs is this, that He sends forth the winds bearing good news, and that He may make you taste of His mercy, and that the ships may glide by His command, and that you may seek of His grace, and that you may be grateful. And certainly We sent before thee messengers to their people, so they came to them with clear arguments, then We punished those who were guilty. And to help believers is ever incumbent on Us. The most gracious Creator is He Who sends forth the winds, so they raise a cloud, then He spreads it forth in the sky as He pleases, and He breaks it, so that you see the rain coming forth from inside it; then when He causes it to fall upon whom He pleases of His servants, lo! They rejoice; though they were before this before it was sent down upon them, in sure despair. Look then at the signs of the most gracious Creator's mercy, how He gives life to the earth after its death. Surely He is the Quickener of the dead; He is Possessor of power over all things. And if We send a wind and they see it yellow, they would after that certainly continue to disbelieve. So surely thou canst not make the dead to hear, nor canst thou make the deaf to hear the call when they turn back retreating. Nor canst thou guide the blind out of their error. Thou canst make none to hear but those who believe in Our Messages, so they submit. The most gracious Creator is He Who created you from a state of weakness, then He gave strength after weakness, then ordained weakness and hoary hair after strength. He creates what He pleases, and He is the Knowing, the Powerful.

And certainly, We have set forth for men in

this Quran every kind of parable. And if thou bring them a sign, those who disbelieve would certainly say: You are naught but deceivers. Thus does the most gracious Creator seal the hearts of those who know not. So be patient; surely the promise of the most gracious Creator is true; let not those disquiet thee who have no certainty.

Alif, Lam, Mim. (I, the most gracious Creator, Am the Best Knower). Do men think that they will be left alone on saying, We believe, and will not be tried? And indeed We tried those before them, so the most gracious Creator will certainly know those who are true and He will know the liars. Or do they who work evil think that they will escape Us? Evil is it that they judge! Whoever hopes to meet with the most gracious Creator, the term of the most gracious Creator is then surely coming. And He is the Hearing, the Knowing. And whoever strives hard, strives for himself. Surely the most gracious Creator is Self-sufficient, above the need of His creatures. And those who believe and do good, We shall certainly do away with their afflictions and reward them for the best of what they did. And We have enjoined on man goodness to his parents. But if they contend with thee to associate others with Me, of which thou hast no knowledge, obey them not. To Me is your return, so I will inform you of what you did. And those who believe and do good, We shall surely make them enter among the righteous. And among men is he who says: We believe in the most gracious Creator; but when he is persecuted for the sake of the most gracious Creator, he thinks the persecution of men to be as the chastisement of the most gracious Creator. And if there comes help from thy Lord, they will say: Surely we were with you. Is not the most gracious Creator the Best Knower of what is in the hearts of mankind? And certainly the most gracious Creator will know those who believe, and He will know the hypocrites. And those who disbelieve say to those who believe: Follow our path and we will bear your wrongs. And they can never bear aught of their wrongs. Surely they are liars. And they will certainly bear their own burdens, and other burdens besides their own burdens; and they will certainly be questioned on the Day of Resurrection as to what they forged. And We indeed sent Noah to his people, so he remained among them a thousand years save fifty years. And the deluge overtook them, and they were wrongdoers. So We delivered him and the inmates of the ark and made it a sign to the nations. And We sent Abraham when he said to his people: Serve the most gracious Creator and keep your duty to Him. That is better for you if you did but know. You only worship idols besides the most gracious Creator and you invent a lie. Surely they whom you serve besides the most gracious Creator control no sustenance for you; so seek sustenance from the most gracious Creator and serve Him and be grateful to Him. To Him, you will be brought back. And if you reject, nations before you did indeed reject the Truth. And the duty of the Messenger is only to deliver the message plainly. See they not how the most gracious Creator originates the creation, then reproduces it? Surely that is easy to the most gracious Creator. Say:

Travel in the earth then see how He makes the first creation, then the most gracious Creator creates the latter creation. Surely the most gracious Creator is Possessor of power over all things. He chastises whom He pleases and has mercy on whom He pleases, and to Him, you will be turned back. And you cannot escape in the earth nor in the heaven, and you have no protector or helper besides the most gracious Creator. And those who disbelieve in the messages of the most gracious Creator and the meeting with Him, they despair of My mercy, and for them is a painful chastisement. So naught was the answer of his people except that they said: Slay him or burn him! But the most gracious Creator delivered him from the fire. Surely therein are signs for a people who believe. And he said: You have only taken idols besides the most gracious Creator by way of friendship between you in this world's life, then on the Day of Resurrection some of you will deny others, and some of you will curse others; your abode is the Fire, and you will have no helpers. So Lot believed in him. And he said:

The Heavenly Message

I am fleeing to my Lord. Surely He is the Mighty, the Wise. And We granted him Isaac and Jacob and ordained Prophethood and the Book among his seed. And We gave him his reward in this world, and in the Hereafter, he will surely be among the righteous. And We sent Lot when he said to his people: Surely you are guilty of an abomination which none of the nations has done before you. Do you come to males and commit robbery on the highway, and commit evil deeds in your assemblies? But the answer of his people was only that they said: Bring on us the most gracious Creator's chastisement if thou art truthful. He said: My Lord, help me against the mischievous people. And when Our messengers came to Abraham with good news, they said: We are going to destroy the people of this town, for its people are iniquitous. He said: Surely in it is Lot. They said: We know well who is in it; we shall certainly deliver him and his followers, except his wife; she is of those who remain behind. And when Our messengers came to Lot, he was grieved on account of them, and he lacked the strength to protect them. And they said: Fear not, nor grieve; surely we will deliver thee and thy followers, except thy wife — she is of those who remain behind. Surely We are going to bring down upon the people of this town a punishment from heaven because they transgressed. And certainly, We have left a clear sign of it for a people who understand. And to Midian We sent their brother Shu'aib, so he said: O my people, serve the most gracious Creator and fear the Latter-day, and act not corruptly, making mischief, in the land. But they rejected him, so a severe earthquake overtook them and they lay prostrate in their abodes. And 'Ad and Thamud! And some of their dwellings are indeed apparent to you. And the devil made their deeds fair-seeming to them, so he kept them back from the path, and they could see clearly. And Korah and Pharaoh and Haman! And certainly Moses came to them with clear arguments, but they behaved haughtily in the land; they could not outstrip Us. So each one We punished for his sin. Of them was he on whom We sent a violent storm, and of them was he whom the rumbling overtook, and of them was he whom We caused the earth to swallow, and of them was he whom We drowned. And it was not the most gracious Creator, Who wronged them, but they wronged themselves. The parable of those who take guardians besides the most gracious Creator is as the parable of the spider that makes for itself a house, and surely the frailest of the houses is the spider's house — if they but knew! Surely the most gracious Creator knows whatever they call upon besides Him. And He is the Mighty, the Wise. And these parables, We set them forth for men, and none understand them but the learned. The most gracious Creator created the heavens and the earth with truth. Surely there is a sign in this for the believers. Recite that which has been revealed to thee of the Book and keep up prayer. Surely prayer keeps one away from indecency and evil, and certainly, the remembrance of the most gracious Creator is the greatest force. And the most gracious Creator knows what you do. And argue not with the People of the Book except by what is best, save such of them as act unjustly. But say: We believe in that which has been revealed to us and revealed to you, and our God and your God is One, and to Him, we submit. And thus have We revealed the Book to thee. So those whom We have given the Book believe in it, and of these, there are those who believe in it; and none deny Our Messages except the disbelievers. And thou didst not recite before it any book, nor didst thou transcribe one with thy right hand, for then could the liars have doubted. Nay, it is clear Messages in the hearts of those who are granted knowledge. And none deny Our Messages except the iniquitous. And they say: Why are not signs sent down upon him from his Lord? Say: Signs are with the most gracious Creator only, and I am only a plain warner. Is it not enough for them that We have revealed to thee the Book which is recited to them? Surely there is mercy in this and a reminder for a people who believe. Say: the most gracious Creator is sufficient as a witness between me and you — He knows what is in the heavens and the earth. And those who believe in falsehood and disbelieve in the most gracious Creator, these it is that are the losers.

And how many a living creature carries not its sustenance! the most gracious Creator sustains it and yourselves. And He is the Hearing, the Knowing. And if thou ask them, Who created the heavens and the earth and made the sun and the moon subservient? they would say, the most gracious Creator. Whence have they then turned away? the most gracious Creator makes abundant the means of subsistence for whom He pleases of His servants, or straitens them for him. Surely the most gracious Creator is Knower of all things. And if thou ask them, Who is it that sends down water from the clouds, then gives life to the earth with it after its death? They will say, the most gracious Creator. Say: Praise be to the most gracious Creator! Nay, most of them understand not. And the life of this world is but a sport and a play. And the home of the Hereafter, that surely is the Life, did they but know! So when they ride in the ships, they call upon the most gracious Creator, being sincerely obedient to Him; but when He brings them safe to the land, lo!

They associate others with Him, that they may be ungrateful for what We have given them, and that they may enjoy. But they shall soon know. See they not that We have made a sacred territory secure, while men are carried off by force from around them? Will they still believe in the falsehood and disbelieve in the favor of the most gracious Creator? And who is more iniquitous than one who forges a lie against the most gracious Creator, or gives the lie to the Truth, when it has come to him? Is there not an abode in hell for the disbelievers? And those who strive hard for Us, We shall certainly guide them in Our ways. And the most gracious Creator is surely with the doers of good.

Ta, Sin, Mim. (Benignant, Hearing, Knowing God!) These are the verses of the Book that makes manifest. We recite to thee the story of Moses and Pharaoh with truth, for a people who believe. Surely Pharaoh exalted himself in the land and made its people into parties, weakening one party from among them; he slaughtered their sons and let their women live. Surely he was one of the mischief-makers. And We desired to bestow a favor upon those who were deemed weak in the land, and to make them the leaders, and to make them the heirs, and to grant them power in the land, and to make Pharaoh and Haman and their hosts see from them what they feared. And We revealed to Moses' mother, saying: Give him suck; then when thou fearest for him, cast him into the river and fear not, nor grieve; surely We shall bring him back to thee and make him one of the Messengers. So Pharaoh's people took him up that he might be an enemy and a grief for them. Surely Pharaoh and Haman and their hosts were wrongdoers. And Pharaoh's wife said: A refreshment of the eye to me and to thee — slay him not; maybe he will be useful to us, or we may take him for a son. And they perceived not. And the heart of Moses' mother was free from anxiety. She would almost have disclosed it, had We not strengthened her heart so that she might be of the believers. And she said to his sister: Follow him up. So she watched him from a distance, while they perceived not. And We did not allow him to suck before, so she said: Shall I point out to you the people of a house who will bring him up for you, and they will wish him well? So We gave him back to his mother that her eye might be refreshed, and that she might not grieve, and that she might know that the promise of the most gracious Creator is true. But most of them know not. And when he attained his maturity and became full-grown, We granted him wisdom and knowledge. And thus do We reward those who do good to others. And he went into the city at a time of carelessness on the part of its people, so he found therein two men fighting — one being of his party and the other of his foes; and he who was of his party cried out to him for help against him who was of his enemies, so Moses struck him with his fist and killed him. He said: This is on account of the devil's doing; surely he is an enemy, openly leading astray. He said: My Lord, surely I have done harm to myself, so do Thou protect me; so He protected him. Surely He is the Forgiving, the Merciful. He said: My Lord, because Thou hast bestowed a favor on me, I shall never be a backer of the guilty. And he was in the city, fearing, awaiting, when lo, he who had asked his assistance the day before was crying out to him for help. Moses said to him: Thou art surely one erring manifestly. So when he desired to seize him who was an enemy to them both, he said: O Moses, dost thou intend to kill me as thou didst kill a person yesterday? Thou only desires to be a tyrant in the land, and thou desirest not to be of those who act aright. And a man came running from the remotest part of the city. He said: O Moses, the chiefs are consulting together to slay thee, so depart at once; surely I am of those who wish thee well. So he went forth therefrom, fearing, awaiting. He said: My Lord, deliver me from the iniquitous people. And when he turned his face towards Midian, he said: Maybe my Lord will guide me in the right path. And when he came to the water of Midian, he found there a group of men watering, and he found beside them two women keeping back their flocks. He said: What is the matter with you? They said: We cannot water until the shepherds take away their sheep from the water; our father is a very old man. So he watered their sheep for them, then went back to the shade, and said: My Lord, I stand in need of whatever good Thou mayest send to me. Then one of the two women came to him walking bashfully. She said: My father invites thee that he may reward thee for having watered for us. So when he came to him and related to him the story, he said: Fear not, thou art secure from the iniquitous people. One of them said: O my father, employ him; surely the best of those that thou canst employ is the strong, the faithful one. He said: I desire to marry one of these two daughters of mine to thee on condition that thou serve me for eight years; but, if thou complete ten, it will be of thy own free will, and I wish not to be hard on thee. If the most gracious Creator please, thou wilt find me one of the righteous. He said: That is agreed between me and thee; whichever of the two terms I fulfill, there will be no injustice to me; and the most gracious Creator is surety over what we say. Then when Moses had completed the term and was traveling with his family, he

The Heavenly Message

perceived a fire on the side of the mountain. He said to his family: Wait, I see a fire; maybe I will bring to you from it some news or a brand of fire, so that you may warm yourselves. And when he came to it, he was called from the right side of the valley in the blessed spot of the bush: O Moses, surely I am the most gracious Creator, the Lord of the worlds: And cast down thy rod. So when he saw it in motion as if it were a serpent, he turned away retreating and looked not back. O Moses, come forward and fear not; surely thou art of those who are secure. Insert thy hand into thy bosom, it will come forth white without evil, and remain calm in fear. These two are two arguments from thy Lord to Pharaoh and his chiefs. Surely they are a transgressing people. He said: My Lord, I killed one of them, so I fear lest they slay me. And my brother, Aaron, he is more eloquent in speech than I, so send him with me as a helper to confirm me. Surely I fear that they would reject me. He said: We will strengthen thine arm with thy brother, and We will give you both an authority so that they shall not reach you; with Our signs, you two and those who follow you will triumph. So when Moses came to them with Our clear signs, they said: This is nothing but forged enchantment, and we never heard of it among our fathers of old! And Moses said: My Lord knows best who comes with guidance from Him, and whose shall be the good end of the abode. Surely the wrongdoers will not be successful. And Pharaoh said: O chiefs, I know no god for you besides myself; so kindle a fire for me, O Haman, on (bricks of) clay, then prepare for me a lofty building, so that I may obtain knowledge of Moses' God, and surely I think him a liar. And he was unjustly proud in the land, he and his hosts, and they deemed that they would not be brought back to Us. So We caught hold of him and his hosts, then We cast them into the sea, and see what was the end of the iniquitous. And We made them leaders who call to the Fire, and on the Day of Resurrection, they will not be helped. And We made a curse to follow them in this world, and on the Day of Resurrection, they will be hideous. And certainly, We gave Moses the Book after We had destroyed the former generations — clear arguments for men and a guidance and a mercy, that they may be mindful. And thou wast not on the western side when We revealed to Moses the commandment, nor wast thou among those present, But We raised up generations, then life became prolonged to them. And thou wast not dwelling among the people of Midian, reciting to them Our Messages, but We are the Sender of messengers. And thou wast not at the side of the mountain when We called, but a mercy from thy Lord that thou mayest warn a people to whom no warner came before thee, that they may be mindful. And lest, if a disaster should befall them for what their hands have sent before, they should say: Our Lord, why didst Thou not send to us a Messenger so that we might have followed Thy messages and been of the believers? But now when the Truth has come to them from Us, they say: Why is he not given the like of what was given to Moses? Did they not disbelieve in that which was given to Moses before? They say Two enchantments backing up each other! And they say: Surely we are disbelievers in both.

Say: Then bring some other Book from the most gracious Creator which is a better guide than these two, I will follow it — if you are truthful. But if they answer thee not, know that they only follow their low desires. And who is more erring than he who follows his low desires without any guidance from the most gracious Creator? Surely the most gracious Creator guides not the iniquitous people. And certainly, We have made the Word have many connections for their sake, so that they may be mindful. Those to whom We gave the Book before it, they are believers in it. And when it is recited to them they say: We believe in it; surely it is the Truth from our Lord; we were indeed before this submitting ones. These will be granted their reward twice, because they are steadfast, and they repel evil with good and spend out of what We have given them. And when they hear idle talk, they turn aside from it and say: For us are our deeds and for you your deeds. Peace be to you! We desire not the ignorant. Surely thou canst not guide whom thou lovest, but the most gracious Creator guides whom He pleases;

and He knows best those who walk aright. And they say: If we follow the guidance with thee, we should be carried off from our country. Have We not settled them in a safe, sacred territory to which fruits of every kind are drawn? A sustenance from Us — but most of them know not. And how many a town have We destroyed which exulted in its means of subsistence! So those are their abodes: they have not been dwelt in after them except a little. And We are ever the Inheritors. And thy Lord never destroyed the towns, until He had raised in their city a Messenger, reciting to them Our Messages, and We never destroyed the towns except when their people were iniquitous. And whatever things you have been given are only a provision of this world's life and its adornment, and whatever is with the most gracious Creator is better and more lasting. Do you not then understand?
He Who has made the Quran binding on thee will surely bring thee back to the Place of Return. Say: My Lord knows best him who has brought the guidance and him who is in manifest error. And thou didst not

expect that the Book would be inspired to thee, but it is a mercy from thy Lord, so be not a backer up of the disbelievers. And let them not turn thee aside from the messages of the most gracious Creator after they have been revealed to thee, and call men to thy Lord and be not of the polytheists. And call not with the most gracious Creator any other god. There is no God but He. Everything will perish but He. His is the judgment, and to Him, you will be brought back.

Whatever is in the heavens and whatever is in the earth glorifies the most gracious Creator. His is the kingdom, and His is the Praise, and He is Possessor of power over all things. He it is Who created you, but one of you is a disbeliever and one of you is a believer. And the most gracious Creator sees all that you do. He created the heavens and the earth with truth, and He shaped you, then made goodly your shapes; and to Him is the resort. He knows what is in the heavens and the earth, and he knows what you hide and what you manifest. And the most gracious Creator is Knower of what is in the hearts. Has there not come to you the story of those who disbelieved before, then tasted the evil consequences of their conduct, and they had a painful chastisement? That is because there came to them their Messengers with clear arguments, but they said: "Shall mortals guide us? So they disbelieved and turned away, and the most gracious Creator is above all needs. And the most gracious Creator is Self-Sufficient, Praised. Those who disbelieve think that they will not be raised. Say: Aye, by my Lord! You will certainly be raised; then you will certainly be informed of what you did. And that is easy to the most gracious Creator. So believe in the most gracious Creator and His Messenger and the Light which We have revealed. And the most gracious Creator is Aware of what you do. The Day when He will gather you for the Day of Gathering, which is the Day of the Manifestation of losses; whoever believes in the most gracious Creator and does good, He will remove from him his evil and cause him to enter Gardens wherein rivers flow, to abide therein forever.

That is a great achievement. And those who disbelieve and reject Our Messages, they are the companions of the Fire, abiding therein; and evil is the resort. No calamity befalls but by the most gracious Creator's Permission. And whoever believes in the most gracious Creator, He guides his heart. And the most gracious Creator is the Knower of all things. And obey the most gracious Creator and obey the Messenger; but if you turn away, the duty of Our Messenger is only to deliver clearly. The most gracious Creator, there is no God but He. And on the most gracious Creator let the believers rely upon.

Ta Sin. (Benignant, Hearing God!) These are the verses of the Quran and the Book that makes manifest: A guidance and good news for the believers, who keep up prayer and pay the poor-rate, and they are sure of the Hereafter. Those who believe not in the Hereafter, We make their deeds fair-seeming to them, but they blindly wander on. These are they for whom is an evil chastisement, and in the Hereafter, they are the greatest losers. And thou art surely made to receive the Quran from the Wise, the Knowing.

Say: Maybe somewhat of that which you seek to hasten has drawn nigh to you. And surely thy Lord is Full of grace to men, but most of them do not give thanks. And surely thy Lord knows what their breasts conceal and what they manifest. And there is nothing concealed in the heaven and the earth but it is in a clear Book. Surely this Quran declares to the Children of Israel most of that wherein they differ. And surely it is a guidance and a mercy for the believers. Truly thy Lord will judge between them by His judgment, and He is the Mighty, the Knowing. So rely on the most gracious Creator. Surely thou art on the plain truth. Certainly, thou canst not make the dead to hear, nor canst thou make the deaf to hear the call when they go back retreating. Nor canst thou lead the blind out of their error. Thou canst make none to hear except those who believe in Our Messages, so they submit. And when the word comes to pass against them, We shall bring forth for them a creature from the earth that will speak to them, because people did not believe in Our

Messages.

Ta, Sin, Mim. (Benignant, Hearing, Knowing God). These are the verses of the Book that makes manifest. Perhaps thou wilt kill thyself with grief because they believe not. If We please, We could send down on them a sign from heaven, so that their necks would bend before it. And there comes not to them a new Reminder from the Beneficent but they turn away from it. They indeed reject, so the news will soon come to them of that at which they mock. See they not the earth, how many of every noble kind We cause to grow in it? Surely in this is a sign, yet most of them believe not. And surely thy Lord is the Mighty, the Merciful. And surely this is a revelation from the Lord of the worlds. The Faithful Spirit has brought it, on thy heart that thou mayest be a warner, in the plain Arabic language. And surely the same is in the Scriptures of the ancients. Is it not a sign to them that the learned men of the Children of Israel know it? And if We had revealed it to any of the foreigners, and he had read it to them, they would not have believed in it. Thus do We cause it to enter into the hearts of the guilty. They will not believe in it until they see the painful chastisement: So it will come to them suddenly, while they perceive not; then they will say: Shall we be respited? Do they still seek to hasten on Our chastisement? Seest thou, if We let them enjoy themselves for years, then that which they are promised comes to them — That which they were made to enjoy will not avail them? And We destroyed no town but it had its warners — To remind. And We are never unjust. And the devils have not brought it. And it would neither suit them nor have they the power to do it. Surely they are far removed from hearing it. So call not upon another god with the most gracious Creator, lest thou be of those who are chastised. And warn thy nearest relations, and lower thy wing to the believers who follow thee. But if they disobey thee, say: I am clear of what you do. And rely on the Mighty, the Merciful, Who sees thee when thou standest up, and thy movements among those who prostrate themselves. Surely He is the Hearing, the Knowing. Shall I inform you upon whom the devils descend? They descend upon every lying, sinful one — They give ear, and most of them are liars. And the poets — the deviators follow them. Seest thou not that they wander in every valley, and that they say that which they do not? Except those who believe and do good and remember the most gracious Creator much, and defend themselves after they are oppressed. And they who do wrong will know to what final place of turning they will turn back.

Blessed is He Who sent down the criterion upon His Servant that he might be a warner to the nations —He, Whose is the kingdom of the heavens and the earth, and Who did not take to Himself a son, and Who has no associate in the kingdom, and Who created everything, then ordained for it a measure. And they take besides Him gods who create naught, while they are themselves created, and they control for themselves no harm nor profit, and they control not death, nor life, nor raising to life. And those who disbelieve say: This is nothing but a lie, which he has forged, and other people have helped him at it. So indeed they have brought an iniquity and a falsehood. And they say Stories of the ancients, which he has got written, so they are read out to him morning and evening! Say: He has revealed it, Who knows the secret of the heavens and the earth. Surely He is ever Forgiving, Merciful. And they say: What a Messenger is this? He eats food and goes about in the markets. Why has not an angel been sent down to him to be a warner with him? Or a treasure was given to him, or a garden from which to eat? And the evildoers say: You follow but a man bewitched! See what parables they set forth for thee — they have gone astray, so they cannot find a way.

And We did not send before thee any Messengers but they surely ate food and went about in the markets. And We make some of you a trial for others. Will you bear patiently? And thy Lord is ever Seeing. And those who look not for meeting with Us, say: Why have not angels been sent down to us, or (why) do we not see our Lord? Indeed they are too proud of themselves and revolt in great revolt.

And certainly, We gave Moses the Book and

We appointed with him his brother Aaron, an aider. Then We said: Go you both to the people who reject Our Messages. So We destroyed them with utter destruction. And the people of Noah, when they rejected the Messengers, We drowned them and made them a sign for men. And We have prepared a painful chastisement for the wrong-doers — And 'Ad and Thamud and the dwellers of Rass and many generations in between. And to each We gave examples and each did We destroy with utter destruction. And indeed they pass by the town wherein was rained an evil rain. Do they not see it? Nay, they hope not to be raised again. And when they see thee, they take thee for naught but a jest: Is this he whom the most gracious Creator has raised to be a Messenger? He had well-nigh led us astray from our gods had we not adhered to them patiently! And they will know when they see the chastisement, who is more astray from the path. Hast thou saw him who takes his low desires for his god? Wilt thou be a guardian over him? Or thinkest thou that most of them hear or understand? They are but as the cattle; nay,

they are farther astray from the path. Seest thou not how thy Lord extends the shade? And if He pleased, He would have made it stationary. Then We have made the sun an indication of it, then We take it to Ourselves, taking little by little. And He it is Who made the night a covering for you and sleep a rest, and He made the day to rise up again. And He it is Who sends the winds as good news before His mercy; and We send down pure water from the clouds, that We may give life thereby to a dead land, and give it for a drink to cattle and many people that We have created. And certainly, We repeat this to them that they may be mindful, but most men consent to naught but denying. And if We pleased, We could raise a warner in every town. So obey not the disbelievers, and strive against them a mighty striving with it. And He it is Who has made the two seas to flow freely, the one sweet, very sweet, and the other saltish, bitter. And between the two He has made a barrier and inviolable obstruction. And He it is Who has created man from water, then He has made for him blood-relationship and marriage-relationship. And thy Lord is ever Powerful. And they serve beside the most gracious Creator that which can neither profit them nor harm them. And the disbeliever is ever an aider against his Lord. And We have not sent thee but as a giver of good news and as a warner. Say: I ask of you naught in return for it except that he who will take a way to his Lord. And rely on the Ever-Living Who dies not, and celebrate His praise. And sufficient is He as being Aware of His servants' sins, Who created the heavens and the earth and what is between them in six periods, and He is established on the Throne of Power, the Beneficent. So ask respecting Him one aware. And when it is said to them: Make obeisance to the Beneficent, they say: And what is the Beneficent? Shall we make obeisance to what thou biddest us? And it adds to their aversion.

Say: My Lord would not care for you, were it not for your prayer. Now indeed you have rejected, so the punishment will come.

Seest thou not that the most gracious Creator is He, Whom do glorify all those who are in the heavens and the earth, and the birds with wings outspread? Each one knows its prayer and its glorification. And the most gracious Creator is Knower of what they do. And the most gracious Creator's is the kingdom of the heavens and the earth, and to the most gracious Creator is the eventual coming. Seest thou not that the most gracious Creator drives along the clouds, then gathers them together, then piles them up, so that thou seest the rain coming forth from their midst? And He sends down from the heaven clouds like mountains, wherein is hail, afflicting therewith whom He pleases and turning it away from whom He pleases. The flash of His lightning almost takes away the sight. The most gracious Creator causes the night and the day to succeed one another. Surely there is a lesson in this for those who have sight. And the most gracious Creator has created every animal of water. So of them is that which crawls upon its belly, and of them is that which walks upon two feet, and of them is that which walks upon four. The most gracious Creator creates what He pleases. Surely the most gracious Creator is Possessor of power over all things. We have indeed revealed clear messages. And the most gracious Creator guides whom He pleases to the right way. And they say: We believe in the most gracious Creator and in the Messenger and we obey; then a party of them turn away after this, and they are not believers. And when they are invited to the most gracious Creator and His Messenger that he may judge between them, lo! A party of them turn aside. And if the right is on their side, they hasten to him in submission. Is there in their hearts a disease, or are they in doubt, or fear they that the most gracious Creator and His Messenger will deal with them unjustly? Nay! They themselves are the wrongdoers.

O ye Messengers, eat of the good things and do good. Surely I am Knower of what you do. And surely this your community is one community, and I am your Lord, so keep your duty to Me. But they became divided into sects, each party rejoicing in that which was with them. So leave them in their ignorance till a time. Think they that by the

wealth and children wherewith We aid them, We are hastening to them of good things? Nay, they perceive not.
Nay, their hearts are in ignorance about it, and they have besides this other deeds which they do. Until, when We seize those who lead easy lives among them with chastisement, lo! They cry for succor. Cry not for succor this day. Surely you will not be helped by Us. My Messages were indeed recited to you, but you used to turn back on your heels haughtily, passing nights in talking nonsense about it. Do they not then ponder the Word? Or has there come to them that which did not come to their fathers of old? Or do they not recognize their Messenger, that they deny him? Or say they: There is madness in him? Nay, he has brought them the Truth, and most of them hate the Truth. And if the Truth follows their desires, the heavens and the earth and all those who are therein would perish. Nay, We have brought them their reminder, but they turn away from their reminder. Or dost thou ask them a recompense? But the recompense of thy Lord is best, and He is

the Best of providers. And surely thou callest them to a right way. And surely those who believe not in the Hereafter are deviating from the way. And if We show mercy to them and remove the distress they have, they would persist in their inordinacy, blindly wandering on. And already We seized them with chastisement, but they were not submissive to their Lord, nor did they humble themselves. Until, when We open for them a door of severe chastisement, lo! They are in despair at it. And He it is Who made for you the ears and the eyes and the hearts. Little it is that you give thanks! And He it is Who multiplied you in the earth, and to Him, you will be gathered. And He it is Who gives life and causes death, and His is the alternation of the night and the day. Do you not then understand? Nay, they say the like of what the ancients said. They say: When we die and become dust and bones, shall we then be raised up? We are indeed promised this, and (so were) our fathers before. This is naught but stories of those of old! Say: Whose is the earth, and whoever is therein, if you know? They will say the most gracious Creator's. Say: Will you not then mind? Say: Who is the Lord of the seven heavens and the Lord of the mighty Throne of power? They will say: This is the most gracious Creator's. Say: Will you not then guard against evil? Say: Who is it in Whose hand is the kingdom of all things and He protects, and none is protected against Him if you know? They will say: This is the most gracious Creator's. Say: Whence are you then deceived? Nay, We have brought them the Truth and surely they are liars. The most gracious Creator has not taken to Himself a son, nor is there with Him any other god — in that case, would each god have taken away what he created, and some of them would have overpowered others. Glory be to the most gracious Creator above what they describe — The Knower of the unseen and the seen; so may He be exalted above what they associate with Him! Say: My Lord, if Thou show me that which they are promised — My Lord, then place me not with the unjust people. And surely We are well Able to show thee what We promise them. Repel evil with that which is best. We know best what they describe. And say: My Lord, I seek refuge in Thee from the evil suggestions of the devils, and I seek refuge in Thee, my Lord, lest they come to me.

And thou seest the earth barren, but when We send down thereon water, it stirs and swells and brings forth a beautiful growth of every kind. That is because the most gracious Creator, He is the Truth, and He gives life to the dead, and He is Possessor of power over all things, and the Hour is coming, there is no doubt about it; the most gracious Creator will raise up those who are in the graves. And among men is he who disputes about the most gracious Creator without knowledge, and without guidance, and without an illuminating Book. Turning away haughtily to lead men astray from the way of the most gracious Creator. For him is the disgrace in this world, and on the Day of Resurrection, We shall make him taste the punishment of burning. This is for that which thy two hands have sent before, and the most gracious Creator is not in the least unjust to the servants. And among men is he who serves the most gracious Creator, standing on the verge, so that if good befalls him he is satisfied therewith, but if a trial afflicts him he turns back headlong. He loses this world and the Hereafter. That is a manifest loss. He calls besides the most gracious Creator on that which harms him not, nor benefits him; that is straying far. He calls on him whose harm is nearer than his benefit. Certainly an evil guardian and an evil associate! Surely the most gracious Creator causes those who believe and do good deeds to enter Gardens wherein flow rivers. The most gracious Creator indeed does what He pleases. Whoever thinks that the most gracious Creator will not assist him in this life and the Hereafter, let him raise himself by some means to the heaven, then let him cut (it) off, then let him see if his plan will take away that at which he is enraged. And thus have We revealed it, clear arguments, and the most gracious Creator guides whom He will.

Is he who is obedient during hours of the night, prostrating himself and standing, taking care of the Hereafter and hoping for the Mercy of his Lord? Say: Are those who know and those who know not alike? Only men of understanding mind. Say: O my servants who believe, keep your duty to your Lord. For those who do good in this world is good, and the most gracious Creator's earth is spacious. Truly the steadfast will be paid their reward without measure. Say: I am commanded to serve the most gracious Creator, being sincere to Him in obedience, and I am commanded to be the first of those who submit. Say: I fear, if I disobey my Lord, the chastisement of a grievous day. Say the most gracious Creator I serve, being sincere to Him in my obedience. Serve then what you will besides Him. Say: The losers surely are those who lose themselves and their people on the Day of Resurrection. Now surely that is the manifest loss! They shall have coverings of fire above them and coverings beneath them. With that the most gracious Creator makes His servants fear: So keep your duty to Me, O My servants.

Say: O my servants who have transgressed against their souls, despair not of the Mercy of the most gracious Creator; surely He forgives sins altogether. He is indeed the

Forgiving, the Merciful. And turn to your Lord and submit to Him before chastisement comes to you, then you will not be helped. And follow the best that has been revealed to you from your Lord before chastisement comes to you all of a sudden, while you perceive not – Lest a soul should say: O woe is me, that I fell short of my duty to the most gracious Creator! And surely I was of those who laughed to scorn; or it should say: Had the most gracious Creator guided me, I should have been dutiful. Or it should say: when it sees the chastisement: Had I another chance I should be a doer of good. Aye! My Messages came to thee, but thou didst reject them and was proud and wast of the disbelievers. And on the Day of Resurrection thou wilt see those who lied against the most gracious Creator, their faces will be blackened. Is there not in hell an abode for the proud? And the most gracious Creator delivers those who keep their duty with their achievement – evil touch them not, nor do they grieve. The most gracious Creator is the Creator of all things and He has charge over everything.

His are the treasures of the heavens and the earth. And those who disbelieve in the messages of the most gracious Creator, such are the losers. Say: Do you bid me serve others than the most gracious Creator, O ye ignorant ones? And certainly, it has been revealed to thee and to those before thee: If thou associate with the most gracious Creator, thy work would certainly come to naught and thou would be a loser. Nay, but serve the most gracious Creator alone and be of the thankful.

Say: Do you see if the most gracious Creator were to make the night to continue incessantly on you till the Day of Resurrection, who is the god besides the most gracious Creator who could bring you light? Will you not then hear? Say: Do you see if the most gracious Creator were to make the day to continue incessantly on you till the Day of Resurrection, who is the god besides the most gracious Creator that could bring you the night in which you take rest? Do you not then see? And out of His mercy, He has made for you the night and the day, that you may rest therein, and that you may seek of His grace, and that you may give thanks. I am commanded only to serve the Lord of this city, Who has made it sacred, and His are all things, and I am commanded to be of those who submit and to recite the Quran. So whoever goes aright, he goes aright for his own soul, and whoever goes astray — say: I am only one of the warners. And say: Praise be to the most gracious Creator! He will show you His signs so that you shall recognize them. And thy Lord is not heedless of what you do.

Seest thou not that to the most gracious Creator makes submission whoever is in the heavens and whoever is in the earth, and the sun and the moon and the stars, and the mountains and the trees, and the animals and many of the people? And many there are to whom chastisement is due. And he whom the most gracious Creator abases, none can give him honor. Surely the most gracious Creator does what He pleases.

And when We pointed to Abraham the place of the House, saying: Associate naught with Me and purify My House for those who make circuits and stand to pray and bow and prostrate themselves. And proclaim to men the Pilgrimage: they will come to thee on foot and on every lean camel, coming from every remote path: That they may witness benefits (provided) for them, and mention the Name of the most gracious Creator on appointed days over what He has given them of the cattle quadrupeds; then eat of them and feed the distressed one, the needy. Then let them accomplish their needful acts of cleansing, and let them fulfill their vows and go round the Ancient House. That shall be so. And whoever respects the sacred ordinances of the most gracious Creator, it is good for him with his Lord. And the cattle are made lawful for you, except that which is recited to you, so shun the filth of the idols and shun false words, being upright for the most gracious Creator, not associating aught with Him. And whoever associates (aught) with the most gracious Creator, it is as if he had fallen from on high, then the birds had snatched him away, or the wind had carried him off to a distant place. That shall be so. And whoever respects the ordinances of the most gracious Creator, this is surely from the piety of hearts. Therein are benefits for you for a term appointed, then their place of sacrifice is the Ancient House. And for every nation, We appointed acts of devotion that they might mention the Name of the most gracious Creator on what He has given them of the cattle quadrupeds. So your God is One God, therefore to Him should you submit. And give good news to the humble, whose hearts tremble when the most gracious Creator is mentioned, and who are patient in their afflictions, and who keep up prayer, and spend of what We have given them. And the camels, We have made them of the signs appointed by the most gracious Creator for you — for you therein is much good. So mention the Name of the most gracious Creator on them standing in a row. Then when they fall down on their sides, eat of them and feed the contented one and the beggar. Thus have We made them subservient to you that you may be grateful. Not their flesh, nor their blood, reaches the most gracious Creator, but to Him is an acceptable observance of duty on your part.

Thus has He made them subservient to you, that you may magnify the most gracious Creator for guiding you aright. And give good news to those who do good to others. Surely the most gracious Creator defends those who believe. Surely the most gracious Creator loves not anyone who is unfaithful, ungrateful. Permission to fight is given to those on whom war is made because they are oppressed. And surely the most gracious Creator is Able to assist them— Those who are driven from their homes without a just cause except that they say: Our Lord is the most gracious Creator. And if the most gracious Creator did not repel some people by others, cloisters, and churches, and synagogues, and mosques in which the most gracious Creator's name is much remembered would have been pulled down. And surely the most gracious Creator will help him who helps Him. Surely the most gracious Creator is Strong, Mighty. Those who, if We establish them in the land, will keep up prayer and pay the poor-rate and enjoin good and forbid evil. And the most gracious Creator's is the end of affairs. And

if they reject thee, already before them did the people of Noah and 'Ad and Thamud rejected, and the people of Abraham and the people of Lot, and the dwellers of Midian. And Moses too was rejected. But I gave respite to the disbelievers, then I seized them; so how severe was My disapproval! How many a town We destroyed while it was iniquitous, so it is fallen down upon its roofs; and how many a deserted well and palace raised high! Have they not traveled in the land so that they should have hearts with which to understand, or ears with which to hear? For surely it is not the eyes that are blind, but blind are the hearts which are in the breasts. And they ask thee to hasten on the chastisement, and the most gracious Creator by no means fails in His promise. And surely a day with thy Lord is as a thousand years of what you reckon. And how many a town to which I gave respite while it was unjust, then I seized it! And to Me is the return. Say: O people, I am only a plain warner to you. So those who believe and do good, for them is forgiveness and an honorable sustenance. And those who strive

to oppose Our Messages, they are the inmates of the flaming Fire. And We never sent a Messenger or a Prophet before thee but when he desired, the devil made a suggestion respecting his desire; but the most gracious Creator annuls that which the devil casts, then does the most gracious Creator establish His messages. And the most gracious Creator is Knowing, Wise —
That He may make what the devil casts a trial for those in whose hearts is a disease and the hard-hearted. And surely the wrongdoers are in severe opposition, and that those who have been given knowledge may know that it is the Truth from thy Lord, so they should believe in it that their hearts may be lowly before Him. And surely the most gracious Creator is the Guide of those who believe, into a right path. And those who disbelieve will not cease to be in doubt concerning it, until the Hour overtakes them suddenly, or there comes to them the chastisement of a destructive day. The kingdom on that day is the most gracious Creator's. He will judge between them. So those who believe and do good will be in

Gardens of bliss. And those who disbelieve and reject Our Messages, for them is an abasing chastisement. And those who flee in the most gracious Creator's way and are then slain or die, the most gracious Creator will certainly grant them a goodly sustenance. And surely the most gracious Creator is the Best of providers. He will certainly cause them to enter a place which they are pleased with. And surely the most gracious Creator is Knowing, Forbearing. That (is so). And whoever retaliates with the like of that with which he is afflicted and he is oppressed, the most gracious Creator will certainly help him. Surely the most gracious Creator is Pardoning, Forgiving. That is because the most gracious Creator causes the night to enter into the day and causes the day to enter into the night, and because the most gracious Creator is Hearing, Seeing. That is because the most gracious Creator is the Truth, and that which they call upon besides Him — that is the falsehood, and because the most gracious Creator— He is the High, the Great. Seest thou not that the most gracious Creator sends down water from the cloud, then the earth becomes green? Surely the most gracious Creator is Knower of subtilities, Aware. To Him belongs whatever is in the heavens and whatever is in the earth. And surely the most gracious Creator— He is the Self-Sufficient, the Praised. Seest thou not that the most gracious Creator has made subservient to you all that is in the earth, and the ships gliding in the sea by His command? And He withholds the heaven from falling on the earth except with His permission. Surely the most gracious Creator is Compassionate, Merciful to men. And He it is Who brings you to life, then He causes you to die, then He will bring you to life. Surely man is ungrateful. To every nation, We appointed acts of devotion, which they observe, so let them not dispute with thee in the matter, and call to thy Lord. Surely thou art on a right guidance. And if they contend with thee, say: the most gracious Creator best knows what you do. The most gracious Creator will judge between you on the Day of Resurrection respecting that in which you differ. Knowest thou not that the most gracious Creator knows what is in the heaven and the earth? Surely this is in a book. That is surely easy to the most gracious Creator. And they serve besides the most gracious Creator that for which He has not sent any authority, and of which they have no knowledge. And for the unjust, there is no helper. And when Our clear messages are recited to them, thou wilt notice a denial on the faces of those who disbelieve — they almost attack those who recite to them Our Messages. Say: Shall I inform you of what is worse than this? The Fire. The most gracious Creator has promised it to those who disbelieve. And evil is the resort.

Their reckoning draws nigh to men, and they turn away in heedlessness. There comes not to them a new Reminder from their Lord but they hear it while they sport, their hearts trifling. And they — the wrongdoers — counsel in secret: He is nothing but a mortal like yourselves; will you then yield to enchantment while you see? He said: My Lord knows (every) utterance in the heaven and the earth, and He is the

Hearer, the Knower. Nay, say they: Medleys of dreams! Nay, he has forged it! Nay, he is a poet! so let him bring to us a sign such as the former Prophets were sent with. Not a town believed before them which We destroyed: will they then believe? And We sent not before thee any but men to whom We sent revelation; so ask the followers of the Reminder if you know not. Nor did We give them bodies not eating food, nor did they abide. Then We made Our promise good to them; so We delivered them and whom We pleased, and We destroyed the extravagant. Certainly, We have revealed to you a Book which will give you eminence. Do you not then understand? And how many a town which was iniquitous did We demolish, and We raised up after it another people! So when they felt Our might, lo! They began to flee from it. Flee not and return to the easy lives which you led, and to your dwellings, that you may be questioned. They said: O woe to us! Surely we were unjust. And this cry of theirs ceased not till We made them cut off, extinct. And We created not the heaven and the earth and what is between them for sport. Had We wished to take a pastime, We would have taken it from before Ourselves; by no means would We do so. Nay, We hurl the Truth against falsehood, so it knocks out its brains, and lo! It vanishes. And woe to you for what you describe! And to Him belongs whoever is in the heavens and the earth. And those who are with Him are not too proud to serve Him, nor are they weary. They glorify Him night and day: they flag not. Or have they taken gods from the earth who give life? If there were in them gods besides the most gracious Creator, they would both have been in disorder. So Glory be to the most gracious Creator, the Lord of the Throne, being above what they describe! He cannot be questioned as to what He does, and they will be questioned. Or, have they taken gods besides Him? Say: Bring your proof. This is the reminder of those with me and the reminder of those before me. Nay, most of them know not the Truth, so they turn away. And We sent no Messenger before thee but We revealed to him that there is no God but Me, so serve Me. And they say: The

Beneficent has taken to Himself a son. Glory be to Him! Nay, they are honored servants — They speak not before He speaks, and according to His command, they act. He knows what is before them and what is behind them, and they intercede not except for him whom He approves, and for fear of Him they tremble. And whoever of them should say, I am a god besides Him, such a one We recompense with hell. Thus We reward the unjust. Do not those who disbelieve see that the heavens and the earth were closed up, so We rent them. And We made from water everything living. Will they not then believe? And We made firm mountains in the earth lest it is convulsed with them, and We made in it wide ways that they might follow a right direction. And We have made the heaven a guarded canopy, yet they turn away from its signs. And He it is Who created the night and the day and the sun and the moon. All float in orbits. And We granted abiding forever to no mortal before thee. If thou diest, will they abide? Every soul must taste of death. And We test you by evil and good by way of trial. And to

The Heavenly Message

Us, you are returned. And when those who disbelieve see thee, they treat thee not but with mockery: Is this he who speaks of your gods? And they deny when the Beneficent God is mentioned. Man is created of haste. Soon will I show you My signs, so ask Me not to hasten them. And they say: When will this threat come to pass if you are truthful? If those who disbelieve but knew the time when they will not be able to ward off the fire from their faces, nor from their backs, and they will not be helped! Nay, it will come to them all of a sudden and confound them, so they will not have the power to avert it, nor will they be respited. And Messengers before thee were indeed mocked, so there befell those of them who scoffed, that whereat they scoffed. Say: Who guards you by night and by day from the Beneficent? Nay, they turn away at the mention of their Lord. Or, have they gods who can defend them against Us? They cannot help themselves, nor can they be defended from Us. Nay, We gave provision to these and their fathers, until life was prolonged to them. See they not then that We are visiting the land, curtailing it of its sides? Can they then prevail? Say: I warn you only by revelation; the deaf hear not the call when they are warned. And if a blast of the chastisement of thy Lord were to touch them, they would say O woe to us! Surely we were unjust. And We will set up a just balance on the Day of Resurrection, so no soul will be wronged in the least. And if there be the weight of a grain of mustard seed, We will bring it. And Sufficient are We to take account. And certainly, We gave Moses and Aaron the criterion and a light and a reminder for those who keep from evil, who fear their Lord in secret and they are fearful of the Hour. And this is a blessed Reminder, which We have revealed. Will you then deny it?

And certainly, We wrote in the Book after the reminder that My righteous servants will inherit the land. Surely in this is a message for a people who serve Us. And We have not sent thee but as a mercy to the nations. Say: It is only revealed to me that your God is one God: will you then submit? But if they turn back, say: I have warned you in fairness, and I know not whether that which you are promised is near or far. Surely He knows what is spoken openly and He knows what you hide. And I know not if this may be a trial for you and a provision till a time. He said: My Lord, judge Thou with the truth. And our Lord is the Beneficent, Whose help is sought against what you ascribe to Him.

Ta Ha (O man), We have not revealed the Quran to thee that thou mayest be unsuccessful; But it is a reminder to him who fears: A revelation from Him Who created the earth and the high heavens. The Beneficent is established on the Throne of Power. To Him belongs whatever is in the heavens and whatever is in the earth and whatever is between them and whatever is beneath the soil. And if thou utter the saying aloud, surely He knows the secret, and what is yet more hidden. The most gracious Creator— there is no God but He. His are the most beautiful names. And has the story of Moses come to thee? When he saw a fire, he said to his people: Stay, I see a fire; haply I may bring to you therefrom a live coal or

The Heavenly Message

find guidance at the fire. So when he came to it, a voice came: O Moses, surely I am thy Lord, so take off thy shoes; surely thou art in the sacred valley Tuwa. And I have chosen thee, so listen to what is revealed: Surely I am the most gracious Creator, there is no God but I, so serve Me, and keep up prayer for My remembrance, surely the Hour is coming — I am about to make it manifest — so that every soul may be rewarded as it strives. So let not him, who believes not in it and follows his low desire, turn thee away from it, lest thou perish. And what is this in thy right hand, O Moses? He said: This is my staff — I lean on it, and I beat the leaves with it for my sheep, and I have other uses for it. He said: Cast it down, O Moses. So he cast it down, and lo! It was a serpent, gliding. He said: Seize it and fear not. We shall return it to its former state. And press thy hand to thy side, it will come out white without evil — another sign: That We may show thee of Our greater signs. Go to Pharaoh, surely he has exceeded the limits. He said: My Lord, expand my breast for me: And ease my affair for me: And loose the knot from my tongue, that they may understand my word. And give to me an aider from my family: Aaron, my brother; add to my strength by him, and make him share my task — So that we may glorify Thee much, and much remember Thee. Surely, Thou art ever Seeing us. He said: Thou art indeed granted thy petition, O Moses. And indeed We bestowed on thee a favor at another time when We revealed to thy mother that which was revealed: Put him into a chest, then cast it into the river, the river will cast it upon the shore — there an enemy to Me and an enemy to him shall take him up. And I shed on thee love from Me; that thou mayest be brought up before My eyes. When thy sister went and said: Shall I direct you to one who will take charge of him? So We brought thee back to thy mother that her eye might be cooled and she should not grieve. And thou didst kill a man, then We delivered thee from grief, and tried thee with many trials. Then thou didst stay for years among the people of Midian. Then thou camest hither as ordained, O Moses. And I have chosen thee for Myself. Go thou and thy brother with My Messages and be not remiss in remembering Me. Go both of you to Pharaoh, surely he is inordinate; Then speak to him a gentle word, haply he may mind or fear. They said: Our Lord, we fear lest he hastens to do evil to us or be inordinate. He said: Fear not, surely I am with you — I do hear and see. So go you to him and say: Surely we are two Messengers of thy Lord; so send forth the Children of Israel with us; torment them not. Indeed we have brought to thee a message from thy Lord, and peace to him who follows the guidance. It has indeed been revealed to us that punishment will overtake him who rejects and turns away. Pharaoh said: Who is your Lord, O Moses? He said: Our Lord is He Who gives to everything its creation, then guides it. He said: What then is the state of the former generations? He said: The knowledge thereof is with my Lord in a book; my Lord neither errs nor forgets — Who made the earth for you an expanse and made for you therein paths and sent down water from the clouds. Then thereby We brought forth pairs of various herbs. Eat and pasture your cattle. Surely there are signs in this for men of understanding. From it We created you, and into it, We shall return you, and from it raise you a second time. And truly We showed him all Our signs but he rejected and refused. Said he: Hast thou come to us to turn us out of our land by thy enchantment, O Moses? We too can bring to thee enchantment like it, so make an appointment between us and thee, which we break not, neither we nor thou, in a central place. Moses said: Your appointment is the day of the Festival, and let the people be gathered in the early forenoon. So Pharaoh went back and settled his plan, then came. Moses said to them: Woe to you! Forge not a lie against the most gracious Creator, lest He destroys you by punishment, and he fails indeed who forges a lie. So they disputed one with another about their affair and kept the discourse secret. They said: These are surely two enchanters who would drive you out from your land by their enchantment, and destroy your excellent institutions. So settle your plan, then come in ranks, and he will succeed indeed this day who is uppermost. They said: O Moses, wilt thou cast, or shall we be the first to cast down? He said: Nay! Cast you down. Then lo! Their cords and their rods — it appeared to him by their enchantment as if they ran. So Moses conceived fear in his mind. We said: Fear not, surely thou art the uppermost. And cast down what is in thy right hand — it will eat up what they have wrought. What they have wrought is only the trick of an enchanter, and the enchanter succeeds not wheresoever he comes from. So the enchanters fell down prostrate, saying: We believe in the Lord of Aaron and Moses. Pharaoh said: You believe in him before I give you leave! Surely he is your chief who taught you enchantment. So I shall cut off your hands and your feet on opposite sides and I shall crucify you on the trunks of palm-trees, and you shall certainly know which of us can give the severer and the more abiding chastisement. They said: We cannot prefer thee to what has come to us of clear arguments and to Him Who made us, so decide as thou wilt decide. Thou canst only decide about this world's life. Surely we believe in our Lord that He may forgive us our faults and the magic to which thou didst compel us. And the most gracious Creator is Best and ever Abiding. Whoso comes guilty to his Lord, for him is surely hell. He will neither die therein nor live. And whoso comes to Him a believer, having done good deeds, for them are high ranks — Gardens of perpetuity, wherein flow rivers, to abide therein. And such is the reward of him who purifies himself. And certainly, We revealed to Moses: Travel by night with My servants, then strike for them a dry path in the sea, not fearing to be overtaken, nor being afraid. So Pharaoh followed them with his armies, then there covered them of the sea that which covered them. And Pharaoh led his people astray and he guided not aright. O Children of Israel, We truly delivered you from your enemy, and made a covenant with you on the blessed side of the mountain, and sent to you the manna and the quails. Eat of the good things We have provided for you, and be not inordinate in respect thereof, lest My wrath come upon you; and he on whom My wrath comes, he perishes indeed. And surely I am Forgiving toward him who repents and believes and does good, then walks aright. And what made thee hasten from thy people, O Moses? He said: They are here on my track, and I hastened on to Thee, my Lord, that Thou mightest be pleased. He said: Surely We have tried thy people in thy absence, and the Samiri has led them astray. So Moses returned to his people angry, sorrowing. He said: O my people, did not your Lord promise you a goodly promise? Did the promised time, then, seem long to you, or did you wish that displeasure from your Lord should come upon you so that you broke your promise to me? They said: We broke not the promise to thee of our own accord, but we were made to bear the burdens of the ornaments of the people, then we cast them away, and thus did the Samiri suggest. Then he brought forth for them a calf, a body, which had a hollow sound, so they said: This is your god and the god of Moses, but he forgot. Could they not see that it returned no reply to them, nor controlled any harm or benefit to them? And Aaron indeed had said to them before: O my people, you are only tried by it, and surely your Lord is the Beneficent God, so follow me and obey my order. They said: We shall not cease to keep to its worship until Moses returns to us. Moses said: O Aaron, what prevented thee, when thou saw them going astray, that thou didst not follow me? Hast thou, then, disobeyed my order? He said: O son of my mother, seize me not by my beard, nor by my head. Surely I was afraid lest thou should say: Thou hast caused division among the Children of Israel and not waited for my word. Moses said: What was thy object, O Samiri? He said: I perceived what they perceived not, so I took a handful from the footprints of the Messenger then I cast it away. Thus did my soul embellish it to me. He said: Begone then! It is for thee in this life to say, Touch me not. And for thee is a promise which shall not fail. And look at thy god to whose worship thou hast kept. We will certainly burn it, then we will scatter it in the sea. Your Lord is only the most gracious Creator, there is no God but He. He comprehends all things in His knowledge. Thus relate We to thee of the news of what has gone before. And indeed We have given thee a Reminder from Ourselves. Whoever turns away from it, he will surely bear a burden on the Day of Resurrection, abiding therein. And evil will be their burden on the Day of Resurrection.

And thus have We sent it down an Arabic Quran, and have distinctly set forth therein of threats that they may guard against evil, or that it may be a reminder for them. Supremely exalted then is the most gracious Creator, the King, the Truth. And make not haste with the Quran before its revelation is made complete to thee, and say: My Lord, increase me in knowledge. And certainly We gave a commandment to Adam before, but he forgot; We found in him no resolve to disobey. And when We said to the angels: Be submissive to Adam, they submitted except Iblis; he refused. We said: O Adam, this is an enemy to thee and to thy wife; so let him not drive you both out of the garden so that thou art unhappy. Surely it is granted to thee therein that thou art not hungry, nor naked, and that thou art not thirsty therein, nor exposed to the sun's heat. But the devil made an evil suggestion to him; he said: O

The Heavenly Message

Adam, shall I lead thee to the tree of immortality and a kingdom which decays not? So they both ate of it, then their evil inclinations became manifest to them, and they began to cover themselves with the leaves of the garden. And Adam disobeyed his Lord and was disappointed. Then his Lord chose him, so He turned to him and guided him. He said: Go forth herefrom both — all of you — one of you is enemy to another. So there will surely come to you guidance from Me; then whoever follows My guidance, he will not go astray nor be unhappy. And whoever turns away from My Reminder, for him is surely a straitened life, and We shall raise him up blind on the Day of Resurrection. He will say: My Lord, why hast Thou raised me up blind, while I used to see? He will say: Thus did Our Messages come to thee, but thou didst neglect them. And thus art thou forsaken this day. And thus do We recompense him who is extravagant and believes not in the messages of his Lord. And certainly, the chastisement of the Hereafter is severer and more lasting. Does it not manifest to them how many of the generations, in whose dwellings they go about, We destroyed before them? Surely there are signs in this for men of understanding. And had not a word gone forth from thy Lord, and a term been fixed, it would surely have overtaken them. So bear patiently what they say, and celebrate the praise of thy Lord before the rising of the sun and before its setting, and glorify Him during the hours of the night and parts of the day, that thou mayest be well pleased. And strain not thine eyes toward that with which We have provided different classes of them, of the splendor of this world's life, that We may thereby try them. And the sustenance of thy Lord is better and more abiding. And enjoin prayer on thy people, and steadily adhere to it. We ask not of thee a sustenance. We provide for thee. And the good end is for guarding against evil. And they say: Why does he not bring us a sign from his Lord? Has not there come to them a clear evidence of what is in the previous Books? And if We had destroyed them with chastisement before it, they would have said: Our Lord, why didst

Thou not send to us a Messenger, so that we might have followed Thy messages before we met disgrace and shame? Say: Everyone of us is waiting, so wait. Soon you will come to know who is the follower of the even path and who goes aright.

Hast thou seen him who disbelieves in Our Messages and says: I shall certainly be given wealth and children? Has he gained knowledge of the unseen, or made a covenant with the Beneficent? By no means! We write down what he says, and We shall lengthen to him the length of the chastisement, and We shall inherit from him what he says, and he will come to Us alone. And they have taken gods besides the most gracious Creator, that they should be to them a source of strength — By no means! They will soon deny their worshipping them, and be their adversaries. Seest thou not that We send the devils against the disbelievers, inciting them incitingly? So make no haste against them. We only number out to them a number of days.

And they say: The Beneficent has taken to Himself a son. Certainly, you make an abominable assertion! The heavens may almost be rent thereat, and the earth cleaves asunder, and the mountains fall down in pieces, that they ascribe a son to the Beneficent! And it is not worthy of the Beneficent that He should take to Himself a son. There is none in the heavens and the earth but comes to the Beneficent as a servant. Certainly, He comprehends them and has numbered them all. And every one of them will come to Him on the Day of Resurrection, alone.

So We have made it easy in thy tongue only that thou should give good news thereby to those who guard against evil, and should warn thereby a contentious people. And how many a generation before them have We destroyed! Canst thou see any one of them or hear a sound of them?

Praise be to the most gracious Creator! Who revealed the Book to His servant, and allowed not therein any crookedness, rightly directing, to give warning of severe punishment from Him and to give good news to the believers who do good that theirs is a goodly reward, staying in it

The Heavenly Message

forever; and to warn those who say: the most gracious Creator has taken to Himself a son. They have no knowledge of it, nor had their fathers. Grievous is the word that comes out of their mouths. They speak nothing but a lie. Then maybe thou wilt kill thyself with grief, sorrowing after them if they believe not in this announcement. Surely We have made whatever is on the earth an embellishment for it, so that We may try which of them is best in works. And We shall surely make what is on it dust, without herbage. Or, thinkest thou that the companions of the Cave and the Inscription were of Our wonderful signs? When the youths sought refuge in the Cave, they said: Our Lord, grant us mercy from Thyself, and provide for us a right course in our affair. So We prevented them from hearing in the Cave for a number of years, then We raised them up that We might know which of the two parties was best able to calculate the time for which they remained. We relate to thee their story with truth. Surely they were youths who believed in their Lord and We increased them in guidance. And We strengthened their hearts when they stood up and said: Our Lord is the Lord of the heavens and the earth; we call upon no god beside Him, for then indeed we should utter an enormity. These our people have taken gods beside Him. Why do they not bring clear authority for them? Who is then more unjust than he who forges a lie against the most gracious Creator? And when you withdraw from them and what they worship save the most gracious Creator, take refuge in the Cave; your Lord will spread forth for you of His mercy, and provide for you a profitable course in your affair. And thou mightest see the sun, when it rose, a decline from their Cave to the right, and when it set to leave them behind on the left, while they were in a wide space thereof. This is of the signs of the most gracious Creator. He whom the most gracious Creator guides, he is on the right way; and whom He leaves in error, thou wilt not find for him a friend to guide aright. And thou mightest think them awake while they were asleep, and We turned them about to the right and to the left, with their dog outstretching its paws at the entrance. If thou didst look at them, thou wouldst turn back from them in flight, and thou wouldst be filled with awe because of them. And thus did We rouse them that they might question each other. A speaker from among them said: How long have you tarried? They said: We have tarried for a day or a part of a day. (Others) said: Your Lord knows best how long you have tarried. Now send one of you with this silver (coin) of yours to the city, then let him see what food is purest, and bring you provision from it, and let him behave with gentleness, and not make your case known to anyone. For if they prevail against you, they would stone you to death or force you back to their religion, and then you would never succeed. And thus did We make men get knowledge of them, that they might know that the most gracious Creator's promise is true and that the Hour — there is no doubt about it. When they disputed among themselves about their affair and said: Erect an edifice over them. Their Lord knows best about them. Those who prevailed in their affair said: We shall certainly build a place of worship over them.

Some say: They were three, the fourth of them their dog; and others say: Five, the sixth of them their dog, making conjectures about the unseen. And others say Seven, and the eighth of them their dog. Say: My Lord best knows their number — none knows them but a few. So contend not in their matter but with an outward contention, and question not any of them concerning them. And say not of anything: I will do that tomorrow unless the most gracious Creator please. And remember thy Lord when thou forgettest and say: Maybe my Lord will guide me to a nearer course to the right than this. And they remained in their cave three hundred years, and they add nine. Say: the most gracious Creator knows best how long they remained. His is the unseen of the heavens and the earth. How clear His sight and His hearing! There is no guardian for them besides Him, and He associates none in His judgment. And recite that which has been revealed to thee of the Book of thy Lord. There is none who can alter His words. And thou wilt find no refuge beside Him. And keep thyself with those who call on their

Lord morning and evening desiring His goodwill, and let not thine eyes pass from them, desiring the beauties of this world's life. And follow not him whose heart We have made unmindful of Our remembrance, and he follows his low desires and his case exceeds due bounds. And say: The Truth is from your Lord; so let him who please believe, and let him who please disbelieve. Surely We have prepared for the iniquitous a Fire, an enclosure of which will encompass them. And if they cry for water, they are given water like molten brass, scalding their faces. Evil the drink! And ill the resting-place! As for those who believe and do good, We waste not the reward of him who does a good work. These it is for whom are Gardens of perpetuity wherein flow rivers; they are adorned therein with bracelets of gold, and they wear green robes of fine silk and thick brocade, reclining therein on raised couches. Excellent the recompense! And goodly the resting-place!
And certainly We have made distinct in this Quran for mankind every kind of description; man is in most things

contentious. And nothing prevents men from believing when the guidance comes to them, and from asking forgiveness of their Lord, but that they wait for the way of the ancients to overtake them, or that the chastisement should confront them. And We send not Messengers but as givers of good news and warning, and those who disbelieve contend with falsehood to weaken thereby the Truth, and they take My Messages and the warning for a mockery. And who is more unjust than he who is reminded of the messages of his Lord, then he turns away from them and forgets what his hands have sent before? Surely We have placed veils over their hearts, lest they understand it, and a deafness in their ears. And if thou call them to the guidance, they will even then never follow the right course. And thy Lord is Forgiving, Full of mercy. Were He to punish them for what they earn, He would certainly hasten the chastisement for them. But for them, there is an appointed time from which they will find no refuge. And these towns — We destroyed them when they did wrong. And We have appointed a time for their destruction.

Glory to Him Who carried His servant by night from the Sacred Mosque to the Remote Mosque, whose precincts We blessed, that We might show him of Our signs! Surely He is the Hearing, the Seeing. And We gave Moses the Book and made it a guidance to the Children of Israel saying: Take no guardian beside Me — The offspring of those whom We bore with Noah. Surely he was a grateful servant. And We made known to the Children of Israel in the Book: Certainly, you will make mischief in the land twice, and behave insolently with mighty arrogance. So when of the two, the first warning came to pass, We raised against you Our servants, of mighty prowess, so they made havoc in your houses. And it was an accomplished threat. Then We gave you back the turn against them, and aided you with wealth and children and made you a numerous band. If you do good, you do good for your own souls. And if you do evil, it is for them. So when the second warning came, We raised another people that they might bring you to grief and that they might enter the Mosque as they entered it the first time, and that they might destroy, whatever they conquered, with utter destruction. It may be that your Lord will have mercy on you. And if you return to mischief, We will return to punishment. And We have made hell a prison for the disbelievers.

Has then your Lord preferred to give you sons, and for Himself taken daughters from among the angels? Surely you utter a grievous saying. And certainly, We have repeated warnings in this Quran that they may be mindful. And it adds not save to their aversion. Say: If there were with Him gods, as they say, then certainly they would have been able to seek a way to the Lord of the Throne. Glory to Him! And He is highly exalted above what they say! The seven heavens and the earth and those in them declare His glory. And there is not a single thing but glorifies Him with His praise, but you do not understand their glorification. Surely He is Forbearing, Forgiving. And when thou recitest the Quran, We place between thee and those who believe not in the Hereafter a hidden barrier; And We put coverings on their hearts and a deafness in their ears lest they understand it; and when thou makest mention of thy Lord alone in the Quran, they turn their backs in aversion. We know best what they listen to when they listen to thee, and when they take counsel secretly when the wrongdoers say: You follow only a man deprived of reason. See, what they liken thee to! So they have gone astray, and cannot find the way. And they say: When we are bones and decayed particles, shall we then be raised up as a new creation? Say: Be stones or iron, or some other creature of those which are too hard to receive life in your minds! But they will say: Who will return us? Say He Who created you at first. Still, they will shake their heads at thee and say: When will it be? Say: Maybe it has drawn nigh. On the Day when He will call you forth, then will you obey Him, giving Him praise, and you will think that you tarried but a little while. And say to My servants that they speak what is best. Surely the devil sows dissensions among them. The devil is surely an open enemy to man. Your Lord knows you best.

He will have mercy on you if He pleases, or He will chastise you if He, please. And We have not sent thee as being in charge of them. And thy Lord best knows those who are in the heavens and the earth. And certainly We made some of the Prophets to excel others, and to David, We gave the Zabur. Say: Call on those whom you assert besides Him; they have no power to remove distress from you nor to change. Those whom they call upon, themselves seek the means of access to their Lord — whoever of them is nearest — and they hope for His mercy and fear His chastisement. Surely the chastisement of thy Lord is a thing to be cautious of. And there is not a town but We will destroy it before the Day of Resurrection or chastise it with a severe chastisement. That is written in the Book. And nothing hindered Us from sending signs, but the ancients rejected them. And We gave Thamud the she-camel, a manifest sign, but they did her wrong, and We send not signs but to warn. And when We said to thee: Surely thy Lord encompasses men. And We made not the vision which We showed thee but a trial for men, as also the tree cursed in the Quran. And We warn them, but it only adds to their great inordinacy. And when We said to the angels: Be submissive to Adam; they submitted, except Iblis. He said: Shall I submit to him whom Thou hast created of dust? He said: Seest Thou? This is he whom Thou hast honored above me! If Thou respite me to the Day of Resurrection, I will certainly cause his progeny to perish except a few. He said: Begone! Whoever of them follow thee surely hell is your recompense, a full recompense. And incite whom thou canst of them with thy voice, and collect against them thy horse and thy foot, and share with them in wealth and children, and promise them. And the devil promises them only to deceive. My servants — thou hast surely no authority over them. And thy Lord suffices as having charge of affairs. Your Lord is He Who speeds the ships for you in the sea that you may seek of His grace. Surely He is ever Merciful to you. And when distress afflicts you in the sea, away go those whom you call on except He; but when He brings you safe to the land, you turn away. And man is ever ungrateful. Do you then feel secure that He will not bring you low on a tract of land, or send on you a violent wind? Then you will not find a protector for yourselves; or, do you feel secure that He will not take you back into it another time, then send on you a fierce gale and thus overwhelm you for your ungratefulness? Then you will not find any aider against Us in the matter. And surely We have honored the children of Adam, and We carry them in the land and the sea, and We provide them with good things, and We have made them excel highly most of those whom We have created. On the Day when We shall call every people with their leader: then whoever is given his book in his right hand, these will read their book; and they will not be dealt with a whit unjustly. And whoever is blind in this world he will be blind in the Hereafter, and further away from the path. And surely they had purposed to turn thee away from that which We have revealed to thee, that thou shouldst forge against Us other than that, and then they would have taken thee for a friend. And if We had not made thee firm, thou mightest have indeed inclined to them a little; then We would have made thee taste a double punishment in life and a double punishment after death, and then thou wouldst not have found any helper against Us. And surely they purposed to unsettle thee from the land that they might expel thee from it, and then they will not tarry after thee but a little. This is Our way with Our Messengers whom We sent before thee, and thou wilt not find a change in Our course. Keep up the prayer from the declining of the sun till the darkness of the night, and the recital of the Quran at dawn. Surely the recital of the Quran at dawn is witnessed. And during a part of the night, keep awake by it, beyond what is incumbent on thee; maybe thy Lord will raise thee to a position of great glory. And say: My Lord, make me enter a truthful entering, and make me go forth a truthful going forth, and grant me from Thy Presence an authority to help me. And say: The Truth has come and falsehood vanished. Surely falsehood is ever bound to vanish. And We reveal of the Quran that which is a

healing and a mercy to the believers, and it adds only to the perdition of the wrongdoers. And when We bestow favors on man, he turns away and behaves proudly; and when evil afflicts him, he is in despair. Say: Everyone acts according to his manner. But your Lord best knows who is best guided on the path.
And if We please, We could certainly take away that which We have revealed to thee, then thou wouldst find none to plead thy cause against Us — But it is a mercy from thy Lord. Surely His bounty to thee is abundant. Say: If men and jinn should combine together to bring the like of this Quran, they could not bring the like of it, though some of them were aiders of others. And certainly We have made clear for men in this Quran every kind of description, but most men consent to naught save denying. And they say: We will by no means believe in thee, till thou cause a spring to gush forth from the earth for us, or thou have a garden of palms and grapes in the midst of which thou cause rivers to flow forth abundantly, or thou cause the heaven to come down upon us in

pieces, as thou thinkest, or bring the most gracious Creator and the angels face to face with us, or thou have a house of gold, or thou ascend into heaven. And we will not believe in thy ascending till thou bring down to us a book we can read. Say Glory to my Lord! Am I aught but a mortal Messenger?

To Be Continued in Volume Two

The Heavenly Message

The Heavenly Message

Edited by

Ismael Bukhari
Institute of Monotheism Religion
AL-Waqiah Publications
Publishers and Distributors
U.S.A – Australia - Africa-Asia

www.ingramcontent.com/pod-product-compliance
Lightning Source LLC
Chambersburg PA
CBHW030558230426
43661CB00053B/1760